"Laying a solid foundation with clear definitions for a preliminary theology of a kind of preaching that enables a transforming encounter with God through the Holy Spirit, Dr. Tyra then seeks in his unique conversational manner to further provide practical application with concrete suggestions for living out the promise of the book. This is a book that will serve well the pastor who preaches as well as the professor who teaches preaching."

—**W. H. DOGTEROM,**
Professor of Pastoral Ministries and Spiritual Formation,
Vanguard University

"Gary Tyra gives us preachers an engaging, encouraging look at preaching as a wonderfully Holy Spirit-induced, sacramental endeavor. Calling in a host of witnesses like Karl Barth, Phoebe Palmer, Augustine, and even me, Tyra shows how preaching is the unique work of Christ loving his people through the frail, human but Spirit-empowered words of us preachers."

—**WILL WILLIMON,**
Professor of the Practice of Christian Ministry, Duke University

"Integrating homiletics and hermeneutics with spiritual formation and pastoral concern, as Paul did, Gary Tyra invites us to go beyond merely devising nice sermons. He summons us to welcome God to speak through us, so that our congregations encounter him in a living way, to preach in a prophetic, Spirit-empowered way that effects transformation."

—**CRAIG S. KEENER,**
F. M. and Ada Thompson Professor of Biblical Studies,
Asbury Theological Seminary

"In recalling a remarkable moment with Jesus, the two men on the road to Emmaus noted that their hearts were 'burning within' as Jesus unpacked the Scriptures to them. Word and Spirit, proclamation and encounter, truth and transformation—could this describe our preaching today? *Sacramental Sermons* is an invaluable answer to that question, written by a friend, scholar, and skilled practitioner."

—**JAMES BRADFORD,**
Lead Pastor, Central Assembly, Springfield, Missouri

"'God really spoke to me today!' Through a sermon? Does the Holy Spirit reveal Jesus in real time? What if congregants could understand theologically what they are actually experiencing through genuinely anointed preaching? And what if preachers would envision their craft as Spirit-anointed sacramental preaching! Gary Tyra invites preachers to prayerfully experience the presence of Jesus during both the preparation of the sermon and its delivery."

—**MARTIN MITTELSTADT,**
Professor of New Testament, Evangel University

"*Sacramental Sermons* provides a welcome alternative to the glut of resources that have reduced preaching to the craft of slick rhetoric more indicative of late-night television than the communication of Eternal Truth. In a post-Christian world that starves people of hope, *Sacramental Sermons* offers a vision of preaching that connects people to a hope-filled encounter with the Living God."

—**BYRON D KLAUS,**
President (1999–2015), Assemblies of God Theological Seminary

"I'm not part of the Pentecostal or Charismatic traditions. However, as a 'cautious continuationist' I still resonated deeply with Gary Tyra's *Sacramental Sermons*. It's theologically rich, historically informed, devotionally warm, and homiletically practical. I heartily commend this book to every preacher of God's word who desires to better understand the work of the Holy Spirit in the preparation, delivery, and impact of our sermons."

—**NATHAN A. FINN,**
Kalos Chair of Intellectual Discipleship, North Greenville University

Sacramental Sermons

WORD AND SPIRIT:

PENTECOSTAL INVESTIGATIONS IN THEOLOGY AND HISTORY

The *Word and Spirit* series will make space for the pneumatological emphasis typical of Pentecostal/charismatic approaches to theology without eclipsing the discernment that comes with the Word of God (that is the Word both christological and scriptural). This series will not be narrowly *Pentecostal* but will include other approaches deemed charismatic as well. Furthermore, the series will also have an ecumenical horizon. Contributors will be encouraged to write in a way that would make these books relevant to other denominational traditions. These books are *Investigations* in that they are scholarly treatments of topics that will seek to remain accessible to pastors as well as seminary and upper division college readers. *Theology* in the series name signals that these are constructive works engaging biblical, systematic, and historical theological discourse, with an eye towards offering contributions of contemporary relevance to the church.

The series will contract academic monographs that offer a solid Pentecostal and ecumenical discussion of key loci, but also of key trajectories in Pentecostal thought and experience.

Sacramental Sermons

Prophetic, Incarnational, and Truly Transformative Preaching

GARY TYRA

CASCADE *Books* • Eugene, Oregon

SACRAMENTAL SERMONS
Prophetic, Incarnational, and Truly Transformative Preaching

Cascade Books
An Imprint of Wipf and Stock Publishers
199 W. 8th Ave., Suite 3
Eugene, OR 97401

www.wipfandstock.com

PAPERBACK ISBN: 979-8-3852-2101-1
HARDCOVER ISBN: 979-8-3852-2102-8
EBOOK ISBN: 979-8-3852-2103-5

Cataloguing-in-Publication data:

Names: Tyra, Gary, author.

Title: Sacramental Sermons : Prophetic, Incarnational, and Truly Transformative Preaching/ Gary Tyra

Description: Eugene, OR: Cascade Books, 2025 | Word and Spirit: Pentecostal Investigations in Theology and History | Includes bibliographical references and index.

Identifiers: ISBN 979-8-3852-2101-1 (paperback) | ISBN 979-8-3852-2102-8 (hardcover) | ISBN 979-8-3852-2103-5 (ebook)

Subjects: LCSH: Jesus Christ—Person and office—Sermons. | Bible—Homiletical use. | Karl Barth, 1886–1968.

Classification: BT203 T97 2025 (paperback) | BT203 (ebook)

VERSION NUMBER 04/06/26

This book is dedicated to the memory of the late Robert P. Meye, professor of New Testament Interpretation and dean of Fuller Seminary's School of Theology, who, having himself studied at the feet of Karl Barth, affirmed a young MDiv student's sense of call to serve the cause of Christ as both a preacher and theologian. Forty years later, I am still living into that ministry vision, ever grateful for Dr. Meye's gracious words of encouragement.

Contents

Acknowledgments

THIS BOOK REALLY WAS a passion project. I have long acknowledged the "sweet torture" entailed in a sincere engagement in the preaching endeavor. It is one thing to come up with an obligatory sermon. It is another to do that which is necessary to prayerfully discern the heart of God for a congregation and then attempt to represent it in a manner that is both coherent and compelling. The call to preach and teach God's word both faithfully and fruitfully week after week is not for those easily distracted or discouraged!

Having striven, for fifty years now, as a pastor and professor to do this, I would like to think I have learned a few things along the way. I am so very grateful to Frank Macchia and Dale Coulter—the editors of the Cascade book series titled "Word and Spirit: Pentecostal Investigations in Theology and History"—for the opportunity to contribute this volume, which focuses on Spirit-empowered preaching. I have enjoyed writing all the books God has allowed me to pen for him. This one was a special delight.

So, many thanks to everyone at Cascade who was involved in its publication. Special thanks to my friend and colleague, Frank Macchia, for his support. And thanks, of course, to my wife, Patti; our kids, Brandon and Megan; their respective spouses, Lindsay and Kevin; and our grandkids, Jacob, Raelyn, Maisey, and Barrett. All of you have inspired and enabled me, once again, to experience another sweet torture: the one involved in discerning the heart of God and then doing one's best to represent it in print.

With that thought in mind, it is my prayer that this literary work works—that many preachers, both novice and veteran, find it to be not only informative, but inspirational as well.

Coram Deo!

Introduction

For since in the wisdom of God the world through its wisdom did not know him, God was pleased through the foolishness of what was preached to save those who believe.

—1 CORINTHIANS 1:21

THOUGH THIS BOOK IS ABOUT HOMILETICS—the art of Christian preaching and teaching, it is much more. It puts forward a rather distinctive theology of preaching—one that can and will underwrite the development and delivery of sermons that may be used by the Holy Spirit to function sacramentally in the life of the church. In other words, I am going to boldly suggest that this book is about the kind of Christian preaching and teaching God always intended!

According to Richard John Neuhaus, "The Latin word *sacramentum* originally referred to an oath or a pledge, especially a soldier's oath of allegiance."[1] After my conversion to Christ as a sophomore in college, I was nurtured in a Protestant, Pentecostal church that acknowledged and celebrated two Christian sacraments: water baptism and the Lord's Table. The good folks in this church viewed the two sacraments (referred to as ordinances) as opportunities to initially profess one's commitment to Christ (baptism), and then to perpetually reaffirm one's commitment to him (the Lord's Table). It was later, while studying church history in seminary, that I became acquainted with the longstanding debate about whether the celebration of the Eucharist is about

1. Neuhaus, *Freedom for Ministry*, 98.

remembering (the Anabaptist view), *receiving* (the Roman Catholic view), or *relating* (the Reformed view).

As a Pentecostal-evangelical reluctant to view the eucharistic rite as salvific (in either a Roman Catholic or Eastern Orthodox sense), I came to embrace the notion that, while the celebration of the Lord's Table does involve a remembrance of what Christ has done for us, thus encouraging an ongoing commitment to him, we should also hope to experience him—his presence—in some special sense during the ritual. In other words, I ended up with a *relational* rather than a merely *memorial* understanding of the Lord's Table.[2] However, looking back, I must admit that for many years, even while serving as a pastor, I was still not certain what this experience of his presence was designed to do in the lives of those participating in the ritual. As a result, the sacrament continued to function mainly as a periodic opportunity for me to remember and give thanks for what Christ has done for me, to signal my ongoing devotion to him, and to appeal to him for strength in this or that area of my walk with him.

Though this was not nothing as far as a sacramental theology goes, I continued to wonder if something might still be missing. I also began to suspect that more than a few of my parishioners and pastoral colleagues were wondering the same thing.

SACRAMENT AS EMPOWERING ENCOUNTER

Over time, several "what if" questions began to form in my mind: What if, while celebrating the Lord's Table (in genuine faith), we not

2. Though I do not identify as a Calvinist, per se, I appreciate the way in which the Swiss Reformer sought to understand the sacraments as "signs" and "seals" in light of the signs and promises God provided Israel in the Old Testament, and Jesus provided his followers in the Gospels. Understood in this light, the sacraments are designed to enable participants to enter into and maintain a spiritually, morally, and missionally faithful relationship with our Trinitarian God. These mandated rituals function as "signs" illustrating the power, purposes, and promises of God, and as "seals" instilling the various graces needed to live fully into them. Because God's endgame is an eternal communion with spiritual progeny who have become capable of loving and trusting him fully and forever, there is a relational dynamic at work in Calvin's understanding of what the sacraments confer. For a thorough discussion of this topic see Wallace, *Calvin's Doctrine of the Word and Sacrament*, 71–81, 133–54.

only offer thanks for what Christ Jesus has done for us, and pledge our ongoing commitment to him, but also, through the Holy Spirit, *encounter*, or actually *commune* with him in real time?[3] And what if these *encounters* with the risen Christ are indeed critical to our spiritual, moral, and ministry formation because they entail the possibility of our genuinely experiencing in our lives those qualities of Jesus that drew his first followers to him: his *wisdom*, *courage*, *compassion*, and *authority?* Furthermore, what if the divinely intended effect of these sacramental *encounters* with the risen Christ is not simply to produce gratitude, but also to *empower* us, his followers, to live as he did—in a God-the-Father pleasing manner, rendering to him a spiritual, moral, and missional faithfulness?[4] Finally, what if the experience of a spiritually enriching, faith-building, ministry-engendering, sacramental *encounter* with Christ is not limited to the Eucharist, but can be experienced throughout the worship gathering, especially the preaching and teaching of God's word?[5]

THE PHENOMENON OF THE SACRAMENTAL SERMON

The premise of this book is that there is a kind of Christian preaching that can be sacramental in the encounter-effecting, faithfulness-producing sense just described. In the introduction to his book *Proclamation and Theology*, mainline Protestant preaching guru William Willimon makes this bold assertion: "The gap, the evangelical distance that ought to concern the preacher, is not one of time—the *historical* space between Jesus and us—nor is it one of communication—the *rhetorical*

3. My Vanguard University colleague, Frank Macchia, writes: "If baptism is the rite of initial union with Christ, the Lord's Supper is the repeated rite of ongoing communion." See Macchia, *Tongues of Fire*, 366.

4. Macchia provides some implicit support for this empowering understanding of the eucharistic rite when he writes: "Christ is present in the sharing of the meal through the Holy Spirit communing with us, bringing us to a deep remembrance of his death, nourishing us afresh by the Spirit, and bringing us to a renewed commitment to the crucified and risen life." See Macchia, *Tongues of Fire*, 368, 373.

5. Such a view, it seems to me, is supported by what the New Testament has to say in an explicit manner about how we come by saving faith (e.g., Rom 10:4–15; 1 Cor 1:21) and receive the Holy Spirit (e.g., Gal 3:2, 5). I will have more to say about this in chapter 3.

space between speaker and listener. The gap that is the main concern of the evangelical preacher . . . is the *theological* space between us and the Trinity."[6]

A few lines later, Willimon shares an equally bold personal anecdote, one that clarifies what a bridging of the theological space between us and God during a preaching event might result in:

> At the front door, as people filed out of the service, some said things like "Nice service," or "Good sermon, preacher." But one young woman shook my hand and said, "Thanks. God really spoke to me today. I really felt a presence. Thanks. I feel like I know what I've got to do next week."
>
> I do not know precisely what happened between that woman and God. I do not know what she heard or what she will do with what she heard. All I know is that, whatever it was, it wasn't silly. It was a surprising, holy miracle, a divine intervention quite beyond the range of my abilities or intentions. She heard the very voice of God. Her name was called. She was addressed, summoned by nothing more spectacular, but certainly nothing less miraculous, than a sermon.[7]

The truth is that many preachers have experienced post-sermon conversations like the one Willimon has described. Thus, my reaction to this story is to ask several additional "what if" questions: What if the kind of preaching that closes the theological space between congregants and the risen Christ was less of a rarity? What if, instead, post-sermon conversations like the one Willimon experienced were something preachers everywhere could routinely hope for? Could it be that there are such things as *sacramental sermons*—that is, prophetic, incarnational, truly transformative preaching that not only points hearers to the hidden mystery of Christ in the text, liturgy, and the world, but also has the effect of enabling hearers through the *Holy Spirit* to sense the risen *Jesus* speaking to them in real time, calling and empowering them to live, as he did, in ways that please our *heavenly Father*?[8] If so, is there

6. Willimon, *Proclamation and Theology*, 4 (emphasis added).

7. Willimon, *Proclamation and Theology*, 5.

8. In chapter 1 of this book I provide nuanced discussions of the manner in which I use the terms "prophetic" and "incarnational" as attributes of genuinely

anything we preachers can do to put ourselves in a position so that the Holy Spirit might genuinely anoint the development and delivery of our sermons in a way that causes them to function in this prophetic, incarnational, truly transformative manner? If even the possibility exists that the answer to the questions presented above might be yes, I would contend that this type of preaching needs not only to be *preferred* but *pursued* as well. That pursuit is what this book is about.[9]

THE NEED FOR SACRAMENTAL SERMONS: A PRELIMINARY WORD

Though I will discuss this topic in more depth in chapter 3, I want to preview here why the church needs to rediscover the kind of Spirit-empowered sacramental preaching we have been discussing.

In the industrialized West, Christian philosophers and theologians lament a widespread post-Christian dynamic that has been energized by deep disappointments people have experienced with the church and Christians. Though some recent polling seems to indicate a possible slowing of this slide away from the faith,[10] the statistics are still

anointed preaching.

9. While readers who are familiar with the work of theologian Hans Boersma will find some tacit support there for what I am proposing here, there are some differences in our respective projects (see especially Boersma, *Sacramental Preaching*, and Boersma, *Scripture as Real Presence*). In particular, I will suggest that my more charismatic understanding of the "sacramental sermon" is a bit more pneumatologically explicit, dependent, and immediate. The focus moves beyond the spiritual/theological exegesis that is presented to the congregation, to the existentially impactful encounter with the risen Christ that results when the Holy Spirit prompts and enables the preacher to speak to the congregation in a prophetic, *Christ-evincing* manner. Thus, while both Boersma and I agree that there is such a thing as sacramental preaching, I suspect we may disagree as to whether an engagement in what he refers to as "sacramental exegesis" is, by itself, capable of producing sermons that function sacramentally in the sense I am proposing. It is my contention that an anointing of the Spirit upon the preparation, presentation, and reception of the sermon is also required—prophetic prompting and enablement by the Spirit of Christ that the preacher and, to some degree, the hearers also, can and must prayerfully cooperate with for the sacramental encounter with the risen Christ to occur. I will have more to say about how my understanding of sacramental sermons differs from Boersma's in succeeding chapters, especially chapter 3.

10. Smith et al., "Decline of Christianity in the U.S. Has Slowed."

concerning. Huge numbers of kids raised in church will, as they emerge into their teen and young adult years, manifest something other than a sincere and pure devotion to Jesus (see 2 Cor 11:3). While some of these spiritually disaffected young people will eventually find their way back to the faith, many will not.[11]

One of the reasons for the post-Christian dynamic just described is the emergence of a despotic social imaginary (cultural ethos)[12] so fiercely and exclusively secular in its orientation that it starves people of the hope they might ever experience anything supernatural. If it is true that hearts and minds are sometimes not just influenced, but determined by their social ethos, we must be concerned that the reigning plausibility structure[13] in contemporary Western societies essentially insists that it is simply not permissible to maintain that there is any good to pursue in life other than temporal human flourishing.[14]

Moreover, though Christianity has not completely disappeared, many Christian theologians and ministry experts lament the current preponderance of a secularized version of the Christian faith, which, they observe, is more influenced by popular, materialistic, therapeutic culture than the Bible. As a result, huge numbers of churchgoers have *not* been discipled in a biblically informed manner. Instead, they are being nurtured toward a lifetime engagement in something some cultural and theological experts refer to as "almost Christianity."[15] In other words: "Houston, we have a problem!"

11. Barna Group, "Six Reasons Young Christians Leave Church."

12. This term refers to "the way we collectively imagine, even pre-theoretically, our social life in the contemporary Western world" (See Taylor, *Secular Age*, 146). Put differently, it is a pervasive understanding (presumption) of the right way for a society to function (see Taylor, *Secular Age*, 172). One gets the sense that a "social imaginary" ends up functioning more broadly as a collective worldview—a shared take on how the world works and the best way for individuals and societies to navigate their way in and through it.

13. See Berger, *Sacred Canopy*, 45–47.

14. See Taylor, *Secular Age*, 18–20.

15. For example, see Dean, *Almost Christian*.

THE PATH AHEAD OF US

What follows is a cursory overview of the several discussions which our homiletical pursuit will entail. The book is divided into three main parts.

A Preview of Part One: The Substance of and Support for Sacramental Sermons

The aim of Part One of the book is to provide the reader with some biblical-theological and historical-theological support for the notion of sacramental sermons. Thus, presented in chapter 1 are two foundation-laying discussions designed to enable a more comprehensive and theologically informed understanding of the Christian sacraments. As well, this chapter explores the phenomenon of genuinely *anointed* Christian preaching. As I have already hinted, I contend that genuinely anointed, sacramental sermons are earmarked by three chief characteristics—they are: *prophetic* in nature, *incarnational* in manner, and *truly transformative* in effect. It is hard to overstate the importance of this chapter to the argument of the book. These initial informational and inspirational discussions truly are foundational to our homiletical pursuit!

Chapter 2 is foundational as well, however. Here our attention shifts to a closer look at the historical-theological support that the notion of sacramental sermons enjoys. Even a cursory survey of the theologies and actual practice of preaching at work in the patristic, medieval, Reformation, post-Reformation, modern, and late-modern eras can be not only inspirational but formational as well. Even if the term "sacramental sermon" is not employed, we should not be surprised to discover in the writings of many of the most influential theologians and preachers in Christian history some significant support for the theological and homiletical dynamics that, when brought together, produce preaching that is prophetic, incarnational, and truly transformative.

A Preview of Part Two: The Need for Sacramental Sermons

Part Two of this work focuses on the need for sacramental sermons. Ironically, the single but hefty chapter that constitutes the midsection of the book provides a substantial examination of that which is necessary to enable church members and their friends, family members, neighbors, and co-workers to escape the tyranny of the secular age in which we currently find ourselves. My hope is that this chapter inspires readers to: (1) take the pursuit of sacramental preaching seriously; and (2) see it through to the end no matter how intimidating a post-Christian, sometimes anti-Christian, cultural zeitgeist might seem. The Christian church must never forget or forgo its God-given responsibility to serve as a sacramental connection between spiritually starved, confused people and Christ, the risen Lord.

A Preview of Part Three: The Process of Sacramental Sermons

The focus of Part Three of the book is the way genuinely anointed, sacramental sermons are developed, delivered, and deliberated upon. In his book *Preaching: Communicating Faith in an Age of Skepticism,* Timothy Keller calls for preachers to develop a "desperate dependence on the Spirit."[16] I could not agree more! Thus, this section is comprised of four important chapters that discuss the various ways preachers, their sermons, and their congregations can and will be impacted by the "desperate dependence on the Spirit" Keller was so keen to emphasize.

The specific focus of chapter 4 is on the preparation (spirituality) of the preacher. It is true that sacramental sermons cannot be manufactured at whim; they are ever and always God's prerogative. That said, the Bible and Christian experience indicate there is an approach to Christian spirituality that dramatically increases the potential for Christian preaching that functions in a prophetic, incarnational, and truly transformative manner. Thus, this chapter will provide readers with: (1) a brief overview of the Pauline, fully Trinitarian, "I-Thou," lifestyle spirituality that enables preachers to live into the Trinitarian realism that sacramental sermons are products of; and (2) a careful consideration

16. Keller, *Preaching,* 207. See also, Chapell, *Christ-Centered Preaching,* 24.

of several specific spirituality practices which will dramatically impact the *logos*, *ethos*, *pathos*, *telos*, and *kairos* of the preaching event, thus enabling sermons that are Spirit-empowered, Christ-evincing, and God-the-Father pleasing (i.e., faithfulness-producing).

In chapter 5 we learn that while prophetic preaching is Spirit-empowered—this does not mean that the preparation of anointed sermons is less arduous. If anything, the development of sacramental sermons is even more demanding, involving as it does several forms of exegesis, all of which must be performed in a prayerful manner. The need for a very real dependence on the Spirit in these exegetical endeavors is indicated by the apostle Paul in his discussion of philosophy, theology, and preaching in 1 Corinthians 1:18–2:5. The need for "faithful listening" during the earliest stages of sermon preparation is also attested to by some reputable theologians and biblical scholars. In this important chapter, we discover that, with the help of the Holy Spirit, preachers can engage in a kind of "hermeneutical hearing" that enables them to discern the heart of God—i.e., the biblically informed, Christ-honoring, missionally faithful message he or she is being called to herald during this or that preaching/teaching event.

Preaching expert William Willimon writes:

> Before preaching can be communication, exhortation, admonition, comfort, or motivation, it must be prayerful listening for the Word of God. . . . Without hearing that Word, preaching has nothing to say. . . . Thus prayer is the first step in sermon preparation, and all subsequent steps of biblical study, sermon construction, and even sermon delivery are aspects of prayer.[17]

This chapter has the potential to be a game-changer for many readers, taking an esoteric topic and making it real.

In chapter 6 we learn that discerning the message through hermeneutical hearing is only the first step in the preparation of sermons. We must also discuss how the prophetic phenomenon impacts several additional traditional *homiletical concerns* related to the *purpose*, *style*, and *mechanics* of this or that sermon.

17. Willimon, *Proclamation and Theology*, 21.

Ultimately, this chapter will provide a list of homiletical moves that have proved to increase the possibility of something prophetic occurring in my own preaching and teaching. While some of the self-reflection questions presented in this discussion might show up in any homiletical textbook, others will be found only in a work like this—one that aims to inspire and enable readers to prepare Spirit-empowered sermons that can, God permitting, play out in a sacramental, encounter-enabling manner.

Finally, chapter 7 discusses a topic of great significance: the process involved in preparing congregations to, with the help of the Holy Spirit, *expect*, *experience*, and then successfully *process* genuinely anointed, sacramental sermons. Put differently, this concluding chapter deals with the elephant in the room: the need for those sitting in the pews to possess hearts that can, like the good soil Jesus described in his parable of the sower, receive the preached word in the manner God intends (Matt 13: 1–23). Thus, this chapter will discuss how pastors can be proactive about encouraging a corporate posture of pneumatological expectancy, and, hence, a capacity for spiritual hearing. In addition, it will suggest some ways the congregation can be enabled to engage in the communal, Spirit-empowered sermon processing I believe is key to church members becoming more than mere hearers of the word, but doers also (Jas 1:22–25).

THE END OF THE BEGINNING

Preaching has always been of paramount importance when it comes to Christian ministry. Sacramental sermons are not everything but they do function as the cornerstone of ecclesial environments that produce the kind of Christian disciples who are "all in" rather than "almost." Prophetic, incarnational, truly transformative preaching is at the heart of gospel ministry that has the power to not only save and sanctify, but also enable churchgoing Christians to become spiritual salt and light—the force for God in the world he desires all of us to be. In the history of Christianity, renewal and revival movements have always begun with prayer. For sure, prayer is key, but a closer look will reveal that what Spirit-anointed prayer movements have nearly always produced are fresh eras of bold anointed preaching that is sacramental, encounter-enabling, life-story shaping in its effect.

I want to conclude this introduction by citing a portion of a course journal entry a student recently submitted. I am hopeful this excerpt will underscore the veracity of the two main suggestions offered already in this work: 1) there is a way to preach and teach that is prophetic, incarnational, truly transformative; and 2) if there was ever time when such fully Trinitarian preaching and teaching is necessary, it is now.

The student had just completed a sixteen-week course titled "Developing a Christian Worldview." The course is a requirement for all students at the Christian university where I teach. As a result, the roster always includes a spectrum of learners whose current level of commitment to Christ ranges from nonexistent to fully devoted. This student began the final entry of his "Worldview Course Journal" indicating that at the beginning of the semester his commitment to Christ was minimal, having been badly damaged, virtually destroyed actually, by disappointing experiences with peers whose professed devotion to Christianity was not backed up by their behavior. We all know the sentiment: "I don't go to church because it's filled with hypocrites." But in this final journal entry, this jaded, cynical, lonely college student wrote the following:

> When I first began this class, I was very skeptical of what I would be learning. In fact, I was dreading entering this class since it felt like "unnecessary" work that was going to pile up with the mountains of work I already have. It was not a personal reason or a pre-conceptualized judgement of the professor, but more of a workload concern.
>
> I would be lying if I would tell you there weren't personal factors involved in my initial reaction to taking the class. I never felt like I fit in [at the] university, I felt like the Christians around me judged me. I have always felt this way in church, that I had a mask on for who I really was.
>
> In the first four weeks I kept a distance relationship with the lecture as I stared blankly into my laptop screen [at] the readings I had to do in other classes. However, as time went on certain speech patterns and words kept drawing my attention.

> I kept trying to resist this attention, but my eyes kept being directed to the lecture as if somebody had softly pulled my chin to point it in the board's direction. I slowly began to transition into enjoying the class. I would sometimes think about the lectures for days and weeks. Of course, there was a handful of content I did not agree with, [but] it was still interesting to learn.
>
> I felt something waken within me once again, a belief for God and ambition for a relationship with Him.
>
> The [things I've taken away from this class have] really opened up my eyes on the perspective of Christianity. I really want to give it another try. I have already incorporated certain practices into my life by being more loyal to God's word. I began to pray more and more as my time in this class went on. I have also decided to read more from the Bible than I would have liked to before, even with the mountains of work I have. I am [now] in the pursuit of a relationship with our Lord and Savior.

This journal entry is illustrative, I propose, of what this book is about. With all due respect to my student's attempt to explain what was happening in the classroom (and his heart), I will suggest that it was not simply some speech patterns and words that drew him in; it was the wooing work of the Holy Spirit, the real presence of the risen Jesus speaking to him through the lectures.

The bottom line is that sacramental encounters with Jesus happen! The risen Christ really will show up if we will take seriously the possibility of prophetic, incarnational, truly transformative preaching and teaching, and do our best to cooperate with the prompting and enabling provided by the Holy Spirit!

But enough introduction. It is time to begin our pursuit of the kind of preaching God always intended.

PART ONE

The Substance of and Support for Sacramental Sermons

1

Sacramental Sermons

Essentials and Earmarks

Pray also for me, that whenever I speak, words may be given me . . .

—Ephesians 6:19

In the conclusion of his most famous sermon—the Sermon on the Mount (Matt 5–7)—Jesus spoke of the importance of foundations (Matt 7:24–27). In the initial chapter of this work on preaching, I want to provide two foundation-laying discussions.

The first of these discussions focuses on what I consider to be the *essentials* of a theology of preaching that can and will underwrite the development and delivery of sacramental sermons. My tack in this initial discussion will be to indicate the developments in my own theological/ministry/spirituality journey that have contributed to the fully Trinitarian, "I-Thou," sacramental theology of preaching at work in this volume. In other words, if there is a "secret sauce" to the preaching of sacramental sermons, the ingredients of that sauce will be made clear in the first half of this chapter!

Then the second half of this chapter will explore the topic of *anointed* preaching. Most ecclesial traditions have room for the phenomenon of sermons that seem to be influenced by the Holy Spirit in an especially powerful manner. There is, however, no mutually agreed upon understanding of how to identify genuinely anointed sermons. Are they *earmarked* by their length, the passion with which they are delivered, the emotional response they engender? Or could it be something more? I have already indicated that I consider the chief characteristics of genuinely anointed preaching to relate to its *prophetic*, *incarnational*, and *transformative* properties. In this chapter I will elaborate upon these three attributes, providing in the process some preliminary biblical and theological support for each.

Together, these two discussions are intended to generate an increased interest in, and commitment to, the homiletical pursuit this book is about. Both are critical to a Spirit-empowered yet biblically faithful theology of preaching: one that is productive of sermons that play out in a sacramental, Christ-encountering manner.

THE THEOLOGY ESSENTIAL TO THE PREACHING OF SACRAMENTAL SERMONS

If, as I have suggested, sacramental sermons are those that play out in an *encounter-effecting* manner, it might be taken for granted that a Christian theology capable of underwriting such preaching would be one which focuses especially on the divine-human *encounter*. Such theologies do exist. For example, in his book, *Truth as Encounter*, the well-known Swiss theologian Emil Brunner boldly and ably argued that the notion that all truth is *encountered* rather than *discovered* or *created*, enables the most biblically faithful understanding of all the theological loci, including one's ecclesiology.[1]

However, long before I read Brunner, I was exposed to the theology of another eminent Swiss theologian, whose theological paradigm, I believe, also supports the notion of sacramental sermons. I am referring, of course, to Karl Barth, whose theology of crisis/encounter[2] was introduced to me many years ago during my graduate and postgraduate days at Fuller Theological Seminary through the mentorship of pastor/theologian Ray Anderson. Of course, there have been other theological

1. Brunner, *Truth as Encounter*.

2. See Barth, *Church Dogmatics* II/1, 23.

influences in my life since my seminary days. But at the end of the day, Barth looms large. I contend here that Barth's theology provides some *essential* support for the conviction that sacramental sermons really are a thing and should be preferred and pursued by those who have received a call to preach.

An Encounter-Oriented Understanding of the Sacramental

The most obvious essential in a theology that enables the kind of preaching God always intended is a particular way of understanding the sacramental dynamic. In truth, it was not my theological paradigm that was influenced by Barth via Ray Anderson, but my ministry and spirituality paradigms as well. Pertinent to the topic of this discussion is my recollection of how intrigued I was when I heard Anderson refer to the sacramental phenomenon as a tangible expression of the grace of God—a point of interpersonal *connection* or *encounter* between a holy God and sinful, imperfect human beings. Anderson, following Barth and his own primary theological mentor, Scottish theologian T. F. Torrance, described Jesus as the "primary sacrament," the primary point of connection between God and man.[3] He went on to speak of the church as the continuing sacramental presence of Jesus Christ: "The church as the body of Christ now lives between the cross and the return of Christ (*parousia*). The original sacramental relation of God to humanity through Jesus Christ is now represented through the enactment of the life of the church itself."[4]

This means that the local church, as the tangible expression or "body" of the resurrected and ascended Christ, is intended by God to function as a point of connection (sacrament) between hurting people and Jesus Christ, who in turn functions as the primary point of connection (sacrament) between them and God. Thus, the local church gathered can and should be a place where hurting people can experience *God the Father* through his *Son, Jesus Christ,* and the working of the *Holy Spirit* in their lives.

3. Anderson, *Soul of Ministry*, 167–69.
4. Anderson, *Soul of Ministry*, 169–70.

A Broadened Understanding of the Sacramental

I resonated with this sacramental understanding of the church itself. But it meant that my understanding of the church's sacraments, especially the Eucharist, would need to be nuanced. First of all, this meant that in addition to viewing the celebration of the Lord's Table as an occasion to *remember* what Christ has done for us, and to provide us with ongoing opportunities to *renew* our faith in, and commitment to, him, it is also possible to see the Eucharist as a way for Christ's followers to, so to speak, reach out in faith and touch the hem of Jesus' garment, *experiencing* through him in real time something very badly needed in their lives (Mark 5:21–32; 6:56).

What is more, if, as Anderson suggested, the *entire* "life of the church" should be a point of contact between hurting people and Christ, I began to suspect that this sacramental dynamic should *not* be limited to the Eucharist, as important as it is. If God intends for local churches to exercise a sacramental function—to be communities of faith where hurting people in the neighborhood can go to seek, find, and encounter the resurrected and ascended Jesus, then not just part of the church's worship gathering, but the whole, should be considered sacramental—encounter-effecting. This would include, in addition to the ceremonial eating and drinking taking place at the Lord's Table, the worshiping, the praying and, very importantly, the preaching that occurs during the assembly.[5]

5. Please note that I do not mean to downplay the importance of the celebration of the Lord's Table. I do, however, want to stimulate deeper thought into the instrumental relationship between the preached word and the Lord's Table. Thus, I contend that we can and should avoid creating a false antithesis between the Eucharist and the sermon. Both are important! The same Jesus who instructed his followers to "do this" with respect to the bread and wine (1 Cor 11:24–25), also admonished them to baptize, preach, and teach (Matt 28:19–20). Common to all these activities is the possibility of existentially impactful (transformative) encounters with the risen Christ, whom Paul refers to as the one true focal point of the faith and life of the church in passages such as Colossians 1:15–20. Moreover, it must be borne in mind that Paul goes on in that passage to emphasize the preached word as the means by which believers continue in Christ and, eventually, become perfect in him (Col 1:21–29)! What this suggests is that there is a primacy to preaching in the sermon/sacrament composite. The manner in which the Reformer John Calvin made this same point will be treated in chapters 2 and 3. Notable as well is the way theologians Karl Rahner and Michael Schmaus are representative of Roman Catholic theologians

And yet, the essentials of a theology that serves to generate sacramental sermons go beyond the broadened way it conceives of the sacramental dynamic. Such a theology will also be fully Trinitarian and realist rather than non-realist in its essence and effect![6]

A Trinitarian Understanding of God

According to Karl Barth, it is a Trinitarian understanding of God that best explains who God is and what he is up to in the world he created. This explains why God's Trinitarian being exercises such a profound influence in every section of Barth's *Church Dogmatics.* One Barthian scholar writes: "Barth understood very clearly at a critical point in the history of Protestant theology that it is from Trinitarian teaching that Christian dogmatics derives not only the entirety of what it has to say about God, but also what it has to say about the *relation* of God and creatures."[7] Again and again in this book I will assert that a critical observation of a Trinitarian understanding of God is that one of his essential attributes is his inherent *relationality*. The Godhead—Father, Son, and Holy Spirit—has existed for all eternity as a loving, trusting, mutually preferring communion. This implies that all the members of the Trinity are personal rather than impersonal, profoundly capable of, and deeply committed to, the dynamic of interpersonal *communion.*[8]

---

who likewise view the preached word as basic to the sacraments. (See Rahner, "Word and the Eucharist," 273–98, and Schmaus, "Word as Salvific Activity in the Church," 16–19.) To be more specific, Schmaus seems to do this when he asserts: "One cannot, strictly speaking, say that the saving activity of the Church includes the proclamation of the word and the use of signs. Rather, the proclamation of the word is the activity of the Church that includes everything else" (Schmaus, "Word as Salvific Activity in the Church," 17). For his part, Rahner seems to provide some implicit support for the thesis of this work when he speaks of an "efficacious preaching of the word of God" [where] "that which is preached takes on the character of an event. It means that the grace of God is not merely spoken of but takes place as an event in this utterance" (Rahner, "Word and the Eucharist," 273).

6. Some support for the ensuing discussion can be found in Griffiths, *Preaching in the New Testament*, 87–89.

7. John Webster in the Foreword to *Trinitarian Theology after Barth,* xi, emphasis added.

8. This commitment to communion entails also a commitment to self-revelation. For more on this and its implications for Christian preaching, see Thompson,

C. S. Lewis drew attention to the fact that the God of the Bible, far from being impersonal, is actually super-personal. Thus, God should be viewed as both hyper-personal and ultra-relational—i.e., radically committed to a personal relationship with those he has created in his image.[9] It stands to reason then that such a God would be very open to making it possible for his image-bearers to encounter him in an empowering manner.

A Fully Trinitarian Understanding of God

Moreover, I have also come to understand how important it is for Christians to be *fully Trinitarian* in our approach to all spirituality and ministry practices. A "fully Trinitarian" approach to any Christian activity is one that acknowledges the critically important role *all three* members of the Godhead play in the endeavor at hand. Thus, no member of the Trinity should be ignored, nor should the role he plays be truncated or downplayed vis-à-vis that of the others. Thus, I will often use the term "fully Trinitarian" as a way of emphasizing the need for Christian spirituality and ministry practices to be Spirit-empowered, Christ-evincing, *and* God-the-Father pleasing in a comprehensive, wholistic manner.

A Realist, "I-Thou" Understanding and Experience of Our Trinitarian God

Going further, behind the sacramental theology of both Karl Barth and T. F. Torrance is a *theological realism* that asserts that because of the incarnation and outpouring of the Holy Spirit, it is possible for God's people to know and *experience* him in real, phenomenal, life story-shaping ways.[10] God is not *merely* a philosophical concept such as the "prime mover" or our "ground of being." Neither is he *simply* a spiritual force that can be accessed/utilized in a formalistic manner. Once again, because the Godhead is, in essence, an interpersonal communion, each member of the Trinity is not just personal and relational but

"Declarative God," 18–33.

9. Lewis, *Mere Christianity*, 160.

10. See Torrance, *Reality and Evangelical Theology*, 23.

hyper-personal and *ultra-relational* in nature. Among other things, this means that God is predisposed toward self-disclosure. In other words, the God of the Bible is a speaking, acting, self-revealing God. [11]

As a result, the way we relate to God must be, as the Jewish philosopher Martin Buber famously argued, "I-Thou" rather than "I-It" in orientation.[12] God is not an "It" we can deconstruct, analyze, master, and utilize as we would a philosophical notion, theological proposition, or spiritual force. Instead, for Christians, the Godhead is an eternally Trinitarian "Thou" who can be known, reverenced, and interacted with in ways that are real, intimate, and life story shaping.

A "Trinitarian realism" goes further to insist that each member of the Trinity—Father, Son, and Holy Spirit—can be known and experienced in the realist manner just described. As a result, a realist, fully Trinitarian approach to any Christian practice is *intentional* about discerning how a theologically real relationship with God the Father, Christ the Son, *and* the Holy Spirit shapes both the mode and motivation of our engagement in the practice. This is yet another game-changing reality as it relates to just about every aspect of Christian spirituality, including our experience of the sacraments. For the sacraments to really accomplish what our Trinitarian God intends, they must be approached in a *fully Trinitarian, theologically real* manner, with an "I-Thou" rather than "I-It" understanding in place. The Christian sacraments are, therefore, best understood as grace-enabled opportunities for hurting people to connect with *God the Father*, as they engage in fresh, timely, *communal encounters* with *his Son* (the primary sacrament), in the power of *his Spirit*.

The Need for a Pneumatologically Real Engagement in the Sacraments

Though I will address this issue again in chapter 3, I will preface that discussion here by boldly asserting the need for a pneumatologically real engagement in the sacraments. It is one thing to engage in the

11. Barth, *Church Dogmatics* I/1, 52, 132.

12. Buber, *I and Thou*.

sacraments in a merely formalistic manner; it is another to approach them in what I refer to as a *pneumatologically real* manner.[13]

It is through the working of the Holy Spirit that Christ's followers encounter/experience the real and risen Jesus (John 16:12–15). In my book *Getting Real: Pneumatological Realism and the Spiritual, Moral, and Ministry Formation of Contemporary Christians,*[14] I suggest that one's *posture* toward Christ's Spirit makes a huge difference in our experience of him. Our *pneumatological posture* is how we approach or relate to the third member of the Trinity. In my experience, church members tend to relate to the Holy Spirit with one of three attitudes in place: *expectancy, presumption, indifference.*

In Ephesians 5:18 the apostle Paul calls for his readers to be continually being filled with the Holy Spirit.[15] Moreover, in Galatians 5:25 we find Paul exhorting church members to "keep in step" with the Spirit. The reality is, however, that not all churchgoers take these fundamental Pauline exhortations seriously. Indeed, many theologians acknowledge that a "pneumatological deficit" is in play in many evangelical as well as mainline Protestant churches.[16] (Even some Pentecostal-Charismatic

13. Some implicit support for the theme of this discussion is provided by Gordon T. Smith when he writes: "[W]e must stress that both baptism and the Lord's Supper are supremely pentecostal acts, acts of the Spirit. Christ is truly and fully present in the celebration of the Lord's Supper, but it is a presence that is effected through the Holy Spirit. Thus we must insist on the *epiclesis*—the prayer for the coming, anointing, and empowerment of the Holy Spirit—when we participate in the celebration of this sacred meal." (See Smith, *Evangelical, Sacramental and Pentecostal*, 42.) And yet, an important implication of the ensuing discussion is that the *epiclesis* must be prayed in what I refer to as a pneumatologically real (rather than merely formalistic) manner!

14. Tyra, *Getting Real.*

15. Commenting on the very fundamental exhortation we find in Ephesians 5:18 to be "filled" with the Spirit, New Testament scholar Francis Foulkes observes: "The tense of the verb, present imperative in the Greek, should be noted, implying as it does that the experience of receiving the Holy Spirit so that every part of life is permeated and controlled by Him is not a 'once for all' experience. In the early chapters of the Acts of the Apostles it is repeated a number of times that the apostles were 'filled with the Holy Spirit.' The practical implication is that the Christian is to leave his life open to be filled *constantly and repeatedly* by the divine Spirit." See Foulkes, *Ephesians*, 152, emphasis added.

16. See Hunsinger, "Mediator of Communion," 177; Tennent, *Invitation to World Missions*, 94; Olson, *Story of Christian Theology*, 521, 523; Kärkkäinen, *Pneumatology*,

churches can suffer from this affliction.) The point is that this less than fully robust understanding and experience of the Spirit can produce ecclesial environments that do not really encourage congregants to take the two Pauline exhortations regarding the Holy Spirit seriously. I will elaborate upon the phenomenon of a pneumatological deficit in chapter 3. For now, I will simply assert that a pneumatologically deficient ecclesial environment makes it possible for congregants to, in effect, become rather *indifferent* toward the working of the Holy Spirit in the life of their church, or, at best, to simply assume that by virtue of their engagement in certain rituals (e.g., baptism and the Lord's Table), his working can be *presumed*. In the face of this I contend that it is only a pneumatological posture of expectancy that will motivate a faithful response to the exhortations found in Ephesians 5:18 and Galatians 5:25.

To be even more specific, one's pneumatological posture will essentially determine one's approach to the Lord's Table. A posture of pneumatological *indifference* does not expect any sort of real, phenomenal encounter with Christ through the Holy Spirit. A posture of *presumption* simply presumes an encounter of some sort because the rite guarantees it. A posture of pneumatological *expectancy*, however, respects the agency and freedom of the Holy Spirit as a divine person who can and must be related to in an "I-Thou" rather than "I-It" manner. Thus, this pneumatological posture will not presume that a genuine encounter with Christ *must* take place simply because one is present for a rite or ceremony. Among other things, this means that those who preside over and participate in the celebration of the Lord's Table must, again and again, humbly, prayerfully invite the Holy Spirit to enable a genuine, life story-shaping encounter with Christ, rather than simply presume that such an encounter can be conjured in a formalistic, automatic, essentially magical manner. In sum, a pneumatologically real approach to the sacraments does not treat the Spirit as an "it" whose working can be presumed upon or controlled by human actions. Instead, the call is for us to be continually being filled with, and to keep in step with the Spirit.

17–18; Loyer, *God's Love through the Spirit*, 1–7; and Moltmann, *Spirit of Life*, 2–3.

Trinitarian Realism and Christian Preaching

Finally, by virtue of my own theological reflection and experiences as a preacher and teacher, I have come to believe that our Trinitarian God always intended for Christian preaching and teaching to function sacramentally. A fully Trinitarian realism is a game-changer when it comes to preaching. It is possible for sermons to enable hearers, through the Holy Spirit, to encounter the risen Christ in real time, genuinely experiencing his beauty (i.e., his remarkable wisdom, courage, compassion, and authority) in our lives, with the result that we experience a life story-shaping empowerment to live as Jesus did, in a God the Father-pleasing—spiritually, morally, and missionally faithful—manner.

I contend that it was never God's intention for the preaching event to serve simply as a counterpoint to the sacrament of the Lord's Table in the worship life of the church. Preaching is not merely a complement to a eucharistic connection with God through Christ and the Holy Spirit, but a critical, integral facilitator of it! Indeed, while Dietrich Bonhoeffer referred to preaching as a third sacrament—the *sacramentum verbi* or "sacrament of the word,"[17] at one point in his theological journey, Karl Barth declared that *preaching grounded on the witness of Scripture* "is the only sacrament left to us."[18] This book is about how we preachers and teachers can responsibly facilitate this sacrament of the word—that is, how we can place ourselves in a position to develop and deliver genuinely anointed sermons that play out in a truly sacramental, encounter-enabling manner.

This leads us to the second foundation-laying discussion I promised for this chapter. Many ecclesial traditions refer to some sermons as being especially "anointed." But what does this mean? How might a biblically informed theology that is imbued with a Trinitarian realism help us discern that which sets genuinely *anointed* sermons apart from others?

17. Bonhoeffer, *Worldly Preaching*, 130.

18. Cited in Currie, *Only Sacrament Left to Us*, 20. The quotation is from Barth, "Need and Promise of Christian Preaching," 114, emphasis added.

THE EARMARKS OF GENUINELY ANOINTED SACRAMENTAL SERMONS

As a young seminarian already pastoring his first church, I was profoundly impressed by the importance Barth, the renowned theologian, placed on preaching.[19] I was also pleasantly surprised by the affinity I sensed between his "event-oriented" conceptions of revelation and proclamation and the Spirit-empowerment that I, as a young Pentecostal-Charismatic, had been encouraged in my pre-seminary days to seek every time I engaged in the preaching task. Thus, I contend that a Trinitarian realism has some huge implications for how we understand the nature of *anointed* preaching. It is when preachers take seriously the fact that Christ's followers can know and experience our Trinitarian God in ways that are real, personal, and phenomenal that they can preach in a manner that is *prophetic*, *incarnational*, and *truly transformative*.

Indeed, these are the three chief characteristics of sacramental, truly anointed sermons. We will explore the historical-theological support for these homiletical dynamics in the chapter which follows. For now, the goal is to provide an overview of these three characteristics along with some of the biblical-theological support they enjoy.

Sacramental Sermons are Prophetic in Nature

The concept of prophetic preaching is not unheard of. However, I am using the term in a very specific way. I am *not* referring to sermons that merely:

- focus on the end times;
- address secret sins and/or spiritual immaturity;
- confront false doctrine;
- or challenge the status quo by inciting hearers to pursue justice and thus change the current social order.

19. See Ott, *Theology and Preaching*, 17.

These are *not* the only ways to understand what it means for preaching to be prophetic. In *Speaking the Truth in Love: Prophetic Preaching in a Broken World*, Philip Wogaman reminds us that

> [t]o be prophetic is not necessarily to be adversarial, or even controversial. The word in its Greek form refers to one who speaks on behalf of another. In Hebrew tradition, a prophet is one who speaks for God. . . . To speak for another is to grasp, first, the mind of the other . . . [G]enuinely prophetic preaching *draws people into the reality of God* in such a way that they cannot any longer be content with conventional wisdom and superficial existence.[20]

As I have argued elsewhere,[21] the coming of the Spirit into the lives of God's people routinely results in the impartation of something I refer to as "prophetic capacity"—that is, the ability to hear God's voice, receive ministry assignments from him, and speak and act into the lives of hurting people at God's behest in a missionally faithful manner. I contend that the story presented in Acts 9:10–20 of Ananias being used by the Holy Spirit to bring Saul of Tarsus into the Christian fold can be viewed as a paradigm for this prophetic capacity thesis. That said, there is abundant biblical support for the thesis throughout both Testaments of the Bible.[22] But rather than rehearse all of this biblical theological research, I will focus attention here on a passage that I did not cite in that previous publication—the verse that serves as the epigraph for this chapter: "Pray also for me, that whenever I speak, words may be given me so that I will fearlessly make known the mystery of the gospel" (Eph 6:19). The truth is that the apostle Paul often requested prayer near the end of his letters—prayers that he might be helped by God to preach the gospel fearlessly, clearly, effectively (e.g., see Col 4:3–4; 2 Thess 3:1). But, as Paul concluded his letter to the Ephesians, his request was more specific. He called for the church members in Ephesus to pray that *words might be "given" him* (Eph 6:19). This petition brings to mind

20. Wogaman, *Speaking the Truth in Love*, 3–4, emphasis added.

21. Tyra, *Holy Spirit in Mission*.

22. For example, see Num 11:25–29; 1 Sam 10:6–11; 19:19–24; 1 Chr 12:18; 2 Chr 24:20; Joel 2:28–29; Luke 1:41–45, 67; 2:25–28; Acts 2:4; 4:8; 8:14–19; 9:17–18; cf. 1 Cor 14:18; 10:44–46; 13:9; 19:6; Eph 5:18–20.

one of the most profound and powerful promises Jesus made to his apostles prior to sending them into the world to proclaim the good news. Having warned them in advance that their ministry on his behalf would sometimes be met with stiff resistance (see Matt 10:18), he went on to say: "But when they arrest you, do not worry about what to say or how to say it. At that time *you will be given what to say*, for *it will not be you speaking, but the Spirit of your Father speaking through you*" (Matt 10:19–20, emphasis added). Luke's version of this same promise is even more striking: "But make up your mind not to worry beforehand how you will defend yourselves. For *I will give you words and wisdom* that none of your adversaries will be able to resist or contradict" (Luke 21:14–15, emphasis added; cf. Acts 6:8–10).

This is the sense in which I refer to preaching that is prophetic. To be clear, I am *not* suggesting that sermons are revelatory in a manner that rivals the authority of sacred Scripture. But I am asserting that there are times when we preachers sense that *both words and wisdom are being given to us*. Sometimes this prophetic phenomenon occurs as we are preparing our sermons. Often it happens in the preaching moment itself. We find ourselves going "off script," as it were, saying things we did not plan to say, communicating things we did not know we knew, and doing so with an eloquence and impact we sense is coming from God himself.[23]

I will elaborate upon this phenomenon in subsequent chapters. For now, the question that seems pressing is this: *Why does this happen?* In the quote above, Philip Wogaman explains that *genuinely prophetic preaching draws people into the reality of God*. Likewise, explaining the homiletical theology of the Pentecostal scholar Frank Macchia, Chris Green writes:

23. One should note that in the final chapter of *Holy Spirit in Mission*, I make the observation that something prophetic can also occur in the classroom as well as the sanctuary. See Tyra, *Holy Spirit in Mission*, 182–83. One should also note how that, in the same work, I clarify that I am not an advocate for the personal "words of knowledge" that some self-professed prophets are wont to proffer. To be honest, I have never had a good encounter with a Christian who referred to himself or herself as a prophet. See Tyra, *Holy Spirit in Mission*, 165–166, 170–72. See also the warning against using sermons to issue public rebukes to individuals in Adam, *Speaking God's Words*, 71.

> Frank Macchia has described Pentecostal preaching as "an event of the Holy Spirit," akin to prophecy, that urges hearers into a transformative engagement with the scriptural text. As the preacher delivers her message, the Spirit generates for the faithful hearers a "present tenseness" of revelation that itself encourages "the faith necessary to experience the God of the Bible as this same God was experienced in 'Bible times.'" As Macchia sees it, preaching holds a special place in the church's relationship to God. He is quite emphatic: more than merely human words are given in a sermon. Under the Spirit's anointing, the sermon is "divine speaking." In worship, the congregation addresses God and in preaching, God speaks back.[24]

Sacramental Sermons Are Incarnational in Manner

My use of the word *incarnational* as an attribute of genuinely anointed preaching also requires some careful nuance. Obviously, I am *not* suggesting that the preacher or sermon is, like the incarnate Christ, ontologically divine and human at the same time, and therefore deserving of adoration. Instead, what I am arguing is that anointed preaching can be incarnational in a functional rather than ontological sense. Incarnational in that it is encounter-enabling. It is possible to experience through a genuinely anointed sermon a fresh instantiation (instance, representation, experience) of the real, spiritual presence of Christ. Channeling John Calvin in the process, Ronald Wallace speaks in support of this contention when, after commenting on the prophetic dynamic at work in preaching, he asserts that "The task of preaching must therefore be undertaken, and the word of the preacher should be heard, in the expectancy that Christ the Mediator will come and give His presence where the Gospel is preached, and cause men to hear his voice through the voice of the minister."[25]

Likewise, in *Theology of Preaching,* Richard Lischer provides support for this thesis when he asserts:

24. Macchia, "Services of the Word," 488–89, as cited in Green, "Transfiguring Preaching," 71.

25. Wallace, *Calvin's Doctrine of the Word and Sacrament,* 83.

> So identified is Jesus the Word with the word of preaching, that the one proclaimed once again becomes the proclaimer. Insofar as preaching rearticulates the themes and offers the life of God in Christ, it is Jesus himself who is the preacher, blessing our sermons with his presence. . . . Christian preaching continues the ministry of Jesus just as surely as it continues the ministry of the apostles. . . . Barth is emphatic about this when he says that preaching does not occur as a spiritual event (or what some theologians have called a word-event), but only in continuity with the fleshly Christ. Bonhoeffer, too, boldly argues that prophetic preaching can be considered incarnational when he insists, "The proclaimed word is the Christ bearing human nature."[26]

In chapter 2 we will examine much more historical-theological support for the dynamic of incarnational, encounter-enabling preaching. But I am pretty sure that most preaching pastors reading this book already know that what I am arguing for here really does happen.

Bud and Sylvia had only been attending the church I was pastoring in West Covina, California for a few months when Sylvia was diagnosed with cancer. Though in my ecclesial tradition water baptisms usually involve full immersion, I baptized Sylvia in the hospital, as she lay on her bed, with a styrofoam cup filled with tap water. And I was there with Bud in that hospital room a few days later when Sylvia, in the wee hours of the morning, passed from this life into the presence of the Lord. In due time, we conducted her funeral. After all the mourners had filed by the casket, paying their last respects to Sylvia and expressing their condolences to her stoic husband, Bud made his way to where I was stationed and threw his arms around me. He is a tall, strong man, whose hold on me that eventful day was firm. Then, with the side of his face pressed against mine, he began to sob deeply. Time passed. More than once I patted him on the back reassuringly. Still, he held on to me, his sobbing unabated. More time passed. I wondered how long this act of grieving would last. Then I sensed Jesus speaking to me, not audibly, but unmistakably, still. He said, "*Don't let go of him, Gary. Hang in there. He's not holding on to you. He's holding on to me.*"

26. Lischer, *Theology of Preaching*, 55–56.

Experiences such as this have convinced me that the phenomenon of the risen Jesus ministering to hurting people—through the words, actions, and presence of his followers—is a thing.[27] It is possible for people to sense Jesus in the room with them during the preaching/ministry moment. It is important for us preachers to never forget our humanity, to never act like we are more holy than we really are. But it is also important for us to show up, our humanity notwithstanding, simply doing our best to discern and obey the ministry promptings graciously provided by the Holy Spirit of God (see Gal 5:25). When we do, the Spirit of Jesus will sometimes make it possible for our hearers to experience a *spiritual* encounter with Christ himself.

Sacramental Sermons are Truly Transformative in Effect

Going further still, I also contend that fully Trinitarian, theologically real preaching is, ultimately, God-the-Father pleasing in its impact. This is because sacramental sermons do not merely inform and/or entertain (cf. Ezek 33:30–33); they leave a mark on those who "hear" them, one way or another (see 2 Cor 2:14–17). Speaking positively, not only can anointed preaching affect people soteriologically (see Rom 10:13–14; 1 Cor 1:21); it can also influence hearers in terms of their devotion (spirituality), sanctification (morality), and commitment to the *missio Dei* (missionality). This is because genuine spiritual encounters with God tend to have this transformative effect.

We find examples of this transformational dynamic throughout the Bible. For example, consider the record of Isaiah's visionary experience as depicted in Isaiah 6:1–12; Peter and James's experience of Jesus as depicted in Luke 5:4–11; and Paul's experience of Christ and the Spirit as depicted in Acts 9:1–22. Each of these encounters with a holy yet merciful God had the effect of enabling a spiritual, moral, and missional faithfulness that was not there before. If it be allowed that anointed sermons can have a sacramental, encounter-enabling effect,

27. See John 14:20; 15:18–20; Rom 18:18; 2 Cor 13:3; Eph 3:20–21; Phil 2:13; 2 Thess 1:1–12; 2 Tim 4:17.

then the upshot would be that such preaching should be expected to be transformative in nature.[28]

The late Tim Keller provided this understanding of why some sermons are truly transformative: "good preaching . . . doesn't tell you to go and change. Rather, it changes you on the spot because you begin to *encounter* something of such beauty that you just desire it and want to become it—you *want* to change."[29] With respect, I will offer that the reason why some sermons (those that are genuinely anointed) are transformative in effect is not simply because they enable hearers to encounter *something* of beauty, but *someone* (cf. Ps 27:4)!

It appears that Keller, himself, understood the personal nature of transformative beauty because of the way he insisted that every sermon must in some way "get to Jesus" for our preaching to be truly biblical, redemptive, transformative. [30] However, I will add that it is possible for those who listen to us preach to not only be confronted with the message about Jesus—all that he has done for us—but to encounter him in real time, in a christologically real manner through the unveiling, revealing, glorifying work of Christ's Spirit![31]

In sum, the apostle Paul knew that it was possible to preach with words given him by the Holy Spirit (Eph 6:19). This is genuinely anointed preaching. This is the kind of preaching God always intended: prophetic in nature, incarnational in manner, and truly transformative in effect.[32]

In the chapter that follows, we will explore whether my contention finds support in the history of preaching. Spoiler alert: it does!

28. Support for the notion that encounters with God are inherently transformative can also be found in Griffiths, *Preaching in the New Testament*, 91–92.

29. Greear, "Tim Keller's Friendship Transformed My Preaching," para. 7, emphasis added.

30. For more on the need for every sermon to get to Jesus and his arresting beauty, see Keller, *Preaching*, 56–63, 161–62.

31. See Matt 18:20; John 14:18; cf. 2 Cor 3:15–18.

32. Some hefty biblical-theological support for the thesis of this discussion can also be found in Griffiths, *Preaching in the New Testament*, 82–94, 125–30.

2

The Right Side of History

More Support for Sacramental Sermons

Until I come, devote yourself to the public reading of Scripture, to preaching and to teaching.

—1 TIMOTHY 4:13

THE SUGGESTION MADE IN the previous chapter that sacramental sermons are the products of genuinely anointed (prophetic, incarnational, truly transformative) preaching, and that this type of preaching is generated by a fully Trinitarian, "I-Thou" theology, is a bold one. If we are to embrace the notion that this is the kind of preaching God always intended, it would certainly help if this audacious thesis enjoyed the support of theologians and preaching practitioners down through the ages. Evidence of such support is precisely what I hope to provide in this chapter.

One might be tempted to think that this would be a simple matter. But the fact is that the genuinely anointed preaching of the word that turned the world upside-down in the first century (Acts 17:6) was not always prioritized by the church following the apostolic era.[1] A thesis put forward by Emil Brunner might explain why.

In *The Misunderstanding of the Church,* Brunner makes the provocative suggestion that the *ecclesia* we read of in the book of Acts and apostolic letters began to experience, in the early era of its existence, a dramatic transformation. What was originally a "spiritual fellowship" or Spirit-animated (charismatic) "communion of persons"[2] gradually morphed into something other, something much less. Brunner believed that something very precious was lost in this historical transformation of the charismatic/communal *ecclesia*—a fellowship energized by the Word and the Spirit—to the early Catholic and then the neo-Catholic church, which he describes in various ways as a very well-organized and salvation-dispensing institution.[3]

At the heart of this transformation, says Brunner, was an important shift in the way the church fathers understood the celebration of the Lord's Table. According to Brunner:

> it is possible to locate a point which might be regarded as the real point of departure for the emergence and crystallization of the new tendencies. That point . . . lies very near to the centre of the New Testament *Ecclesia,* and the change which takes place here consists in a very slight shift of emphasis which can be characterized by saying that what was very near to the centre becomes itself the centre: namely the sacred meal, the Eucharist. From being an act, perpetually repeated according to the Word of the Lord, by which the community seeks to realize itself as a fellowship with and in Christ, the festal meal becomes the essence of salvation itself and the thing which constitutes the community's life. While the Lord had given

1. For more on the preaching/teaching that occurred in the earliest days of the church, see Harrison, *Apostolic Church*, 159–66.

2. See Martin, *Worship in the Early Church*, 130–32; Harrison, *Apostolic Church*, 154–57.

3. "Neo-Catholic" is the way Brunner often referred to the Roman Catholic (Papal) Church that the early Catholic Church (which included Greek Orthodoxy) eventually morphed into. For a brief history of this transition from the *ecclesia* of the New Testament to the "church of the papacy" and then the Reformation, see Brunner, *Misunderstanding of the Church*, 94–96.

> it in order to emphasize the Word and Spirit through which He Himself is present, it now became the real decisive self-disclosure of the divine, depriving the Word of its centrality and therefore to an ever-increasing extent imparting to the meal itself the character of a holy thing; a process in the course of which the substantial physical elements, which originally had no independent significance and were only signs having a meaning merely as the material basis of the rite, became the real media of God's self-communication. In such a way the holy meal first became the "sacrament" and so the focal point of faith.[4]

In other words, Brunner's thesis was that it was not simply the gnostic heresies, imperial persecutions, and rapid growth of the movement that caused the *ecclesia* to, over time, morph into the institutional church, but that it was the way the ceremony of the Lord's Table became not just a rallying point for the emerging fellowship, but the means of saving grace (salvation) for each individual and then, the very reason for the existence of the church as a salvation-dispensing institution. We must note that Brunner presents a careful and thorough argument for how this shift from meal to sacrament explains the eventual emergence of priests, ordination, bishops, and canon law. His explicit concern is how this shift at the center has resulted in a rather dramatic loss of: (1) the charismatic and communal dynamics which the New Testament witnesses to in its depictions of church life; as well as (2) the apostolic emphasis we find in the New Testament on the preaching of the gospel. Brunner's summary of this institutional transformation and its effect on Christ's body merits a slow, careful reading:

> The episcopal administration of a sacramental grace places the Christian community in the position of a receiving laity; episcopal apostolic authority makes of them subjects who owe obedience. Only through this twofold dependence upon the Church ruled by bishops and priests can the individual attain salvation. Out of the "mystical" brotherhood rooted in the Word and the Spirit, out of the Body of Christ whose head is Christ Himself alone, and whose members therefore

4. Brunner, *Misunderstanding of the Church*, 74–75.

> are of equal status, out of the royal priesthood and holy nation has grown the Church—a totality composed of individual communities, each of which comes under the ecclesiastical jurisdiction of a bishop, who as administering priest stands opposed to the receiving laity because he controls the sacrament, the food of salvation, the sacral thing which holds together the individual components and makes them into a solidary collective.[5]

I draw attention to Brunner's thesis because it may explain, at least in part, why, in the writings of some church fathers, we find, on balance, more rhapsodizing over the Eucharist than theologizing regarding the preaching task.[6] Still, throughout the history of the Christian movement we find reasons to believe that the apostolic commitment to a fully Trinitarian, "I-Thou," theology which produces a prophetic, incarnational, and transformative manner of preaching was not completely lost, the supposed institutionalization of the church notwithstanding.[7]

Though the phrase "sacramental sermons" may not appear on every page, the history of homiletical theology is rife with allusions to preaching that, because it is grounded in a fully Trinitarian, "I-Thou" theology produces sermons that are prophetic in nature, incarnational in manner, and truly transformative in effect. In the next several pages I will curate for the reader a slew of these allusions. It is my hope that a perusal of these supportive references and insinuations will not only inform our theology of preaching, but also inspire us toward an eager, faithful pursuit of genuinely anointed preaching.

5. Brunner, *Misunderstanding of the Church*, 83.

6. The theologies of both Irenaeus and Ignatius, for example, have been described as Eucharist-centered. (See Hahn, "Eucharistic Theology of Early Church Fathers," paras. 4–16.) Support for the notion that early apostolic preaching morphed into something different in the dawn of the second century can be found in Carroll, *Preaching the Word*, 21–62.

7. For an excellent, book-length discussion of the apostolic-charismatic-prophetic preaching we find in the New Testament era, see Griffiths, *Preaching in the New Testament*.

ANOINTED PREACHING IN THE PATRISTIC ERA

My sense is that the early church fathers were especially concerned about church order, polemics, and theology in general rather than homiletical theology in particular. For example, while Irenaeus (ca. 130–202) wrote a book titled *On the Apostolic Preaching*, it was an explication of the message preached by Christ's apostles rather than a theology of preaching per se.[8] Moreover, church historian Henry Chadwick reports that, after the Montanist controversy played out, the church became so resistant to the idea that revelation was still occurring that Irenaeus was the last writer who could "still think of himself as belonging to the eschatological age of miracle and revelation."[9] That said, there are allusions to some church fathers who seemed to demonstrate an interest and passion in continuing the apostolic commitment to the Spirit-empowered preaching of the gospel we read about over and over again in the epistolary corpus of the New Testament.

Melito of Sardis (100–180 AD)

For example, one of the preachers of this era, Melito of Sardis, is said to have possessed a "reputable and prophetic character (one who was led in the Spirit),"[10] and was so Christocentric in his approach to preaching that he employed the stratagem of "speaking on behalf of Christ in the first person through direct appeal, beckoning the hearer to respond.[11] This might at first glance strike us as presumptive and overly enthusiastic. Or it could be that Melito had sensed Christ speaking through him and other preachers, making his appeal through them in an especially powerful, personal manner. While I am not in the habit of speaking for Christ in the first person, I think I know what Melito may have been referring to.

8. See Irenaeus, *On the Apostolic Preaching*.

9. Chadwick, *Early Church*, 53.

10. Hartog, "Melito of Sardis," 5.

11. Hartog, "Melito of Sardis," 77.

Basil of Caesarea (330–379 AD)

Apparently, so did Basil of Caesarea, who taught that "those who preach the gospel are the 'lips of Christ.'"[12] By this he meant that not only should "preachers possess virtuous character consistent with the virtues they preach," but they should also be committed to the idea that "to preach the Scriptures is to preach Christ," doing so in a way that "draws hearers to deeper worship of God and a passion for becoming more like God."[13]

John Chrysostom (347–407 AD)

Pressing on, something akin to an implicit pneumatological realism seems to have been at work in the much renowned preaching of John Chrysostom (the Golden Mouth), who believed and taught that "The Word, vivified by the Spirit, must be applied in the present situation and to the issues of the day. For this reason, the congregation should pray for the preacher and invoke the Spirit's empowerment."[14] One scholar sees evidence of Chrysostom's pneumatologically real reliance on the Spirit in the prayer that he uttered prior to preaching: "Almighty God, unto whom all hearts are open, all desires known, and from whom no secrets are hid; cleanse the thoughts of our hearts by the inspiration of your Holy Spirit, that we may perfectly love you, and worthily magnify your holy name, through Christ, our Lord."[15]

Saint Augustine (354–430 AD)

Augustine greatly influenced the preaching dynamic of his and succeeding eras by championing the idea that while the Bible provides the content, it is classical rhetoric that should dictate the "form and style" of

12. Morgan, "Basil of Caesarea," 123.

13. Morgan, "Basil of Caesarea," 123.

14. Wainwright, "Preaching as Worship," 325–36, as cited in Hartog, "John Chrysostom," 133.

15. Volz, "Genius of Chrysostom's Preaching," para. 5.

sermons.[16] However, we must also note that Saint Augustine was committed to preaching that is transformative in effect. Preaching scholar Paul Hartog says of Augustine: "While defending the use of rhetorical strategies in preaching, he was clear that eloquence was not the desired end but that changed lives were."[17] Hartog goes on to quote Augustine: "The very reason we teach is that it be acted upon. It is useless simply to persuade people about the truth of what we are talking about, and useless simply to entertain them by the way we speak, if what is said is not acted upon."[18]

These references give the impression that the earmarks of genuinely anointed preaching presented earlier in this work were in evidence in the preaching of the patristics. The question is: *can we find evidence of a commitment to genuinely anointed preaching in the succeeding generations?* Our survey continues.

ANOINTED PREACHING IN THE MEDIEVAL ERA

Providing some implicit support for Emil Brunner's provocative thesis, the editors of the helpful work *A Legacy of Preaching: Apostles to the Revivalists* acknowledge that during the medieval era "the reading and preaching of the Scriptures took a back seat to liturgical symbols."[19] At the same time, however, there were some preachers who resisted this move, seeking to revive a mode of preaching we might describe as genuinely anointed.

Bernard of Clairvaux (1090–1153 AD)

For example, we read that the sermons of Bernard of Clairvaux focused on "the experiential relationship between God and humanity,"[20] and

16. Long, "And How Shall They Hear?" 170–73, as cited in Willimon, *Conversations with Barth*, 47.

17. Smither, "Augustine of Hippo," 153.

18. Augustine, *Teaching Christianity*, as cited in Smither, "Augustine of Hippo," 153.

19. See Forrest et al., eds., *Legacy of Preaching*, 158.

20. See Hoare, "Bernard of Clairvaux," 179.

that his preaching beautifully exemplified a "heartfelt desire to be at one with God,"[21] which involved being "existentially present in Christ."[22] Language such as this implies a Trinitarian realism and an encounter-effecting sermonic aim.

Francis of Assisi (1181–1226 AD)

Another medieval preaching titan was St. Francis of Assisi. For years I have labored to counter the canard that Francis downplayed the importance of preaching. I was heartened, therefore, in the course of my research, to read the following:

> One popular quip about preaching, frequently attributed to Francis, is that preachers should "Preach the Gospel every day, and use words if necessary." While there is something to commend here about the emphasis on the life of the preacher as a tool for communicating the gospel, there is no evidence Francis ever said this. It is important to recognize this because, while he does commend the importance of living well, it contradicts the gospel message to which Francis was so committed. Living virtuously gives credibility to our spoken words, but teaching people to act nicer through our example will not save their souls, and this was the concern of Francis. He recognized that salvation came through an understanding and submission to the truth of Christ and his offer of grace told in the communication of the gospel.[23]

Due to the dramatic nature of Francis's conversion, and the fact that his theology flowed from his conversion experience,[24] I get the feeling that his theology was very definitely theologically real and "I-Thou," rather than "I-It" in nature. So was his "theology of preaching." Thomas of Celano, an early Franciscan disciple and the author of one of the earliest biographies of St. Francis, describes his preaching in this succinct manner: "His words were neither hollow, nor ridiculous, but

21. Hoare, "Bernard of Clairvaux," 181.

22. Hoare, "Bernard of Clairvaux," 185.

23. Holder, "Francis of Assisi," 194–95.

24. Horn, "Will the Real St. Francis Please Stand Up?," para. 13.

filled with the power of the Holy Spirit, penetrating the marrow of the heart so that listeners were turned to great amazement."[25] Moreover, Thomas of Celano also indicates that when instructing those in the order who were given permission to preach, St. Francis admonished them, "The preacher must first draw from secret prayers what he will later pour out in holy sermons. He must first grow hot within before he speaks words that are in themselves cold."[26]

It is no wonder, then, that Francis's sermons had the effect of producing life-transforming spiritual encounters with the risen Christ. Evidence for this assertion can be found in the writings of Ugolino Brunforte, yet another early Franciscan friar who collected some of the earliest traditions about Saint Francis. Referring to a sermon Francis once preached in Assisi, Brunforte reported:

> Saint Francis ascended the pulpit and began to preach in so wonderful a way on holy penance, on the world, on voluntary poverty, on the hope of life eternal, on the nakedness of Christ, on the shame of the passion of our blessed savior, that all those who heard him, both men and women, began to weep bitterly, being moved to devotion and compunction. And in all Assisi, the passion of Christ was commemorated as it never had been before.[27]

Here is the upshot: it would certainly seem that the preaching of St. Francis was genuinely anointed, and that in the manner defined in the previous chapter of this work!

John Huss (1369–1415 AD)

Near the end of the medieval era, preachers—such as John Huss in Prague and Girolamo Savonarola in Florence—evidenced in their preaching a return of the apostolic, prophetic voice, which would deeply affect, a century later, the pulpit ministries of Reformers such as Martin Luther, Ulrich Zwingli, John Calvin, and John Knox. Regarding

25. Horn, "Will the Real St. Francis Please Stand Up?," para. 9.
26. Horn, "Will the Real St. Francis Please Stand Up?," para. 14.
27. Horn, "Will the Real St. Francis Please Stand Up?," para. 15.

Huss in particular, one preaching scholar remarks: "Preaching a sermon is one thing: having something worthwhile to say in that sermon is another. John Huss was not only a preacher; he was a man with a message."[28] And where did that message come from? The Scriptures for sure, but there was also some pneumatological realism at work in Huss's homiletics. Another scholar reports this quote from Huss: "I preach the sacred Scriptures—not I, but principally the Holy Spirit."[29]

I cannot help but offer here that it makes all the difference in the world when we approach the preaching/teaching event believing to the core of our being that God is up to something in the lives of the people gathered, and he has made us a party to it. As for Huss, this sense was ongoing. We read of him that "Influenced and challenged by the writings of John Wycliffe, buoyed by a firm resolve to preach the Scripture, and determined to preach in the language of the people, Huss was no longer an obscure peasant—he became a thundering voice calling for biblical fidelity, moral purity, and ecclesiastical reform."[30] And yet, it was also true that, while Huss could preach from God's Word as someone who bore a Spirit-enabled, prophetic anointing, his concern was genuinely doxological and pastoral as well.[31] Once again, I will offer an experience-based perspective: a pulpit presence that is both prophetic and pastoral at the same time is not just intriguing but winsome. Such a presence is Christ-evincing; it reminds folks of Jesus of Nazareth!

ANOINTED PREACHING IN THE REFORMATION ERA

I have already indicated how that the preaching of the principal Reformers during this important era in the history of Christianity was influenced by pre-Reformation preachers such as Huss. This is why we find in the Reformation era an unvarnished attempt to recapture

28. Howell, "John Huss," 252.

29. Fudge, "Hussite Theology and the Law of God," 90, as cited in Schwanda, "Legacy of John Huss," para. 33.

30. Howell, "John Huss," 249.

31. Spinka, *John Hus at the Council of Constance*," 63, as cited in Howell, "John Huss," 254.

a theology and approach to preaching vividly reminiscent of that witnessed to in the New Testament.

Martin Luther

Of Luther we read that his theology changed dramatically in the course of his life, becoming much more personal, real, "I-Thou" in nature. This remarkable shift occurred because he had come to recognize "that this person, the God who had revealed himself in and as Jesus Christ, is a speaking God, and his speaking creates—and in forgiving sins, recreates—children out of sinners."[32]

This shift in Luther's theology from law to grace—from God as essentially impersonal to radically relational—significantly impacted his theology of preaching. His conviction that the preaching and teaching of God's word is "the most important part of the divine service" is well known.[33] But the theological basis for this conviction is too important not to highlight. One Luther scholar seems to echo aspects of Brunner's provocative thesis and my own when he suggests that Luther's new

> appraisal of public preaching rested on his understanding of God as a being who is in conversation with his human creatures, a conversation that creates the community that links them to him and to each other. Luther regarded God's Word as the instrument or agent of his creative and sustaining will. As God had spoken the worlds into existence in Genesis 1, so also the Word of the gospel in Jesus Christ created sinners anew, refashioning them into his children. He also believed that God's Word, and thus his saving activity, takes place through oral, written, and sacramental forms of the Word. God was truly present as coauthor when the prophets and apostles wrote the Scriptures, and he is present in its use as the Holy Spirit guides its proclamation throughout the history of the church. For Luther, the sermon was one of the most vital instruments of the Holy Spirit's fostering of repentance, bestowing forgiveness of sins, and empowering the godly life

32. See Kolb, "Martin Luther," 282.

33. Kolb, "Martin Luther," 286.

> of the reborn child of God. His sermons made clear that God was at work in his hearers' minds and hearts as the Word came from the pulpit.[34]

Surely this excerpt is evocative of the elements and earmarks of genuinely anointed preaching proffered in the previous chapter.

John Calvin

The homiletical theology of another magisterial Reformer, John Calvin, also provides support for the thesis of this book. Reminding his readers that the Second Helvetic Confession states that "the preaching of the Word of God *is* the Word of God," Calvin scholar Anthony Lane clarifies that while Calvin never made this assertion himself, he would have agreed with it.[35] Lane then goes on to indicate Calvin's high view of preaching by asserting that, though the Reformer saw a parallel between preaching and the sacraments (i.e., the word preached and the word made visible via ceremony), he did not view them as equal in terms of ministry importance. Referring to the importance of the "sacramental word," says Lane, Calvin offered that, since the ceremony requires the word in order to function as a sacrament, "it is wrong to celebrate the sacraments without explanatory preaching, but it is all right to preach without celebrating a sacrament."[36] Lane also draws attention, more specifically, to Calvin's support for the phenomenon of prophetic preaching by citing Calvin: "God chooses to speak to us not directly, not through angels, but through human beings. This is a singular privilege that he deigns to consecrate to himself the mouths and tongues of men in order that his voice may resound in them."[37] In sum, we find in Calvin an especially hearty endorsement for the prophetic

34. Kolb, "Martin Luther," 287.

35. See Lane, "John Calvin," 352.

36. Lane, "John Calvin," 352–53, citing in the process Calvin, *Institutes of the Christian Religion*, 4:14:1–6. I will have more to say about Calvin's view of the relation of preaching to the sacraments in chapter 3. See also Larson, "John Calvin On the Sacraments," 2, 11.

37. Lane, "John Calvin," 353, citing Calvin, *Institutes of the Christian Religion*, 4:1:5.

nature of genuinely anointed preaching and, hence, the phenomenon of sacramental sermons.

ANOINTED PREACHING IN THE POST-REFORMATION ERA

At the risk of oversimplification, and with the assistance of the *Encyclopedia Britannica*, I offer that, after the Reformation era (1517–1648), Protestantism developed in several different directions. *Protestant Orthodoxy* understood Christianity as essentially a system of doctrines, and thus its emphasis was on "right doctrine." [38] There were both Lutheran and Reformed versions of Protestant Orthodoxy, which is also referred to as Protestant scholasticism. *Pietism*, on the other hand, was a "religious reform movement that began among German Lutherans in the 17th century. It emphasized personal faith against the main Lutheran church's perceived stress on doctrine and theology over Christian living."[39] A third movement, *Puritanism*, was much influenced by German Pietism but can be understood more precisely as "a religious reform movement in the late 16th and 17th centuries that sought to 'purify' the Church of England of remnants of the Roman Catholic 'popery' that the Puritans claimed had been retained after the religious settlement reached early in the reign of Queen Elizabeth I."[40] Finally, elements and aspects of both Pietism and Puritanism converged in the eighteenth and nineteenth centuries into yet another movement known as *Revivalism,* which can be understood as "a movement in some Protestant churches to revitalize the spiritual ardour of their members and to win new adherents," but which also emphasized "personal religious experience, the priesthood of all believers, and holy living, in protest against established church systems that seemed excessively sacramental, priestly, and worldly."[41] All this to say that in this next section of our survey, we will discover some more evidence for my suggestion that

38. "Protestant Orthodoxy," para. 1.
39. "Pietism," para. 1.
40. "Puritanism," para. 1.
41. "Revivalism," para. 1.

sacramental, encounter-effecting sermons, really is the kind of preaching God always intended.

William Perkins (1558–1602)

In his tremendously influential book *The Art of Prophesying*, Puritan preacher William Perkins advised that the best sermons are those where the Spirit's empowerment is apparent. He explained: "The 'demonstration of the Spirit' (1 Cor 2:4) becomes a reality when, in preaching, the minister conducts himself in such a way that everyone—even those who are ignorant of the gospel and are unbelievers—recognize that it is not so much the preacher who is speaking but the Spirit of God in him and by him."[42]

John Owen (1616–1683)

Another famous Puritan churchman, John Owen, also provided some salient support for this book's thesis that genuinely anointed sermons can and will be encounter-enabling in their effect. In a chapter titled "John Owen: Preaching for the Glory of God," Henry M. Knapp says about Owen: "Reflecting again his Puritan roots, public worship in Owen's mind was never merely a question of correct form or the performance of specific rites; rather, true worship is intertwined with the worshipper's experience of God."[43] Then Knapp proceeds to indicate Owen's commitment to the idea that fostering an encounter-rich experience of Christian worship is what Christian preaching is all about. He avers that, according to Owen:

> True communion with the triune God—and, hence, communion with the divine Persons—is best expressed by his people in and through their worship together. The primary benefit of worship is the believer's communion with God, and this communion-in-worship goal directs true preaching. True biblical preaching, as part of godly worship, is manifest in

42. Perkins, *Art of Prophesying*, 73, as cited in Millioni, "William Perkins," 374.
43. Knapp, "John Owen," 400.

> one's communion with God, and any preaching which does not foster this divine experience, no matter how rigorous or doctrinally attentive, is false worship.[44]

Knapp summarizes his treatment of Owen's approach to preaching thusly: "committed to a heart-warming, experiential communion with his God, Owen's preaching wove together the most prevalent themes of his era. Led always by the Spirit, attentive to the needs of the flock and beginning in his or her heart and life, the pastor proclaims the Word in worship, for communion with the triune God and for his glory."[45]

Philipp Jakob Spener (1635–1705)

Eventually the writings of English Puritans reached the European continent and gave rise to a Dutch Pietism, which then produced a German Pietism.[46] When, as a young pastor/seminarian, I was introduced to the book *Pia Desideria* or "Pious Desires" by Philipp Jakob Spener, it hugely affected my philosophy of ministry. First, I found Spener's critique of the training of ministers in the German universities to be both bold and incisive. As a seminarian who loved my graduate studies, I needed to be reminded of the need for my preaching to be genuinely anointed rather than merely erudite. Author, pastor, and musician Julian Pace explains the situation Spener was reacting to:

> It was not that the clergy were poorly educated. Indeed, the average Lutheran clergyman had received rigorous training in Biblical languages, systematic theology, and logical reasoning, yet for all this training and knowledge, the preaching of many a Lutheran clergyman during Spener's day was dull and ineffective.
>
> Sermons had become highly academic affairs where pastors would wax eloquent over the most minor of theological matters. They would often lapse into long soliloquys [*sic*] in foreign languages the common people [had] little hope of understanding. Sermons were often seen as opportunities for the

44. Knapp, "John Owen," 400.
45. Knapp, "John Owen," 408
46. "Pietism," para. 3.

> pastor to show off their rhetorical prowess with little thought given to whether the sermon would be of any practical value to the laity. Sermons were primarily informational and rarely transformational.[47]

Thus, it can be argued that it was a commitment to the notion that genuinely anointed sermons can and will be truly transformative that caused Spener to veritably beg the Lutheran church to overhaul the training of its ministers. This concern might indicate an awareness on his part of a major earmark of genuinely anointed preaching.

With this thought in mind, the second way in which *Pia Desideria* hugely impacted me was Spener's call for churches to gather members into "conventicles" or small groups so that members might engage in "communal Bible reading, prayer and mutual support, and admonition."[48] To be more specific, however, these small group meetings were more than generic Bible studies. For Spener, their actual purpose was to encourage and enable church members to meet and engage in a prayerful discussion of the Sunday sermon (and the biblical passage[s] it was based on) so as to actually apply it to their lives (see Jas 1:22–25)! For reasons that I will discuss in chapter 7, I am convinced of the very real importance of helping congregation members engage in a regular, prayerful, communal processing of the sermons their Lord inspires their church leaders to deliver. Early in my theological journey, the Lord used Spener and *Pia Desideria* to form this conviction in me.

As it happens, Pietism as a religious phenomenon is not viewed by everyone in a positive manner. Still, I contend that, while a focus on personal piety can lead to something I refer to as "Christian Pharisaism," it need not. When grounded in the message of grace, and therefore pursued in a theologically real, prayerful, communal manner, it can result in a grace-embracing and grace-extending lifestyle that renders to God the spiritual, moral, and missional faithfulness he desires and deserves.[49]

47. Pace, "On Pietists and Preaching," paras. 4–5.

48. Olson and Winn, *Reclaiming Pietism*, 39.

49. For more on Christian Pharisaism and how to avoid it, see Tyra, *Defeating Pharisaism*.

Jonathan Edwards (1703–1758)

Is there any indication that the preaching of the eighteenth-century revivalists in America and England also aimed at being prophetic, incarnational, and truly transformative? Not surprisingly, there is!

Jonathan Edwards scholar Gerald McDermott offers that this famous instigator of the Great Awakening in America was thoroughly committed to the concept of anointed preaching, describing him as having believed that it "was necessary that the preacher beg God's Spirit to inspire his preparation and enliven his words," and that "Power came from God's blessing, without which even labored preparation and enthusiastic delivery would produce no lasting results."[50]

John Wesley (1703–1791)

For his part, John Wesley's preaching has been described as "missional" even though it occurred long before that term came into vogue. One scholar suggests that Wesley's conversion to a "living faith," which was productive of what I have referred to as a pneumatological posture of expectancy (rather than presumption or indifference), tremendously influenced not only the message but also the manner of Wesley's pulpit ministry. Michael Pasquarello opines: "This eighteenth-century form of missional preaching was accompanied by surprising manifestations of God's power, as listeners were awakened and moved to vital faith by the work of the Spirit through the ministry of the Word."[51] More specifically, it is reported that the preaching of both John Wesley and George Whitefield at times produced the phenomenon of speaking in tongues.[52]

In addition to this dynamic type of proclamation, Wesley was led by the Spirit to encourage converts to engage in several types of communal meetings (society, class, and band) as a "necessary means of cultivating a faith active in love for God and love for neighbor—holiness

50. McDermott, "Jonathan Edwards," 463.

51. Pasquarello, "John Wesley," 481.

52. Bridgers, *American Religious Experience*, 8.

of heart and life."[53] Well known is the role the pietism of the Moravians played in Wesley's conversion toward an evangelical faith.[54] Even though it may be true that Wesley "in his own mind, lived and died an Anglican,"[55] I will humbly suggest that we see in Wesley the effect of what might be described as an inexorable, Spirit-prompted pull away from an overly institutional/ceremonial conception of the church toward the more charismatic/communal *ecclesia* of the Apostolic era. I will have more to say about Wesley's impact on my understanding of the need to help congregants prayerfully, communally process the preaching and teaching they receive in the final chapter.

ANOINTED PREACHING IN THE NINETEENTH CENTURY

The volume of support in the nineteenth century of the Christian era for preaching that can be described as prophetic, incarnational, and truly transformative is significant, as the following citations and quotations will indicate.

Phoebe Palmer (1807–1874)

Phoebe Palmer was a game-changer in several ways. She was not only a powerful woman preacher but a pioneer in evangelical social action. One description of her ministry legacy reads:

> During her life . . . Palmer spoke to over 100,000 people about Jesus and sparked a revival that brought nearly a million people into the church. Her influential theology paved the way for such modern holiness denominations as the Church of the Nazarene and the Church of God (Anderson, Indiana), and for Pentecostalism as well. . . . But Palmer did more than talk about Jesus. She put his love into action in New York

53. Pasquarello, "John Wesley," 481.

54. Pace, "Pietist Credentials of John Wesley," paras. 1, 7.

55. Marsh, "Was Wesley an Anglican?," 203–4.

> City's worst slum, pioneering a new kind of incarnational philanthropy.[56]

Another summary of Palmer's life says of her that she "was profoundly influential on the way many people, both in Methodism and beyond, thought about the Christian life. She is seen as someone who links the 18th-century 'revival preaching' associated with John Wesley, with the 20th-century Pentecostalism that began at Azusa Street in 1905."[57] Palmer's Trinitarian realism, and the effect it had on her ministry, is evident in her testimony, which included these words:

> I know that the Holy Spirit, the Comforter has come! And has taken up His abiding residence in my heart—inciting me ceaselessly to every good word and work, and giving me a longing desire for the spiritual benefit of those around me—enabling me also to call upon God with a confidence heretofore unknown or unfelt, being assured that it is the principle of holy life within me, [giving expression to] my petitions and enabling me to exercise faith for the fulfillment of the promises. Glory be to the Triune God for such a salvation![58]

There is little doubt that Phoebe Palmer's preaching effused the aroma of the "special sauce" at work in genuinely anointed preaching.

Catherine Booth (1829–1890)

The same can be said about the preaching of groundbreaking female preacher Catherine Booth, co-founder, along with her husband, William, of the Salvation Army. It was said of Catherine that "Her authority for preaching came from the prompting of the Holy Spirit in her life. And the thousands who heard her preach recognized that authority."[59] Citations such as this provide support for my contention that it is not only the wisdom, courage, and compassion of Jesus that the Holy Spirit

56. White, "Holiness Fire Starter," para. 2.

57. John, "Heroes of the Faith," para. 8.

58. Palmer, *Way of Holiness with Notes by the Way*, 89, as cited in "Phoebe Palmer," para. 4.

59. Green, "Catherine Booth," 90.

will enable his followers to embody, but in some sense his authority as well.

B. H. Carroll (1843–1914)

It may surprise some to discover that B. H. Carroll, the founder of Southwestern Baptist Theological Seminary, also seemed to know a thing or two about prophetic preaching. He once opined: "An inspired man, when he speaks, does not speak his will: when he writes, he does not write his will, but he speaks and writes for God, being moved by the Holy Spirit."[60] As a result, a duo of preaching history scholars have written: "In Carroll's understanding, the preacher was God's spokesperson. They [*sic*] literally spoke for God and represented God on earth. Therefore, what the preacher said and did was as God's representative."[61]

ANOINTED PREACHING IN THE TWENTIETH CENTURY

It is acknowledged by many today that the "secularization theory," which asserted that, due to the increasing influence of modernization, religiosity would diminish, has proved not to be true.[62] In this section we may be stumbling upon at least one of the reasons why: genuinely anointed preaching. The support in the contemporary era for my understanding of the kind of preaching God always intended is especially vibrant.

Karl Barth (1886–1968)

It is well known that, as a young pastor, Karl Barth experienced what can be referred to as the "preacher's dilemma," the desperate need to not only have something to say but "something pressing, interesting,

60. Carroll and Cranfill, *Sermons and Life-Sketch of B. H. Carroll,* 110 as cited in Matz and Sutton, "B. H. Carroll," 262.

61. Matz and Sutton, "B. H. Carroll," 263.

62. Thuswaldner , "Conversation with Peter L. Berger," paras. 1–2.

and engaging to say."[63] Deeply disappointed at the support many of his liberal theological mentors gave to the Kaiser's aggressive war policy,[64] and the way his liberal theological training in Germany had not adequately prepared him to engage in the preaching task, he "began a fresh reading of the Bible."[65] He discovered what he referred to as: "the strange new world of the Bible." He began to see that "the Bible is the rumbling of an earthquake, the thundering of ocean waves. . . . This "strange, new world" did not simply want to speak to our world; it wanted to destroy and rebuild our world by the inbreaking of 'the world of God.'"[66] If this is true, then the preaching of God's word cannot help but possess a prophetic element. Commenting on the understanding of God that Barth's fresh reading of the Bible produced in him and his preaching, William Willimon writes:

> "Prophetic," in a biblical sense, means more than simple expressionistic "disruption" of the present order. It means disruption of the present order by the invasion of a specific presence, a God who has an identity and specific demands, a God whom we cannot make into anything we please, a God with a name and a face, Jesus. The remedy against the tendency toward idolatry is not the vague and mysterious, generic "God" who is no God but rather a vision of and a receptivity to the true and real God who comes to us in complex but specific triunity. . . . Without God as an active agent, preaching, biblical preaching really is impossible.[67]

A more passionate exponent of the importance of a Trinitarian realism to preaching is hard to imagine! Moreover, Willimon continues:

> Barth thundered forth that preaching is interesting, as a form of communication, for primarily theological rather than rhetorical reasons. Preaching is the Word of God. As preachers, we must speak God's word. That is a frightening task, particularly

63. Willimon, *Conversations with Barth*, 14. See also Ott, *Theology and Preaching*, 17.

64. Baum, *Twentieth Century*, 9.

65. Willimon, *Conversations with Barth*, 14.

66. Willimon, *Conversations with Barth*, 14.

67. Willimon, *Conversations with Barth*, 34.

> on a weekly basis. Yet we must not begin with the preacher, with the preacher's words, or with our fears. We must begin in faith, specifically, faith in a God who speaks.[68]

We must also, I contend, embrace the reality that because of the incarnation of Christ, and the working of the Holy Spirit, we cannot only *understand* God in an "I-Thou" manner but *experience* him thusly as well.[69] As it happens, I have written elsewhere about the implicit support I see in the work of Karl Barth for the notion of prophetic preaching that plays out in a sacramental manner.[70] My argument is that, while Barth never professed a Pentecostal experience, his theology provides Pentecostals with some implicit support for the notion of prophetic preaching that is sacramental in effect. Here I will only highlight some of the foundational components of that argument.

First, Barth's pneumatological realism can be discerned in passages that indicate the importance of the Holy Spirit to the task of theology. Here's but one example:

> Only the Spirit himself can rescue theology! He, the Holy One, the Lord, the Giver of Life, waits and waits to be received anew by theology as by the community. He waits to receive from theology his due of adoration and glorification. He expects from theology that it submit itself to the repentance, renewal, and reformation he effects. He waits to vivify and illuminate its affirmations which, however right they may be, are dead without the Spirit.[71]

In other places, Barth spoke directly to the importance of the Holy Spirit to Christian living. For example:

> To receive the Spirit, to have the Spirit, to live in the Spirit *means being set free and being permitted to live in freedom.* . . .To have inner ears for the Word of Christ, to become thankful for His work and at the same time responsible for

68. Willimon, *Conversations with Barth*, 47.

69. See Torrance, *Reality and Evangelical Theology*, 23.

70. See Tyra, "From Sola Scriptura to the Sacramental Sermon,"141–81; Tyra, "Revelation as Encounter."

71. Barth, *Evangelical Theology*, 57.

> the message about Him and, lastly, to take confidence in men for Christ's sake—*that is the freedom which we obtain, when Christ breathes on us, when He sends us His Holy Spirit*. If He no longer lives in a historical or heavenly, a theological or ecclesiastical remoteness from me, *if He approaches me and takes possession of me*, the result will be that I hear, that I am thankful and responsible and that finally I may hope for myself and for all others; in other words, that *I may live in a Christian way*. It is a tremendously big thing and by no means a matter of course, to obtain this *freedom*. We must therefore every day and every hour pray *Veni Creator Spiritus* [Come, Creator Spirit] in listening to the word of Christ and in thankfulness. That is a closed circle. We do not 'have' this freedom; it is again and again given to us by God.[72]

Second, there is also evidence in Barth's writings for his belief that preaching can and must rise above the level of mere human discourse. There is a kind of preaching that is *prophetic* in the sense that it creates the possibility of a personal *encounter* between the sermon's hearers and a speaking God. Barth wrote:

> Proclamation is human speech in and by which God Himself speaks like a king through the mouth of his herald, and which is meant to be heard and accepted as speech in and by which God Himself speaks and therefore heard and accepted in faith as divine decision concerning life and death, as divine judgment and pardon, eternal Law and eternal Gospel both together.[73]

Third, this prophetic understanding of preaching derives from Barth's view of revelation as an *encounter*. Barth scholar Trevor Hart explains: "Revelation, as Barth never tires of reminding his readers, is an event; it is something which happens, something which God does, and something in which we are actively involved."[74] Moreover, when God, in his freedom, graciously speaks in a self-revelatory

72. Barth, *Dogmatics in Outline*, 138–39, emphasis added.

73. Barth, *Church Dogmatics* I/1, 52. See also "Word of God in Biblical Theology" in Griffiths, *Preaching in the New Testament*, 9–16.

74. Hart, "Revelation," 45.

manner to his creatures, this results not simply in instruction—cognitive knowledge—but *encounter*—relational knowledge, a "personal knowing of God."[75]

Fourth, Barth also insisted that the encounter-effecting Word of God takes three forms: the living, the written, and the proclaimed.[76] Much more will be said about this important Barthian assertion in subsequent chapters but for now the point is that it suggests that the Word of God real or living (Christ) can be experienced not only through the Bible but through biblical preaching as well.

Fifth, the Word of God proclaimed—i.e., genuinely anointed preaching—can be sacramental in the way it plays out. Early in his career, Barth wrote: "The best preaching is as such an equivalent to the kerygma that the Roman Catholic church offers every day in the form of the sacrament of the altar."[77] Barth scholar Aaron T. Smith interprets Barth thusly: "Whereas for Rome, the presence of God is mediated in the Eucharist, *that presence is encountered in Reformation theology in the event of the sermon*."[78] Meanwhile, as I pointed out in chapter 1, another Barth scholar, Thomas Christian Currie, interprets Barth in a very similar manner, saying:

> Barth describes this proclamation event in . . . *sacramental* language. Any reference to sacrament does not begin with the Lord's supper or baptism, Barth maintains, but begins with *Jesus Christ and his ongoing presence* in the life of the Christian community *through the work of the Spirit*. This broader view of sacramental presence, not only includes Scripture and preaching, but renders baptism and the Lord's Supper dependent on the gospel, on the proclaimed and heard Word of God.[79]

Finally, sixth, for Barth, true proclamation involves something akin to the phenomenon of *incarnation* (at least, in a functional,

75. Hart, "Revelation," 42.

76. Barth, *Church Dogmatics* I/1, 88–124.

77. Barth, *Göttingen Dogmatics*, 31, as cited in Smith, *Theology of the Third Article*, 85.

78. Smith, *Theology of the Third Article*, 85, 114–15.

79. Currie, *Only Sacrament Left to Us*, 20. Quotation is from Barth, "Need and Promise of Christian Preaching," 114, emphasis added.

encounter-enabling sense).[80] At the very least, his language is certainly evocative of the incarnation when he writes of preaching:

> The willing and doing of proclaiming man, however, is not in any sense set aside in real proclamation. As Christ became true man and remains true man to all eternity, real proclamation becomes an event on the level of all other human events. . . . But as Christ is not just true man, so it is not just the willing and doing of proclaiming man. It is also and indeed it is primarily and decisively the divine willing and doing. Precisely for this reason the human element is not set aside. What seems to be the burning question of the nature of the co-existence and co-operation of the two factors is a highly irrelevant question. God and the human element are not two co-existing and co-operating factors. The human element is what God created. Only in the state of disobedience is it a factor standing over against God. In the state of obedience it is service of God. Service of God does not have to be removed in order that God Himself may be honoured in it.[81]

Obviously, neither the preacher nor his or her sermon is ontologically divine. But that does not rule out the possibility that something divine may be occurring during genuinely anointed preaching—the Spirit of Jesus making it possible for sermon auditors to encounter the spiritual presence of Jesus in and through the preaching event.

These are only highlights of my argument that Barth's theology lends some implicit support for the notion of Spirit-empowered, prophetic preaching that is sacramental in the sense of being encounter-enabling in its effect.

Dietrich Bonhoeffer (1906–1945)

I contend that, perhaps due to the direct influence of Barth, the homiletical theology of German pastor/theologian Dietrich Bonhoeffer was also very supportive of the notion of sacramental sermons. In one of his own homilies, Bonhoeffer revealed the Trinitarian realism at work

80. Barth, *Church Dogmatics*, I/1, 94.

81. Barth, *Church Dogmatics* I/1, 94.

in his theology, and therefore, his essentially prophetic understanding of preaching:

> This is what makes a sermon something unique in all the world, so completely different from any other kind of speech. When a preacher opens his Bible and interprets the Word of God, a mystery takes place, a miracle: the grace of God, who comes down from heaven into our midst and speaks to us, knocks on our door, asks questions, warns us, puts pressure on us, alarms us, threatens us, and makes us joyful again and free and sure. When the Holy Scriptures are brought to life in a church, the Holy Spirit comes down from the eternal throne, into our hearts, while the busy world outside sees nothing and knows nothing about it—that God could actually be found here.[82]

Moreover, in one of his lectures on preaching, delivered in his underground seminary, Bonhoeffer explained:

> *The sermon derives from the incarnation of Jesus Christ and is determined by the incarnation of Jesus Christ.* It does not derive from some universal truth or emotional experience. The word of the sermon is the incarnated Christ. The incarnate Christ is God. Hence the sermon is actually Christ. God *as* human being. Christ *as* the word. As the Word, Christ walks through the church community."[83]

D. Martyn Lloyd-Jones (1899–1981)

Pressing on, we also see a Trinitarian realism and embrace of an as encounter-enabling preaching in the homiletical theology of the well-known British evangelical preacher D. Martyn Lloyd-Jones. His view of the purpose of preaching has been described thusly: "Conversion was vital, as was the transformation of the individual through the

82. Bonhoeffer, *London, 1933–1935*, as cited in Clements, "Dietrich Bonhoeffer," 311.

83. Bonhoeffer, *Theological Education at Finkenwalde, 1935–1937*, 509–510, emphasis original, as cited in Clements, "Dietrich Bonhoeffer," 311.

presence of God mediated via the proclaimed Word in the Power of the Spirit."[84] Indeed, Lloyd-Jones placed much importance on the "unction" provided by the Holy Spirit. In his book *Preaching and Preachers*, he boldly explained the effect of a Spirit-enabled unction:

> It gives clarity of thought, clarity of speech, ease of utterance, a great sense of authority and confidence as you are preaching, an awareness of a power not your own thrilling through the whole of your being, and an indescribable sense of joy. You are a man possessed, you are taken hold of, and taken up. I like to put it like this—and I know of nothing on earth that is comparable to this feeling—that when this happens you have a feeling that you are not actually doing the preaching, you are looking on. You are looking at yourself in amazement as this is happening. It is not your effort; you are the instrument, the channel, the vehicle: and the Spirit is using you, and you are looking on in great enjoyment and astonishment. There is nothing that is in any way comparable to this. That is what the preacher himself is aware of.[85]

Though some have viewed this description of Spirit-enabled unction with not just reserve but actual disdain,[86] I will humbly offer my amen to it. Many times, have I experienced precisely what Lloyd-Jones spoke of. What is more, I am convinced that, if we let him, the Holy Spirit will deign to provide this preaching unction time and again. While it cannot be conjured, it is something we preachers can and should hope to experience as we allow our sense of pneumatological expectancy (rather than presumption or indifference) to influence the way we approach the preaching task.[87]

John Stott (1921–2011)

The need for a sense of expectancy in the heart of the preacher and the congregation was something that another British churchman

84. Trueman, "D. Martyn Lloyd-Jones," 328.
85. Trueman, "D. Martyn Lloyd-Jones" 326.
86. Trueman, "D. Martyn Lloyd-Jones" 330.
87. For more on this see Gambo, *Spirit-Empowered Witness*, 126–29.

and scholar John Stott also believed in wholeheartedly. In a sermon about preaching, the ever evangelical Stott defined the endeavor this way: "To preach is to open up the inspired text with such faithfulness and sensitivity that God's voice is heard and God's people obey him."[88] Later in that same sermon, Stott revealed the theological realism that was at work in his understanding of the homiletical task, as well as the importance of a posture of pneumatological expectancy rather than presumption or indifference:

> How different it is when both preacher and people are expecting to hear the voice of God and they've come to church in order to hear God's voice addressing them. Why then the whole situation is transformed and the atmosphere becomes electric. The people bring their Bible to church, and when they open it for the lesson or for the sermon, they sit on the edge of their seats or pew hungrily waiting for the Word of God. And the preacher also prepares in such a way that he is expecting God to speak. He prays beforehand in his study that God will come and address His people. He prays again before he enters the pulpit. He prays again, maybe, before he begins to preach. And then when the sermon is finished, he prays again that God will speak to the congregation, that the Holy Spirit will move from person to person to person, addressing them with His own still, small voice.[89]

Once again, I will have more to say later on about how preachers might be intentional about enabling congregations to approach the preaching moment with a sense of hopeful anticipation. At this point, I will simply observe that, apparently, one does not have to be a professing Pentecostal or Charismatic to intuitively recognize the importance of a fully Trinitarian, "I-Thou" approach to the preaching task. No wonder the secularization theory foundered!

88. Stott, "Privilege of Preaching," para. 6.

89. Stott, "Privilege of Preaching," para. 38.

ANOINTED PREACHING IN THE TWENTY-FIRST CENTURY

The veracity of the observation presented above is demonstrated, I believe, in the way at least one prominent preaching expert in our contemporary era, who, even though he does not identify as a Pentecostal-Charismatic, still seems to know a thing or two about the special sauce crucial to genuinely anointed preaching. The preacher I have in mind is William Willimon, a theologian who has also served as a bishop in the United Methodist Church, professor of Christian ministry at Duke University, and dean of Duke Chapel. I will conclude this historical survey with some citations from Willimon's very helpful book titled *Proclamation and Theology*, published in our own era.

Early in this book, Willimon, having described the powerful preaching of John Wesley, essentially lays his cards on the table with respect to the topic at hand:

> If you have never had your soul seized by God in a sermon, if you have never been surprised that through the frail, inadequate, poorly delivered, not fully comprehensible words of an ordinary woman or man preaching your life was changed, if you have never been swept away by the rush of divine revelation coming to you in a homily, then you may think that this talk about God speaking in preaching sounds silly.
>
> Yet for the multitudes, which no one can number—who have been enlisted in God's great movement to take back the world, all those who heard their name called by God through a preacher, all those who risked life itself on the basis of nothing more than words heard in a sermon, the saints who have gone before us and who even now stand among us—the preached word has been, still, the very Word of God.[90]

Then, as if to make his message sure and certain, Willimon continues:

> I'm saying that God in Christ became incarnate in John Wesley's sermons. The Almighty God, who hung the stars and flung the planets in their courses, came close to humanity in

90. Willimon, *Proclamation and Theology*, 9.

> the preaching. The evidence for that outrageous claim is not in Wesley's sermons. The evidence is in the people he produced through his preaching, or more accurately, in the undeniable work God did though a preacher named Wesley. Our God talks, and talks a great deal, mainly through preaching.[91]

Apparently, Willimon believes in the possibility of sermons functioning in a prophetic, incarnational, truly transformative manner!

And yet, I believe it is possible to be even more specific. First, let us focus on the prophetic aspect of genuinely anointed preaching. As a former bishop in the United Methodist Church, we would expect Willimon to be a fan of the preaching of Wesley, but early in *Proclamation and Theology* Willimon also refers appreciatively to the way John Calvin, in one of his sermons, "dared to speak of contemporary pastors as prophets."[92] Then, in an ensuing chapter titled "The Prophetic Word," Willimon cites still other Christian theologians (such as Martin Luther and Karl Barth)[93] to make his case for the phenomenon of prophetic preaching. He then states boldly that

> we contemporary preachers are heirs to the great prophetic tradition of Israel and the church. Prophets in the Bible are not those who peer into the future and predict events that other people don't see (which is how they are mischaracterized by some in evangelical Christianity and pop culture). Nor are prophets carping social critics a bit to the left of the Democratic Party (as they are misconstrued by some in liberal Christianity). Prophets are those who have been assaulted by, and are now obsessed with, the truth of God. Prophets are those who have unusual gifts for discernment into the purposes of God and who are unusually bold in bringing those purposes to speech.[94]
>
> Rarely are divine words directly spoken. Most of the time they require an intermediary, some human being to speak for God. This God rarely works solo. Rather, this God tends to summon

91. Willimon, *Proclamation and Theology*, 9.
92. Willimon, *Proclamation and Theology*, 16.
93. Willimon, *Proclamation and Theology*, 19.
94. Willimon, *Proclamation and Theology*, 22.

> and enlist ordinary women and men to speak for God. Those who are thus summoned are called prophets.[95]

Once again, allow me to be clear: this emphasis on the "prophetic" in preaching does not in any way suggest an experience of divine revelation that bypasses or downplays the importance of the written word. The idea is the word and Spirit in balanced ministries. Or, put differently, it is possible to approach the preaching task with a theologically real, "I-Thou" understanding of God and his word in place. Here is how Willimon expressed this synergistic dynamic that lies at the heart of the sacramental sermon phenomenon:

> Every preacher, in turning toward Scripture as a source for a sermon, is turning toward a living, speaking personality in documentary form that opens its arms toward us and rushes out to meet us in order to speak to us, through us, so that the church might be lifted up and transported to where God is.[96]

But I am arguing that anointed preaching is not only prophetic in nature, but incarnational in manner. Is there any evidence that Willimon embraces this notion as well? There is. Later in *Proclamation and Theology,* he explains:

> The Incarnation is the great mystery that makes preaching possible. As we have stressed earlier, preaching is a divinely wrought, miraculous act. Preaching is God's speech. Preaching is God's chosen means of self-revelation. If a sermon "works," it does so as a gracious gift of God, a miracle no less than the virginal conception of Jesus by the Holy Spirit. One reason why Christians tend to believe in the likelihood of miracles like the virgin birth of Jesus or the resurrection of Christ is that we have experienced miracles of a similar order, if not similar magnitude, in our own lives as we have listened to a sermon. Something has come to us from afar; something has been born in us that we ourselves did not conceive. A word has been heard that is not self-derived. It's a mysterious, undeserved gift. It's a miracle. Thus preaching is theological not

95. Willimon, *Proclamation and Theology*, 23.

96. Willimon, *Proclamation and Theology*, 35.

> only in its substance but also in its means. Preaching is not only talk about God but miraculous talk by God.[97]

Though Willimon is careful to provide some badly needed nuance—a reminder that "at the same time, preaching is an utterly human, mundane, carnal, and fleshly thing"—the fact remains that prophetic, Christ-evincing preaching happens![98] Again, I contend we must be careful to distinguish between an ontological understanding of such incarnation and one that is functional. The latter means not that preachers and sermons are ontologically divine in the sense that Jesus was, but that, driven by the same impulse at work in Christ's incarnation, God comes near again and again via genuinely anointed sermons, near enough to effect powerful spiritual encounters between people with ears to hear and the risen Jesus.

Then, Willimon pulls all the loose ends together when he states plainly that, just as the purpose of Christ's incarnation was not simply to identify with us, but to heal our humanity, ultimately, the goal of sacramental sermons is changed, transformed, empowered lives.

> In Jesus of Nazareth, we have experienced God among us in a way that is sacramental. Even as bread and wine become signs of God's self-giving, the Body and Blood of Christ as received in the congregation, so the sermon is a sort of sacrament of the Word. . . . We preachers long to connect the Word with the hearts and minds of our congregations because it is of the nature of this God to connect. Our pastoral care and pastoral visitation among our people is thus related to our preaching. The Christian faith is never some disembodied spiritual affair. The Word is meant to be heard, embodied, performed, and enfleshed. Bonhoeffer's most eloquent sermon was preached from the Nazi gallows.
>
> Therefore we preachers, in our sermons, perform the word—seeking through our words, movements, gestures, and tone of voice to incarnate the biblical word—so that our congregations might embody the Word and the Word might dwell

97. Willimon, *Proclamation and Theology*, 55–56.
98. Willimon, *Proclamation and Theology*, 56.

> in them richly. That means that every sermon is meant to be a summons, a call, a vocation toward Incarnation. . . . Through our illustrations, stories, references, and connections, we demonstrate that One who was fully God and fully human means fully to be with us as we are so that we might become as he is, so that the Word might be embodied even in us. . . . We preachers seek to perform the Word in our sermons so that the congregation might perform the Word in the world.[99]

This survey has demonstrated, I trust, that throughout the history of the Christian movement there have been theologians and preachers who, despite the process of ecclesial institutionalization, were moved by the Holy Spirit to engage in preaching that is prophetic, incarnational, and truly transformative. I contend such preaching can be considered sacramental, and wonder if this is not the kind of preaching God always intended.

In the final (third) section of this book, we will explore further the difference which the elements and earmarks of genuinely anointed preaching will make in the planning and delivery of sermons that aim at hearing and honoring the heart of God. But before we do that, we need to wrestle with another important matter: the very real need for contemporary preachers to dedicate themselves to the kind of preaching this book is about.

99. Willimon, *Proclamation and Theology*, 60–61.

PART TWO

The Need for Sacramental Sermons

3

Sacramental Sermons and Our Secular Age

I would like to learn just one thing from you: Did you receive the Spirit by the works of the law, or by believing what you heard?

—Galatians 3:2

Several years ago, I was working in the second-floor office of the church I was pastoring when my secretary alerted me that a woman was downstairs, hoping to see me though she did not have an appointment. I instructed my secretary to send the woman up. Greeting this visitor at the top of the stairs, I ushered her into my office and offered her a seat.

After introducing herself to me, this mature woman with a kind smile and intelligent eyes came straight to the point. Leaning forward in her chair, she said, "Pastor, I've been to a lot of churches that could tell me about God. I'm wondering if this is the kind of church that can help me experience him."

In response to this very honest, straightforward query, I smiled and said, "I'd like to think so." Thus began a yearlong mentoring relationship that resulted in the baptism and spiritual formation of a retired community college professor who, though part of a post-Christian culture, was at the same time very hungry for an authentic, personal, *experiential* relationship with God. I did not realize it at the time, but what occurred in this woman's life was a sort of prison break—a breaking out of a culturally pervasive state of mind that the Canadian philosopher Charles Taylor refers to as the "immanent frame."

Though the secularization theory referred to in the previous chapter has been found wanting by some prominent sociologists and theologians (e.g., Peter Berger, Harvey Cox),[1] this does not mean that secularization in the sense of cultural pressure to focus on mundane rather than spiritual realities does not happen. Indeed, it does. The question is: *Is secularity in the sense just described invincible, or can people caught in its grip be delivered from it?* I am reminded of G. K. Chesterton's observation: "At least five times, therefore, with the Arian and the Albigensian, with the Humanist sceptic, after Voltaire and after Darwin, the Faith has to all appearance gone to the dogs. In each of these five cases it was the dog that died."[2] What I hope to do in this chapter is discuss the role that genuinely anointed preaching can play in helping people, like the woman referred to above, break free of our culture's current commitment to the notion that nothing matters but the natural, the temporal, the material, the secular.

AN OVERVIEW OF CHARLES TAYLOR'S ARGUMENT

In his highly lauded opus *A Secular Age*, Charles Taylor masterfully explores the root and fruit of contemporary secularity. In doing so, Taylor laments the disenchanting of reality he attributes at least in part to the Protestant Reformation's promotion of rationalism over against the mysticism associated with Roman Catholicism. According to Taylor, the radically secular age we currently inhabit is due in large part to this overcorrection.

Rather than presume that all the readers of this work are familiar with Taylor's prodigious analysis of modern secular culture, I will provide here a brief synopsis of it, doing my best, whenever possible, to retain (and explain) Taylor's iconic verbiage.

1. See Reaves, "Peter Berger and the Rise and Fall of the Theory of Secularization," para. 1. See also Cox, *Fire from Heaven*, 104–5.

2. Chesterton, "Five Deaths of the Faith," para. 10.

Excarnation is the term by which Taylor refers to the denial in the modern era that "embodied feeling"—one's emotions, intuitions—can be a way in which persons sense or experience "something higher," something transcendent (e.g., God).[3] More specifically, excarnation refers to "the transfer of our religious life out of bodily forms of ritual, worship, practice so that it comes more and more to reside 'in the head.'"[4] In other words, some professing Christians overintellectualize the faith. Such a de-sacramentalizing, de-spiritualizing, philosophizing move, says Taylor, along with Protestantism's emphasis on the freedom of the individual conscience, set in motion the eventual emergence of the Enlightenment, deistic religion, modern science, and our contemporary secular age where everyone exists as a "buffered self" within an "immanent frame."

Taylor's *immanent frame* refers to "a constructed social space, where instrumental rationality is a key value, and time is pervasively secular . . ." Thus, the ambiance of our existence as moderns is completely secular rather than sacred; "this frame constitutes a 'natural' order, to be contrasted to a 'supernatural' one, an 'immanent' world over against a possible 'transcendent' one."[5]

Meanwhile, the *buffered self* is the condition of people who, because they exist in a modern, enlightened world that has been disenchanted, are no longer "open and porous and vulnerable to a world of spirits and powers."[6] Put simply, *in a secular age people are constrained to think of themselves as purely material beings existing in a purely material world.*[7]

3. Taylor, *Secular Age*, 288, 293, 554–55.

4. Taylor, *Secular Age*, 613.

5. Taylor, *Secular Age*, 542.

6. Taylor, *Secular Age*, 27.

7. And yet, it is important to note at this point that "Taylor argues that the meaning of the word secular has at least three different senses in our contemporary context. The first two are obvious enough—'a sphere differentiated from the sacred, as when the church is separated from the state,' or 'the results of the historical process of secularization, such as a decline in belief in God or religious practice.'" But there is also a third sense of secular: "a cultural context in which religious belief has come to be understood as one contested option among others." (See Keane, "Philosopher for a Secular Age," para. 2.) I take this to mean that, according to Taylor, it is "permissible" to be piously devoted to a variety of ideas and causes as long as (1) the beliefs

However, says Taylor, while it is true our current *social imaginary*[8] (in the industrialized West) is earmarked by a rather strident commitment to an *exclusive humanism*,[9] many of us, even the most irreligious of us, the truth be known, can be haunted, afflicted by a deeply felt malaise due to the absence in our lives of anything transcendent.[10] In other words, even though our current, culturally pervasive (collective) worldview has embraced the notion that human flourishing here and now should be one's main if not only focus, many members of our society are haunted by the nagging feeling that there is (or should be) something more to our existence than the laws of nature.

Without a belief in an *enchanted universe*, (a world that has room for the supernatural),[11] this haunting has produced two versions of an *expressive individualism*—i.e., two ways for moderns to be religious in a secular way—endeavoring in a rational manner to fully realize their humanity within the immanent frame. Romanticism's quest for *authenticity*[12] calls for us to lean into our authentic (animal) self, understood as

driving this piety/devotion are rational rather than irrational, and (2) one does not insist that one's beliefs are true in an objective rather than subjective manner.

8. To be more precise, this term refers to "the way we collectively imagine, even pre-theoretically, our social life in the contemporary Western world" (Taylor, *Secular Age*, 146). Put differently, it is a pervasive understanding (presumption) of the right way for a society to function (Taylor, *Secular Age*, 172). One gets the sense that a "social imaginary" ends up functioning more broadly as a collective worldview—a shared take on how the world works and the best way for individuals and societies to navigate their way in and through it.

9. Exclusive (or self-sufficing) humanism occurs when the goal of human flourishing becomes a person's or culture's exclusive focus and does so without the person or culture imagining that any other ultimate concern might be a possibility. See Taylor, *Secular Age*, 18–20.

10. Taylor describes the *haunting* as "a sense in our culture that with the eclipse of the transcendent, something may have been lost" with the result that "our actions, goals, achievements, and the like have a lack of weight, gravity, thickness, substance. There is a deeper resonance which they lack, which we feel should be there." Taylor, *Secular Age*, 307.

11. To be more precise, an *enchanted view of the universe*, says Taylor, allows for a world "filled with spirits, some of whom are malign." Taylor, *Secular Age*, 27.

12. Taylor describes the *culture of "authenticity"* as "the understanding of life which [suggests] . . . that each of us has his/her own way of realizing our humanity, and that it is important to find and live out one's own, as against surrendering to conformity with a model imposed on us from outside, by society, or the previous generation, or religious or political authority." The call here is to "find yourself,

a pleasure-seeking, pain-avoiding creature of nature. The other option involves a search for a personal, transcendent sense of meaning and fulfillment via a fervent commitment to one or more activist causes.[13] So, the idea seems to be that many people living in our secular age—not religious in a spiritual sense but still haunted by the possibility of, and need for, some sense of meaning and purpose in their lives—have either turned inward, seeking to find and give expression to their true, authentic selves, or have devoted themselves in a quasi-religious, even fundamentalist, manner to an activist cause or movement bigger than themselves. I suspect that most of us know of folks—friends, family, neighbors, co-workers—who fall into one or the other of these two categories. Sadly, they are very fervent in their pursuit of existential meaningfulness yet lack the sense of shalom (genuine inner peace) that only a sincere, personal faith in Christ brings (Rom 5:1). This creates a sense of drivenness that resembles religious obsession. What is more, their devotion to their socially approved-of pursuit(s) threatens to make them impervious to the notion of finding their true selves in Christ, since this requires faith in the traditional pre-Enlightenment sense. Moreover, the post-Christian sensibility of being "over" Christianity and "done" with the church can be especially pungent in the case of those who have history with the faith but have been disappointed by the church and/or individual Christians.

Secularism is here to stay, says Taylor, but he also speaks of those in history who "broke out of the immanent frame; people who went through some kind of 'conversion.'"[14] Thus, there is a way *not* to be secular, our current cultural milieu notwithstanding. Taylor's method of choice for this liberation seems to involve a conversion back to "a social imaginary that animated Europe in the past."[15] He implies as much when he makes the following assertion: "The hold of the former Christendom on our imagination is immense, and in a sense, rightly

realize yourself, release your true self, and so on." See Taylor, *Secular Age*, 475.

13. Taylor, *Secular Age*, 696–97. See also the discussion of two forms of nonreligious fundamentalism currently at work in our culture—a disenchanted model of social justice and a disenchanted form of social preservation—in Johns, *Re-Enchanting the Text*, 51–53.∂

14. Taylor, *Secular Age*, 728.

15. See James K. A. Smith, *How (Not) to be Secular*, 134.

so. So the sense can easily arise, that the task of breaking out of the dominant immanentist orders today is already defined by the model of Christendom."[16]

Though this is not all that Taylor is about, it would seem that he is suggesting that the way forward is to head backward, to re-embrace the Christianity of the pre-Reformation era: not all its doctrines, mind you, but its mystique, its rites and rituals that convey to us an experience of the transcendent. More specifically, because of the way Taylor attributes the dynamic of *excarnation* to the Protestant Reformation,[17] which eventually resulted in a "de-communioned," "de-ritualized," and "disembodied" version of religion,[18] it is possible to hear in Taylor an implicit call for a *reconversion* to a sacramentalism, at the center of which is a fully *incarnated* eucharistic observance.

PROTESTANT RESPONSES TO TAYLOR'S DIAGNOSIS

Interestingly, Taylor's cultural diagnosis has been very influential among many Protestant theologians and church leaders. From James K. A. Smith's *How (Not)* to *Be Secular: Reading Charles Taylor*, to Andrew Root's *Faith Formation in a Secular Age: Responding to the Church's Obsession with Youthfulness,*[19] to an anthology edited by Collin Hansen and produced by the Gospel Coalition titled *Our Secular Age: Ten Years of Reading and Applying Charles Taylor,*[20] Protestant theologians and churchmen have interacted with Taylor's massive tome in a critically appreciative manner, hoping in the process to help contemporary Christians in the West escape the influence of the *secularity* so very pervasive in the current era, and then encourage their cultural peers to do likewise.[21]

16. Taylor, *Secular Age*, 734–35.

17. Taylor, *Secular Age*, 611, 614.

18. See Smith, *How (Not) to be Secular,* 58. It should be noted that Smith goes on to associate this de-ritualized version of Christianity with "much contemporary Protestantism," especially the "liberal stream" and "progressive evangelicals." See also Taylor, *Secular Age*, 614.

19. Root, *Faith Formation in a Secular Age.*

20. Hansen, ed., *Our Secular Age.*

21. Once again, I direct the reader's attention to some recent Pew Research

For example, James K. A. Smith suggests that we evangelicals must recover a sacramentalism that, while not necessarily *re-incarnated*, has been *re-inspired* and is therefore *inspiring*. For sure, this is only part of Smith's response to Taylor, but referring to this as a "Reformed catholicity,"[22] Smith suggests that having recognized "the disenchantment and excarnation of evangelical Protestantism" while at the same time rejecting the "Christianized subtraction stories of liberal Christianity" and feeling "the pull of more incarnational spiritualities," evangelicals might "move toward more Catholic expressions of the faith." This is key, according to Smith, precisely because "these expressions of the faith will actually exert more pull on those who have doubts about their 'closed' take on the immanent frame"[23] than scholastic apologetic approaches that essentially focus merely on rationalistic (intellectual) argumentation.[24] In other words, Smith contends that, rather than continue to engage in a logic-based apologetics, a return to a more mystical, sacramental, liturgical approach to worship is the critical missional move evangelical Christians must make if we want to push back against the stranglehold the immanent frame has on so many of our secular contemporaries. According to one reviewer of Smith's seminal work, *Desiring the Kingdom: Worship, Worldview, and Cultural Formation*, at the heart of Smith's argument are these assertions:

- "man is a loving thing before he is a thinking thing";
- an apologetic based on rational arguments "is flawed because man is not primarily a thinker";
- since "man's loves are shaped by the bodily," not by the conceptual, it is through a regular engagement in rituals—embodied practices—that our affections are formed;

Center polling which suggests that the post-Christian dynamic referred to in these pages may be slowing. (See Smith et al., "Decline of Christianity in the U.S. Has Slowed.") Still, I contend that the concerns of the many Protestant theologians and church leaders alluded to above are valid, and that our current ministry context in the West should be considered essentially post-Christian. The question is: how best to respond to it?

22. Wax, "Mission in a Secular Age," para. 17.

23. Smith, *How (Not) to be Secular*, 138–39.

24. See Wax, "Mission in a Secular Age," paras. 19–22.

- on the one hand "the historic liturgies of the church are a way to regularly train our affections and loves for the kingdom of God";
- on the other hand, "the world also trains our loves by means of liturgies"—e.g., "going to the mall" or "singing the national anthem"—that can produce commitments to things and ideas that compete with the kingdom of God (e.g., consumerism or nationalism);
- this is why "the gathering of the church is to be a place where the true story is told in such a way that it . . . counter-forms us so that we desire the kingdom of God rather than the kingdom of this world with its multitude of competing idols";
- "the church does this through its liturgies and not just by giving information . . . What is needed to counter-form us is not just a shaping of the intellect (although that may be part of it), but rather a shaping of our loves that is inculcated in part by the physical aspects of the church's liturgies."[25]

Furthermore, toward the goal of a "re-inspired" sacramentalism, a growing number of contemporary voices are insisting that such a move requires not only a re-enchanted understanding of Christian worship, but the world as well. For his part, Smith interprets Taylor thusly: "While the Reformers rightly sought to reject superstition, the result was that they sort of de-sacramentalized creation and Christian worship. The world become [*sic*] ontologically 'flat' rather than, as Gerard Manley Hopkins put it, 'charged with the grandeur of God.'"[26] This perspective lies at the heart of the call for a *sacramental ontology* of creation.

Space will not allow for a thoroughly nuanced discussion of the various approaches Protestant theologians have taken toward an understanding of the natural world as sacramental. At the risk of oversimplification, one view holds that the world is sacramental in the sense that the real presence of God can be experienced through it because it owes its existence to, points to, and participates in divine realities.

25. Kelley, "James K. A. Smith," 4–6.

26. Justin Taylor, "Interview with James K. A. Smith," para. 22. See also Smith, *Desiring the Kingdom*, 143–44.

Another view goes further, and holds that the world is essentially sacred itself, thoroughly infused and animated by the Spirit of God. According to both of these approaches, a reinspired sacramentalism that reliably effects genuine, transformative encounters with God's presence will necessarily entail post-Enlightenment ontology that does not deny the supernatural or even drive too deep of a wedge between the natural and the supernatural. A sacramental ontology is necessary if, absent an embrace of the Roman Catholic doctrine of transubstantiation, contemporary Christians are to experience Christ's real presence via natural sacramental media (water, wine, bread, etc.).[27]

To be honest, because of my embrace of an *evangelical* (evangel- or gospel-centered) understanding of how we come by grace, and my predilection toward a relational rather than magical understanding of the way sacraments work, I am a bit ambivalent about the need for a sacramental ontology that underwrites the robust sacramentalism of Roman Catholicism, Eastern Orthodoxy, and a growing number of other Protestants (including Pentecostals). Instead, my focus is on the way a *pneumatological realism* underwrites the ability of Christians to embody or "live into" a Pauline, fully Trinitarian, "I-Thou" *lifestyle spirituality*, and the role *sacramental sermons* play in that process.

ANOTHER WAY (NOT) TO BE SECULAR

Though I believe Taylor is right about the fact that not all the results of the Reformation have been advantageous, I contend the problem lies deeper than an "excarnation" dynamic that elevated the rational over the liturgical, turned God into a concept, and reduced faith to mere mental assent. Another profoundly fundamental issue is the *pneumatological deficit* that was referred to my Introduction. This critical theological deficiency was codified by the scholastic Reformers and is still present in many churches (even some Pentecostal-evangelical ones).[28] Thus, I contend that the first step in helping church members break

27. For a concise yet accessible and helpful discussion of the differences between these two approaches to a sacramental ontology, see Johns, *Re-Enchanting the Text*, 55–80, 86–87.

28. For more on this see Tyra, *Getting Real*, 53–55.

free of the immanent frame, becoming less secular and consumerist in their faith and much more missionally impactful as a result, is to help them *live into* a biblically informed, Christ-honoring doctrine of the Holy Spirit, forging an existentially impactful, *lifestyle spirituality* in the process. For sure, an engagement in liturgy/sacraments can aid in helping church members cultivate this spirituality. However, for such an engagement to effect a genuine, transformative encounter with Christ, genuinely anointed preaching is required.[29] And, foundational to genuinely anointed preaching is the embrace of a pneumatological realism.

Once again, at the heart of my proposal for a pneumatological realism is the contention that it is possible for Christ's followers to experience the Spirit of God in ways that are real—i.e., personal, interactive, and phenomenal—rather than merely theoretical, conceptual, or ritualistic. Moreover, these interactions with the Spirit can and will prove to be both *epistemologically helpful*—i.e., revelatory in terms of God's love, will, and purposes (Eph 1:17; 3:16–19; Col 1:9; 1 Cor 2:6–16)—and *existentially impactful*—i.e., transformative, life story-shaping, and ministry-engendering (Gal 5:22–23; Col 1:10–12).[30]

However, due to the tendency in some theologies to overly immanentize the Spirit, conceptualize the Spirit, and radically minimize the role the Spirit plays in Christian discipleship, it is not uncommon for contemporary church members to view the Holy Spirit merely as a sanctifying force they can simply *presume* to be at work in their lives because they have engaged in this or that religious ritual (e.g., baptism, confirmation, the laying on of hands, the Lord's Table). "Traditioning" apart from a realist understanding and experience of the Spirit makes it possible for church members to refer to the third person of the Trinity

29. Commenting on the "anointing" referred to in 1 John 2:20, biblical scholar I. Howard Marshall opines that the apostle had this in mind. (See Marshall, *Epistles of John*, 153.) Moreover, Marshall is careful to indicate that "It is unlikely that the picture of anointing was derived from some actual act of anointing with oil, whether at the baptism of new converts or at some later point, although there is evidence that this practice developed at a later stage." (See Marshall, *Epistles of John*, 153–54.) It would seem, then, that John had a realist, immediate rather than a ceremonially-mediated experience of the Holy Spirit in mind when he spoke of this anointing.

30. For more on this, see Tyra, *Getting Real*, 21–22. For a discussion of the connections between a pneumatological realism and ones that are philosophical and more generally theological in nature, see Tyra, *Getting Real*, 16–33.

when reciting the creed, singing hymns, and so forth, while at the same time possessing an attitude of *presumption* (or even *indifference*) toward him. Indeed, speaking practically, a presumptive posture toward Christ's Spirit can occur even in ecclesial settings where a sacramental ontology is officially given the nod. What is missing in an ecclesial environment influenced by an essentially non-realist pneumatology is an adequate, practical understanding of:

- the Holy Spirit's personhood and relationality;
- the Holy Spirit's agency;
- the Spirit's immediacy;
- how important the Spirit is to absolutely *every* aspect of the Christian life;
- why Christ's followers can and should *expect* to experience the Spirit in ways that are sometimes *phenomenal* in nature (i.e., immediate, and evident to the senses);
- why church members can hope to, through the Spirit, interact with the risen Christ in existentially impactful, life story-shaping ways; and
- the pivotal role the Holy Spirit plays in empowering a bold, prophetic, faithful, and fruitful Christian witness.[31]

While these truths must be taught as well as caught, it *can* happen. The history of Christian preaching and teaching tells us so. Indeed the New Testament itself bears witness to the instrumental connection between preaching and the experience of Christ's Spirit. The epigraph for this chapter reads: "I would like to learn just one thing from you: Did you receive the Spirit by the works of the law, or by believing what you heard?" (Gal 3:2).

When you think of it, a *realist* understanding and experience of the Holy Spirit is the antithesis of a buffered self, existing in an immanent frame within a disenchanted world. This, by itself, should be reason enough to conclude that the key to helping church members *not*

31. For a book-length treatment of the Holy Spirit's role in Christian witness, see Tyra, *Holy Spirit in Mission*.

be secular is ultimately pneumatological in nature. And yet, I will go on here to drill down a bit more deeply into why this is so.

Harvey Cox, Pentecostalism, and the Failure of the Secularization Theory

Early in his career, Harvey Cox—the Hollis Research Professor of Divinity at the Harvard Divinity School—had welcomed the "great secularization" that was expected to occur once modernity had arrived. In his book *The Secular City: Secularization and Urbanization in Theological Perspective,* Cox essentially applauded the impending demise of religiosity, celebrating "the advent of secular urban civilization and the retreat of traditional Christianity."[32] Cox insisted that this development would "liberate men from the religious superstitions of the past and turn their attention, as the God of Genesis intended, to fashioning the world around them."[33]

However, Cox would eventually recognize that something else occurred during the twentieth century that made possible a *resurgence of religion.* Even as more and more people were becoming increasingly disenchanted with traditional religion, they were also losing faith in the alternative: "the pseudoreligions of technical advancement and rational enlightenment." Not content with either secularization or traditional religion but still feeling "a desperate need for credible values and a spiritual center," many of the "urbanized masses" of the world began to search for a third alternative.[34]

In his *Fire from Heaven: The Rise of Pentecostal Spirituality and the Reshaping of Religion in the Twenty-First Century,* Cox elaborates upon the nature of this third alternative:

> These traumatic cultural changes created a radically new religious situation. Most churches fumbled their efforts to respond to it. Conservatives dug in and insisted that dogmas were immutable and hierarchies indispensable. Liberals tried

32. Tedeschi, "Religion in the Secular City, by Harvey Cox," para. 1. This article is a critical review of Cox, *Secular City.*

33. Tedeschi, "Religion in the Secular City, by Harvey Cox," para. 1.

34. Cox, *Fire from Heaven,* 104.

> to adjust to the times but ended up absorbing so much of the culture of technical rationality that they no longer had any spiritual appeal. But the pentecostals, almost by accident it sometimes seems, found a third way. They rebelled against creeds but retained the mystery. They abolished hierarchies but kept ecstasy. They rejected both scientism and traditionalism. They returned to the raw inner core of human spirituality and thus provided just the new kind of "religious space" many people needed.[35]

Cox is obviously making a connection here between Pentecostalism's emphasis upon spiritual experience and the kind of spirituality most conducive to the conditions on the ground during the era of late modernity. Indeed, in *Fire from Heaven*, Cox makes the provocative suggestion that, given the cultural changes that have transpired in the West in recent years, Pentecostal spirituality may be the best hope for the reshaping of religion in our time and the future. Commenting in an affirming manner on the spread of Pentecostalism around the world, he asserts,

> Pentecostalism has succeeded because it has spoken to the spiritual emptiness of our time by reaching beyond the levels of creed and ceremony into the core of human religiousness, into what might be called "primal spirituality," that largely unprocessed nucleus of the psyche in which the unending struggle for a sense of purpose and significance goes on.[36]

Put differently, Cox believes that there exists at the core of human beings a very basic, profound need to encounter something transcendent to their creaturely existence—i.e., God. Endeavoring to explain why so many discontented people are inspired by the story of the first Pentecost, Cox writes:

> It is about the experience of God, not about abstract religious ideas, and it depicts a God who does not remain aloof but reaches down through the power of the Spirit to touch human hearts in the midst of life's turmoil. It should come as

35. Cox, *Fire from Heaven*, 104–5.

36. Cox, *Fire from Heaven*, 81.

> no surprise, therefore, that in our present time of social and cultural disarray . . . pentecostalism is burgeoning nearly everywhere in the world.[37]

According to Cox, Pentecostalism affects its adherents in a way that is very important. It provides a *primal spirituality* that includes a capacity for: *primal speech*—the ability to speak to God from the heart bypassing the constrictions of human language (a post-postmodern experience of ultimate Reality if you will); *primal piety*—the ability to experience the presence of God and express devotion to him in deeply satisfying ways that disregard modern societal conventions; and *primal hope*—the ability to maintain "an unshakable expectation of a better future" despite all rational indications (or cynical fears) to the contrary.[38] The implication is that many people living in this late-modern era, haunted by the desire to experience some sort of transcendence, have and are experiencing it through a form of Christian faith that takes Spirit-empowerment seriously.

Cox seems to present some significant support for what Pentecostalism may contribute to the "overcoming-secularity" conversation. And yet, with respect, I believe that Cox has it only partly right. In truth, it is not simply a *primal spirituality* that a pneumatological realism can help church members experience, but a *fully Trinitarian, "I-Thou," lifestyle spirituality* as well! And this is certainly *not* a distinction without a difference! There is a biblically informed, Christ-honoring, and Spirit-empowered spirituality that cultivates within practitioners the holy habit of praying again and again: "Ok, God, what are you up to now and how can I cooperate with you in it?" This is the very opposite of being trapped within an immanent frame!

The Key to Embodying a Pneumatological Realism in Everyday Life

What is more, the spirituality of which I speak is not based upon the latest fad but on the letters penned by the apostle Paul in which we may

37. Cox, *Fire from Heaven*, 5.

38. Cox, *Fire from Heaven*, 81–82.

discern the basic *convictions*, *commitments*, and *customs* that animated the spirituality he himself practiced and promoted. This understanding of Paul's spirituality begins with a consideration of how he prayed for the readers of his letters. For instance, in his letter to the Colossians Paul wrote:

> For this reason, since the day we heard about you, we have not stopped praying for you. We continually ask God to fill you with the knowledge of his will through all the wisdom and understanding that the Spirit gives, so that you may live a life worthy of the Lord and please him in every way: bearing fruit in every good work, growing in the knowledge of God . . . (Col 1:9–10)

As indicated in a previously published work, my contention is that *the practice of Christian spirituality can and should involve our learning how to live into (embody) this Pauline prayer.* It is not about obeying a particular list of rules, observing a particular collection of rituals, or engaging in a particular register of practices. The focus is, instead, on an ongoing Holy Spirit-enabled "I-Thou" interaction with Christ the Son which results in a *lifestyle* or *way of being in the world* that pleases God the Father.

Talk about embodiment! Just imagine for a moment the possibility of a *lifestyle spirituality* that enables church members to render to God the spiritual, moral, and missional faithfulness he desires and deserves. Such a spirituality is radically transformative not only in the lives of practitioners but to the regnant social imaginary as well.

In Part Three of this book, I will have more to say about the why, what, and how of this Pauline lifestyle spirituality and the way it can and will affect the preaching task. In what remains of this chapter, we will consider the way its practice can enable us to help our cultural peers escape the immanent frame.

TOWARD A SPIRIT-EMPOWERED, MISSIONALLY IMPACTFUL RESPONSE TO OUR SECULAR AGE

What do we do with the possibility that many of our cultural peers might, like the retired community college professor who came to see me in my office, be eager to *experience* a kind of Christianity that enables an intimate, interactive relationship with God? While a commitment to *traditioning* them via a re-inspired engagement in the sacraments and liturgical worship is certainly an option, I am convinced that the deliberate cultivation of ecclesial environments that engender a pneumatological expectancy (rather than presumption or indifference) is key to helping people break free of the immanent frame and enter into a vibrant, Spirit-empowered, missionally impactful walk with Christ.

Taylor argues that when our cultural contemporaries convert from belief to unbelief, it is not because of the scientific evidence; rather it is because the story science tells, presented as not only a more sensible one, but more mature as well, is more attractive for psychological reasons. Who does not want to sit among the adults at family holiday gatherings? Who does not want to take "the stance of maturity, of courage, of manliness, over against childish fears and sentimentality"?[39] The current crop of "evangelistic" atheists not only attempt to make the case for naturalism; they also belittle and demean the Christian faith at every turn. The main message of their "subtraction stories" is this: you must be either a psychological weakling or a moron to believe what the Christian church is selling. This "framing" of the stories has implications, says Taylor. "If our faith has remained at the stage of the immature images, then the story that materialism equals maturity can seem plausible."[40] Commenting on this theme, James K. A. Smith helpfully explains:

> Such tales of maturity and "growing up" to "face reality" are stories of courage—the courage to face the "fact" that the universe is without transcendent meaning, without eternal purpose, without supernatural significance. So, the convert to unbelief has "grown up" because she can handle the truth

39. Taylor, *Secular Age*, 365.

40. Taylor, *Secular Age*, 365.

> that our disenchanted world is a cold, hard place. At the same time, the claim is that there can be something exhilarating in this loss of purpose and teleology. If nothing matters, and we have the courage to face this, then we have a kind of Epicurean invulnerability. While such a universe might have nothing to offer us by way of comfort, it is also true that "in such a universe, nothing is demanded of us." Now the loss of purpose is also a liberation: "*we* decide what goals to pursue." God is dead; *viva la revolution!*[41]

Then Smith concludes:

> If Taylor is right, it seems to suggest that the Christian response to such converts to unbelief is not to have an argument about the data or "evidences" but rather to offer an alternative story that offers a more robust, complex understanding of the Christian faith. The goal of such witness would not be the minimal establishment of some vague theism but the invitation to *historic, sacramental* Christianity.[42]

I am convinced, along with Smith, that Taylor is right about the fact that something more is needed than intellectual arguments if we are going to reach our secular, post-Christian peers. (Harvey Cox is saying the same thing!) I also support any Spirit-enabled, biblically informed approach to Christian worship that succeeds in helping church members cultivate a Christ-honoring *habitus* or way of being in the world.[43] And yet, I will go on to humbly wonder aloud whether some of the calls for a focus on liturgical traditioning are not in need of some fine-tuning. More specifically, it is the dyadic pairing of "historic" and "sacramental" that I feel the need to nuance. Perhaps what is needed is a missional "embodiment" of a Christianity that is not only *historic* and *sacramental* but *pneumatologically real* as well.

41. Smith, *How (Not) to be Secular*, 77–78, emphasis original. Quotation is from Charles Taylor, *Secular Age*, 367.

42. Smith, *How (Not) to be Secular*, 77, emphasis added.

43. Smith, *Imagining the Kingdom*, 140.

Needed: A Both-And Versus Either-Or Approach

My proposal regarding another way to help folks break free of the immanent frame does not mean to suggest that an enthusiastic engagement in the sacraments and pneumatological realism are mutually exclusive. They most certainly are not. However, I believe it is possible to practice a sacramentalism in a way that lacks a sufficient degree of pneumatological expectancy. Smith seems to acknowledge this himself when he quotes Taylor's admission that the same poetic language that can stir those within the immanent frame to wonder about the possibility of something transcendent can cease to do so. "The language may go dead, flat, become routinized, a handy tool of reference, a common place, like a dead metaphor, just unthinkingly invoked."[44] Smith then continues: "The same risk attends religious, liturgical language: the prayers 'can become dead, routine.'"[45]

Moreover, some liturgical theologians point out that the prevailing social imaginary can actually affect the manner in which the church's liturgies are experienced, "attaching a meaning to them which is not their plain or original meaning."[46] For example, liturgical theologian Alexander Schmemann has drawn attention to the fact that, prior to the Constantinian establishment of Christianity, the social imaginary of the empire was deeply influenced by paganism. More than just the worship of idols, it was "a cosmic feeling" which permeated "the whole fabric of the social, political and economic life of the times."[47] Schmemann then points out how this still-influential cultural ethos affected the way the Christian liturgy was experienced at the time, and the way it developed as a result. Summarizing Schmemann's analysis of this liturgical development, Alastair Roberts writes:

> Although the church's worship may have remained much the same in its objective form, as the church filled the place in the

44. Smith, *How (Not) to be Secular*, 136. The quote is from Charles Taylor, *Secular Age*, 759.

45. Smith, *How (Not) to be Secular*, 136. See also Green, *Toward a Pentecostal Theology of the Lord's Supper*, 251.

46. Schmemann, *Introduction to Liturgical Theology*, 97.

47. Schmemann, *Introduction to Liturgical Theology*, 112.

> social imaginary that paganism had vacated, the meaning of its liturgical practice became severely distorted as it was refracted through the "mysteriological" piety of paganism.
>
> The effect of this mysteriological piety was to cast the liturgy as a sanctifying cult, akin to the mystery cults' mode of religion. The mystery religions offered saving cults with the dramatically re-enacted myths that served them, whereas Christianity presented a saving faith that answered to the once-for-all work of Christ in history. The mystery cults served as means of "sanctification," separating the sacred and the profane, conferring sacred status through ceremonies and rituals, whereas Christian liturgy was the faithful action of the church, by which the eschatological character of Christ was manifested.
>
> Under the influence of mysteriological piety, Christian worship was subtly yet markedly transformed. Clergy and cult, by which the desired sanctification was effected, began to eclipse the congregation and liturgy as the "work of the people." Buildings came to be regard[ed] as sacred and sanctifying, and cults began to develop around particular holy sites. As they were perceived and approached differently, ceremonies became increasingly elaborate and grand, embellished with accretions of many attendant rites, all designed to produce a more awe-inspiring liturgical drama to answer the desire for sanctifying rite.[48]

Roberts then suggests that the same is happening today and that Taylor's cultural analysis might help church leaders discern and be on guard against the manner in which our current social imaginary—our secular age—might skew the way contemporary churchgoers experience the church's liturgies. For instance, focusing on the "expressive individualism" that Taylor suggests is a widespread response to the current social imaginary, Roberts warns that

> the return to traditional liturgy that one finds in some circles can be driven by the same underlying forces of expressive individualism. Rather than a submission to authority, tradition

48. Roberts, "Liturgical Piety," 64–65.

> can be an attractive consumer choice for those in search of "authenticity" in a society where many options on offer seem to lack the weight and beauty of long-established custom. Attending a church with a higher liturgy can be a worshiper's means of signaling refinement, elevated aesthetic judgment, ecclesiastical pedigree, and socio-economic class. In such cases, tradition may be valued principally for its vintage feel or ancient dignity, rather than for the truth that first animated its creation.[49]

Roberts then articulates this rather startling conclusion:

> That the liturgy will, with sufficient repetition, bring the imagination around to an appropriate understanding is not self-evident. Would not evidence suggest that, with an imagination lacking the appropriate modes and postures of receptivity to its images, the practice of the liturgy can fail to exert its intended transformative power—indeed that it might become a process of *malformation*? Repetition of etiolated liturgy may not be able to counteract the effect of a misguided liturgical piety by itself.[50]

I will add to this discussion the reminder that the apostle Paul wrote to the Corinthian church twenty centuries ago castigating them for the way their observance of the Lord's Table, impacted by their current social imaginary, was causing them to do the very opposite of pledging themselves to, and actually experiencing, true communion with Christ and his body—their fellow believers (1 Cor 11:17–34)!

Where does this leave us? On the one hand, there is the increasingly popular conviction that the "strange rituals of Christian worship" are the *only* thing that will reach our cultural peers because of their ability to provide them with a better "answer to their most human aspirations."[51] On the other hand, there is biblical, theological, and historical evidence that suggests that sacraments and liturgies by

49. See Chauvet, *Symbol and Sacrament,* as cited in Roberts, "Liturgical Piety," 69.

50. Roberts, "Liturgical Piety," 71–72.

51. Smith, *How (Not) to be Secular*, 139.

themselves may not actually help our cultural peers escape the immanent frame.

I deeply appreciate the missional impulse behind many calls for an evangelical sacramentalism. My concern, however, is that, if we are not careful, what we may end up appearing to endorse is just another false antithesis, this time between a *hyper-rationalized* version of the Christian faith on the one hand, and a *hyper-ritualized* version on the other. To be sure, I have spoken with many young adults (some of whom were nurtured in a Pentecostal-evangelical environment) who express tremendous appreciation for the sacramentalism and liturgical approach to worship they have come to embrace. I am genuinely happy for those who have found that the "strange rituals" of the church help them experience the Holy Spirit in their lives. At the same time, I am concerned about the possibility of an overcorrection: i.e., the notion that the *only* way to experience the Spirit is through the sacraments/liturgy.[52]

I can attest to the fact this type of overcorrection does happen despite the fact that, as we have already noted, it was through genuinely anointed preaching that the first followers of Christ experienced the Spirit (Gal 3:2; Eph 1:13) and entered the faith (Rom 15:17–19; 1 Thess 4:5; 1 Pet 1:12; cf. Heb 2:3–4; 1 John 2:20). Moreover, some prominent theologians have insisted that an anointed preaching of the word is necessary for our engagement in the sacraments to be effectual—i.e., encounter-effecting and relationship-enabling! For instance, in *Calvin's Doctrine of the Word and Sacrament,* Ronald Wallace summarizes Calvin's commitment to the primacy of preaching:

> "The Word which gives life to the sacraments is . . . a clear and distinct voice which is addressed to men and avails to beget faith in them." These conditions can best be fulfilled through the preaching of a sermon, and thus it is that Calvin urges that the sacrament if it is to be properly administered should be preceded by preaching—"a word which preached, makes us understand what the visible sign means." In the use of the sacraments it is of the utmost importance not only that the

52. For more on how to avoid this either-or dilemma, see Wilson, *Spirit and Sacrament,* and Tomberlin, *Pentecostal Sacraments.*

> Word be given but that those who participate attend first to the Word and then relate the sacramental action to the Word that has been spoken, otherwise the sacraments will lose their value. . . . The sacramental activity of the Church must not be preferred to the Word, for neither can be ultimately separated from the other.[53]

Interestingly, a Roman Catholic contemporary of Calvin, the Dutch theologian, Desiderius Erasmus (1469–1536), likewise spoke to the importance of preaching vis-à-vis baptism and the Eucharist. In a work titled *Ecclesiastes sive concionator evangelicus* (*On the Art of Preaching*), Erasmus opined:

> The most important function of the priest is teaching by which he may instruct, admonish, chide, and console. A layman can baptize, all the people can pray. The priest does not always baptize, he does not always absolve, but he should always preach. What good is it to be baptized if one has not been catechized, what good to go to the Lord's Table if one does not know what it means?[54]

Though it is possible to overcorrect with respect to the Protestant Reformation and embrace a sacramentalism that diminishes the importance of preaching, it is neither necessary nor wise to do so. If anything, preaching in general must be awarded primacy, and sermons that play out in a sacramental manner should be prayerfully pursued!

This being said, I am not sure that any of the disenchanted Pentecostals with whom I have interacted over the years had been genuinely exposed to the type of pneumatological realism and sacramental sermons I am advocating for. This possibility finds some support in an indictment that practical theologian Andrew Root levels at a segment of contemporary Pentecostal-evangelicalism. Says Root:

53. Wallace, *Calvin's Doctrine of the Word and Sacrament,* 137. The first quote in this citation is from Calvin, "Commentary on Exodus 24:5" in the *Corpus Reformatorum,* 25:75. The second quote is from Calvin, *Institutes of the Christian Religion,* 4:14:4.

54. Erasmus, *On the Art of Preaching,* as cited in Edwards, *History of Preaching,* 275.

> While these charismatic evangelicals continued talking about a personal relationship with Jesus and seeking ecstatic experiences in worship, they nevertheless made faith formation about commitment to the idea of Jesus, stripping formation, ironically, of its transcendent encounter with divine action, making conversion an epistemological shift rather than an ontological encounter."[55]

To the degree Pentecostal-evangelical churches have done this—have blended a routinization of charisma with an overly rational, philosophical version of the Christian faith—a correction is indeed called for. But we must avoid an *overcorrection* that involves a conflating of sacramentalism and liturgical worship with the dynamic of keeping in step with the Spirit (Gal 5:25). The "disruptive witness of art" notwithstanding, it is not merely the phenomenon of beauty that should enliven us spiritually, but an intimate, interactive, life story-shaping relationship with the God behind the beauty.[56] For this we need a truly *re-inspired* engagement in the sacraments, one that is animated by a collective embrace of a pneumatological realism, and the sacramental sermons produced by it.

In his *Spirit and Sacrament: An Invitation to Eucharismatic Worship*, Andrew Wilson seems to be describing a healthy, balanced, pneumatologically real version of liturgical worship when he writes:

> Imagine a service that includes healing testimonies and prayers of confession, psalms, hymns and spiritual songs, baptism in water and baptism in the Spirit, creeds that move the soul and rhythms that move the body. Imagine young men seeing visions, old men dreaming dreams, sons and daughters prophesying, and all of them coming to the same Table and then going on their way rejoicing.
>
> Can you see it? That's what it means to be Eucharismatic.[57]

55. Root, *Faith Formation in a Secular Age*, 83.

56. For more on the "disruptive witness of art," see Noble, "Disruptive Witness of Art."

57. Wilson, *Spirit and Sacrament*, 15–16.

While I could wish that this description by Wilson of a Eucharismatic worship gathering included an explicit reference to genuinely anointed preaching, I do see it. What is more, I believe the apostle Paul would support it (1 Cor 9:20–22). Not simply because it is liturgical, however, but because it encourages a posture of pneumatological expectancy, and is, therefore, sacramental in the prophetic sense that it will enable an ever-increasing number of our spiritually disenchanted cultural peers to conclude that God really is among us (1 Cor 14:24–25)! Put simply, not *only* a "more robust, complex *understanding* of the Christian faith" is needed, but a more robust, compelling, pneumatologically real *experience* of it as well.

And, yes, we can do this! We can enable our cultural peers, like the spiritually weary woman referred to at the beginning of this chapter, to not only know about God but experience him also! It is possible to escape from the immanent frame that earmarks our secular age. We can cultivate Christian communities that function in a sacramental manner, connecting hurting, haunted people with the risen Christ, the primary sacrament (1 Tim 2:5). I pray this chapter, and the book as a whole, will prompt readers to recognize that genuinely anointed, sacramental sermons play a key role in helping this happen.

The next section of the book will focus on some practical things we can do to cooperate with the Holy Spirit in the production of sermons that play out in a sacramental manner. It is time to talk turkey. Our pursuit of the kind of preaching God always intended continues.

PART THREE

The Process of Sacramental Sermons

4

The First Step

The Preacher's Preparation

Our gospel came to you not simply with words but also with power, with the Holy Spirit and deep conviction. You know how we lived among you for your sake.

—1 THESSALONIANS 1:5

WE ALL KNOW THAT not all sermons are created equal. But it can be argued that the qualitative difference between them may be due more to the preacher's experience of God than his or her intelligence or personality. In *Freedom for Ministry,* Roman Catholic theologian and cleric Richard John Neuhaus made this astute observation:

> Whether he speaks in tones stentorian or is barely audible, whether he is accompanied by grand gestures or with a crouch of intense concentration, it is soon evident that *here* is a preacher. Here is no smooth therapist, no peddler of religious palmsmanship, no friendly pusher of spiritual highs, no aspiring social critic, no seven o'clock news commentator on

> portentous events. No, here is a preacher who has been visited by the seraphim with a burning coal from the altar.[1]

Because you are still reading this work, the chances are good that you may be resonating with its main theme: it is possible for sermons to be sacramental in the sense that they are encounter-enabling. We have looked at the biblical and theological support for such a conviction, and the great need for us to act upon it for our own sake and that of our cultural peers. Now the question is: *How are we to proceed?*

The first step in the actualization of sacramental sermons is the preparation (spirituality) of the preacher. In previous chapters I have referred to the possibility of, and need for, a Pauline, fully Trinitarian, "I-Thou," lifestyle spirituality.[2] My aim here is to explore how such a spirituality can impact the preaching dynamic. I contend that the convictions, commitments, and customs of the lifestyle spirituality I believe Paul himself practiced and promoted will dramatically impact the *logos* (meaningfulness), *ethos* (trustworthiness), *pathos* (winsomeness), *telos* (needfulness), and *kairos* (timeliness) of our sermons in such way as to greatly increase the likelihood that they play out in a sacramental, encounter-enabling manner. For sure, sacramental sermons are not something we preachers can conjure or manufacture in our own strength. But they do happen, and there are things we can do, with the help of the Holy Spirit, to put ourselves in a position to deliver them. As the title of this chapter suggests, the most needful thing is to attend to our own spirituality.

THE CONNECTION BETWEEN PAUL'S SPIRITUALITY AND SACRAMENTAL SERMONS

I have become convinced that it is possible to discern in the letters penned by the apostle Paul the basic *convictions*, *commitments*, and *customs* that animated the spirituality he himself practiced and promoted. My understanding of Paul's spirituality begins with a consideration of

1. Neuhaus, *Freedom for Ministry*, 161.

2. For a book-length treatment of this spirituality, see Tyra, *Introduction to Spirituality*.

how he prayed for the readers of his letters. For instance, in his letter to the Colossians Paul wrote:

> For this reason, since the day we heard about you, we have not stopped praying for you. We continually ask God to fill you with the knowledge of his will through all the wisdom and understanding that the Spirit gives, so that you may live a life worthy of the Lord and please him in every way: bearing fruit in every good work, growing in the knowledge of God . . . (Col 1:9–10)

My thesis is that *the practice of a biblically informed Christian spirituality can and should involve our learning how to live into this Pauline prayer.* It is not just about obeying a particular list of rules, observing a particular collection of rituals, or engaging in a particular register of practices. The focus is, instead, on an ongoing Holy Spirit-enabled interaction with Christ the Son that results in a *lifestyle* or *way of being in the world* that pleases God the Father.

In *Introduction to Spirituality,* I refer repeatedly to a Pauline, fully Trinitarian, "I-Thou," lifestyle spirituality that is Spirit-empowered, Christ-honoring, and pleasing to God the Father precisely because of the way it engenders within us the spiritual, moral, and missional faithfulness he desires and deserves. My goal here is to address something not touched on explicitly in that work: *how the convictions, commitments, and customs of this Christian spirituality can facilitate the kind of sacramental sermons described in this book.*

Well known is the fact that in his *On Rhetoric: A Theory of Civic Discourse,* Aristotle famously argued that public speaking that is effective (persuasive) possessed three key attributes: (1) *logos*—the message must be intelligible, meaningful, plausible; (2) *ethos*—the speaker and the message need to be credible; and (3) *pathos*—the message must affect listeners in a visceral manner. Some contemporary experts in leadership and communication have suggested that we would also do well to pay attention to what Aristotle had to say about two other aspects of effective oral presentations: (4) *telos*—the goal, purpose, essential needfulness of the message; and (5) *kairos*—the message's propriety or timeliness.[3]

But also well-known is the way the apostle Paul seemed to minimize the importance of human wisdom and rhetoric (especially that promoted by the Sophists) to *his* preaching of the gospel (see 1 Corinthians 2:1–5).[4] Does this mean that Christian preachers must eschew the study and use of all communication theory and skills? In *The Imperative of Preaching,* John Carrick suggests that a demonization of all rhetoric would constitute an overcorrection. There is such a thing as a *sacred* (Spirit-enabled) *rhetoric,* exemplified in the preaching of Paul himself, that is not only appropriate but necessary for faithful Christian preaching.[5]

So, the question I want to address is: *What if we discovered that the convictions, commitments, and customs that make up a Pauline, fully Trinitarian, "I-Thou," lifestyle spirituality work together to facilitate truly anointed preaching precisely because of the way they impact the* logos, ethos, pathos, telos, *and* kairos *of the messages Christian ministers deliver?* The rest of this chapter endeavors to explain why I believe all Christian preachers need to take the question just posed very seriously.

PAUL'S SPIRITUALITY IN A NUTSHELL

I contend that Paul's own spirituality can be discerned in the way he called for the readers of his letters to devote themselves to the cultivation of a Spirit-empowered, Christ-honoring, God-the-Father–pleasing, lifestyle spirituality. Why would Paul exhort the members of the churches he cared for so deeply to live in a manner he himself did not employ? Instead, we find Paul encouraging his readers to imitate his way of life (1 Cor 4:15–16; 11:1; Phil 4:9). Thus, we can discern at least the broad contours of the apostle's spirituality in passages where he:

3. For example, see Rodriguez, *Amplify Your Influence,* 27–39.

4. Carrick, *Imperative of Preaching,* 3.

5. Carrick, *Imperative of Preaching,* 4.

indicates that Christian discipleship should go beyond sin management toward the experience of personal transformation (Rom 12:1–2; 2 Cor 3:18);

announces the possibility of church members experiencing an entirely "new" (*kainos*) kind of life (Rom 6:4; 2 Cor 5:17) as they "put off" or "take off" their previous way of being in the world and "put on" or "clothe" themselves in a way more in keeping with the way of Christ (Eph 4:22–24; Col 3:7–10; cf. Rom 13:12–14; Col 3:12–14);

encourages his readers to be careful to avoid a spirituality that is preoccupied with, driven by, or limited to the observance of religious festivals and celebrations linked to certain days, months, seasons, and years (Gal 4:8–11; Col 2:16);

instructs readers to engage in the primary spiritual practices (prayer and thanksgiving) in a continual, perpetual, ongoing manner (e.g., Rom 12:12; Eph 6:18; Phil 4:6; Col 4:2; 1 Thess 5:17);

exhorts his readers to be continually being filled with the Holy Spirit (Eph 5:18) and to "keep in step with the Spirit" (Gal 5:25);

urges his readers to devote themselves to a way of being in the world that pleases God (Rom 8:8; Col 1:10; 1 Thess 2:4; 4:1; Titus 2:1–3).

All of these passages suggest that Paul viewed Christian spirituality as an ongoing rather than occasional activity, and that his call was for Christ's followers to join him in the cultivation of a Spirit-empowered, Christ-honoring, God-the-Father pleasing, lifestyle spirituality.

It was with this end in mind that Paul communicated in his letters a set of *convictions*, *commitments*, and *customs* that should be considered essential to the spirituality just described. Paul's spirituality affected the entirety of his walk with Christ, including his preaching. I am convinced it can make a difference in our pulpit ministry as well!

HOW OUR SPIRITUALITY CONVICTIONS CAN CONTRIBUTE TO SACRAMENTAL SERMONS

The writings of Paul contain several references to a Spirit-enabled *mindset* that is necessary if Christ's followers are to live in a way that pleases God.[6] For instance, here are a couple of passages where we see Paul making this point:

> Do not conform to the pattern of this world, but be transformed by *the renewing of your mind*. Then you will be able to test and approve what *God's will* is—his good, pleasing and perfect will. (Rom 12:2, emphasis added)
>
> You were taught, with regard to your former way of life, to put off your old self, which is being corrupted by its deceitful desires; *to be made new in the attitude of your minds*; and to put on the new self, created to be *like God* in true righteousness and holiness. (Eph 4:22–24, emphasis added)

Commenting on these two passages, biblical scholars Bruce Barton, David Veerman, and Neil Wilson explain,

> The Greek word for "transformed" (*metamorphousthe*) is the root for the English word *metamorphosis*. Believers are to experience a complete transformation from the inside out. And the change must begin in the *mind*, where all thoughts and actions begin. . . . One of the keys, then, to the Christian life is to be involved in activities that renew the mind. *Renewing* (*anakainosei*) refers to a new way of thinking, a mind desiring to be conformed to God rather than to the world. We will never be truly *transformed* without this *renewing* of our mind.[7]

Though it may be true that who and how we are in the world is determined more by what we love than what we believe, as it relates to a lifestyle spirituality productive of a truly God-pleasing life, Paul was convinced that our foundational beliefs about who God is and what he is about matter big time!

6. See Rom 8:6; 12:2; 1 Cor 2:16; Eph 4:20–24; Phil 3:17–21; Col 2:18; 3:1–4, 7–8; 1 Tim 6:3–5; cf. 1 Pet 4:7; 5:8.

7. Barton et al., *Romans*, 231 (emphasis original).

The historical context of those passages where Paul calls for Christ's followers to, essentially, think differently than they did before makes clear that the renewing of the mind Paul himself had experienced and then prescribed for others had to do with some new paradigm-impacting theological beliefs that were generated by his own life-changing experience with the risen Christ and the Holy Spirit during and after his experience on the road to Damascus (see Acts 9:1–22). Far and away, the most important change in the apostle's theology was his embrace of the Trinitarian realism referred to in this book's Introduction. In Paul's case, his new theological realism insisted that, rather than conceive of God the way many Greeks in his day did—merely as a philosophical notion (e.g., a first-cause or one's ground of being)—or as many of his contemporaneous Jewish rabbis might have—as an austere lawgiver and judge—Paul came to realize that the Christian Scriptures portray the Creator as a very real, hyper-personal, and ultra-relational divine being who, because of the incarnation of Christ and outpouring of his Spirit, can be personally known and experienced in an intimate and interactive manner as a holy yet loving heavenly Father. Going further still, I will argue that, for Paul, a "Trinitarian realism" veritably mandated the necessity of intimate, interactive, life-story-shaping relationships with the risen Christ and the Holy Spirit as well. All these possibilities were ones personally realized by the apostle Paul as the book of Acts and his writings reveal. Put simply, Paul came to know and experience our Trinitarian God in an "I-Thou," rather than "I-It" manner.[8]

Now because I have already focused some attention in this work on a theological realism in general and pneumatological realism in particular, I want to devote a few lines here to what it meant for Paul to experience a christological realism. I contend that a careful consideration of the pneumatology presented in John 14–16 provides support for the notion that one of the primary tasks of the Holy Spirit is to make it possible for Christian disciples to experience the ongoing mentoring relationship with Christ that John 15 exhorts us toward.[9]

8. This distinction between "I-Thou" and "I-It" is a prominent theme in Buber, *I and Thou*, as well as Brunner, *Truth as Encounter*.

9. For more on this, see Tyra, *Christ's Empowering Presence*, 99. See also Tyra,

It is not just a memory or an example of Christ that will drive a vibrant Christian spirituality, but the risen Jesus interacting with his followers in real, personal, life-story-shaping ways. When we pray to or worship Christ, we must be careful to "realize" his presence. In this way, we avoid merely talking at or singing toward the *idea* of him. A christological realism creates in us an attitude or posture of *expectancy* with respect to his real presence. He might at any time, through the Spirit, break into our reality, bringing comfort or providing us with some crucial wisdom or guidance.[10] Though we do not presume that we have the power to conjure or command his presence, we have learned to take the promise of Matthew 28:20 at face value and understand him to be perpetually "with" us. Through the mediatorial work of the Holy Spirit, we have come to know and experience Christ as risen, real, and really committed to an ongoing mentoring relationship with his disciples. As I will indicate below, a christological realism is not only a game-changer with respect to our everyday spirituality, but our preaching as well.

In addition to a Trinitarian realism, Paul's theology proper—i.e., his understanding of who God is and what he is about—was also greatly impacted by his conversion experience. I contend that Paul wanted his readers to conceive of *charity*, *sanctity*, and *missionality* as three *prime traits* of the God of the Bible. It is not that the concepts of charity, sanctity, and missionality were unknown to Paul before his life-changing encounter with Christ, but the way they could be *understood* and *lived into* in a theologically real manner was a radically new development.

In my *Introduction to Spirituality*, I treat each of these divine traits, demonstrating their prominence in passages where we find the apostle

- *reflecting* on his own spiritual and ministry journey (i.e., his personal experience of these three traits);
- *exhorting* his readers to think, believe, or act in ways that are in keeping with these cardinal characteristics; and
- *informing* his readers about how he is *praying* for them with these divine traits in mind.

"Proclaiming Christ's Victory over Sinful Personal Desires."

10. See, e.g., Acts 18:9–11; 22:17–21; 23:11; 26:15–18; 2 Tim 4:17.

Though space will not allow for a reprise of these three in-depth discussions, I will offer here that a thorough examination of how the Pauline corpus supports the notion that Paul's theological paradigm (or mindset) really did seem to focus on God's *charity*, *sanctity*, and *missionality*.[11]

Moreover, Paul's letters also support the hugely important notion that he equated *pleasing God* with *proving faithful* (e.g., 1 Cor 4:2, 17; Gal 5:22; Eph 1:1; 6:21; Col 1:2, 7; 4:7, 9; 1 Tim 2:7). Indeed, it is passages such as these that prompt me to suggest, more specifically, that Paul was convinced that a vibrant Christian spirituality will be one that engenders within its adherents a spiritual, moral, and missional faithfulness.

Thus, in a nutshell, these are the convictions that formed the root system of Paul's spirituality. This is the renewed thinking Paul considered necessary for Christ's followers to experience genuine spiritual transformation.

The question is: How do these theological convictions, and the spirituality they spawn, affect the kind of sermons we preachers might, with an anointing provided by Christ's Spirit, deliver?

For one thing, by itself, a theologically real, "I-Thou" spirituality increases the likelihood that the nature of our sermons might be genuine "messages" from God rather than eloquent presentations born of our own creative genius. Though I do not encourage preachers to refer to their own sermons in a cavalier manner as "messages from God," I believe it is possible for genuinely anointed sermons to, in fact, communicate God's heart to hearers in a faithful, powerful way.

Pressing further, if we, like Paul, become convinced that God's essential attributes are an eternal *relationality* (love), *sanctity* (holiness), and *missionality* ("sendingness"),[12] we should not be surprised to find that the sermons we feel prompted by the Spirit to deliver tend to focus on the *spiritual*, *moral*, and *missional* faithfulness of the those to whom

11. For a through discussion of how Paul's letters refer to: God's charity, see Tyra, *Introduction to Spirituality*, 39–42; God's sanctity, see Tyra, *Introduction to Spirituality*, 43–46; God's missionality, see Tyra, *Introduction to Spirituality*, 46–49.

12. Hunsberger, "Starting Points, Trajectories and Outcomes." See also Van Gelder and Zscheile, *Missional Church in Perspective*, 52–53; Flett, *Witness of God*, 5.

we preach. In other words, these three forms of faithfulness derive from, and are the appropriate response to, God's essential attributes: relationality, sanctity, and missionality. This emphasis in our preaching on the threefold faithfulness God desires and deserves is hugely important if our goal, as loving shepherds, is to help our congregants someday hear Jesus say to them "Well done, good and faithful servant" (Matt 25:21, 23)!

Moreover, the spirituality Paul practiced and promoted can enable sermons, genuinely prompted by the Spirit, to evidence the spiritual wisdom he referred to as the "mind of Christ"—a divinely enabled understanding of who God is and what he is up to in the world (see 1 Cor 2:6–16).[13] When this is the case, our preaching will necessarily possess a profound sense of meaningfulness (*logos*) for those with ears to hear. Indeed, it has been my experience that when the Christian communicator is engaged in a fully Trinitarian, "I-Thou" form of spirituality, even Sunday school lessons, small group presentations, and classroom lectures can end up possessing a special, inherent, significant degree of divinely inspired meaningfulness, trustworthiness, winsomeness, needfulness, and timeliness.

Put differently, it has been my experience that in the case of a *sanctified rhetoric*, there is an interplay between the *logos, ethos, pathos, telos,* and *kairos* qualities of the preacher and his or her sermon. For example, I suggest that a prophetic, genuinely meaningful word or message (*logos*) from God will necessarily possess the timeliness and propriety (*kairos*) referred to in Proverbs 25:11 (NASB): "Like apples of gold in settings of silver is a word spoken in right circumstances." Such a communique will also prove to be especially compelling at a visceral level (*pathos*) to those with ears to hear. A christologically and pneumatologically real understanding of those passages in John 10 where Jesus talks about the sheep recognizing and following his *voice* not only allows for this suggestion but argues for it!

These are just some of ways in which our *convictions* regarding who God is and what he is about will shape the nature and effect of not just our spirituality, but our sermons as well!

13. See Keener, *Mind of the Spirit*, 195–99.

HOW OUR SPIRITUALITY COMMITMENTS CAN CONTRIBUTE TO SACRAMENTAL SERMONS

That said, the preacher's embrace of Paul's theological realism, informed by a Spirit-enabled understanding of God's essential attributes, does not, by itself, guarantee that the process of sermon formulation will be impacted. This is why it is necessary to acknowledge that Paul's spirituality, founded on his new theological convictions, also comprised several crucial *commitments*. Paul specifically encouraged the readers of his letters to:

1. keep in step with Christ's Spirit (i.e., be continually filled with and led by the Holy Spirit);
2. cultivate a passionate, perpetual pursuit of Christ's empowering presence; and
3. engage in a lifelong prosecution of God's missional purposes for his creation.

My contention is that these three Pauline spirituality commitments, when addressed in a pneumatologically, christologically, and theologically real manner, will contribute to a spiritual, moral, and missional faithfulness before God. Because this threefold faithfulness is so important to our walk with Christ, and therefore Paul's spirituality, I want to be even more precise regarding the way it works.

To begin, according to Paul, to be *spiritually faithful* is to "continue" in Christ and one's faith in him as God's messiah (see, e.g., Rom 11:22; Col 1:21–23; 2:6–7), and in so doing to avoid even the possibility of apostasy.[14] It is accomplished through our abiding or remaining in Christ (see John 15:1–8) by means of both a *volitional-intellectual* connection (Gal 1:6–9; 2:6–7; 2 Cor 11:3–4) and a *mystical-experiential* communion (Gal 2:20; Col 3:1–4).[15] Thus, one's commitment to keep

14. See Rom 11:17–22; 1 Cor 9:24–10:12; 15:1–2; 16:13; 2 Cor 1:24; 11:2–3; Gal 4:8–20; 5:2–6; Col 1:21–23; 1 Thess 3:5; 1 Tim 1:18–19; 3:6–7; 4:1–10; 5:8; 6:9–12, 20–21; 2 Tim 2:11–13, 16–21, 24–26; 4:7–8.

15. For more on this both-and understanding of what it means to abide in Christ, see Tyra, *Christ's Empowering Presence*, 101–3; Tyra, *Getting Real*, 62–72; Tyra, *Introduction to Spirituality*, 69–83, 127–43.

in step with Christ's Spirit augurs toward the *spiritual faithfulness* God is looking for.

Second, to be *morally faithful* as Christ's followers involves our learning to make ethical decisions and form moral opinions the same way Jesus did, by allowing the Holy Spirit to help us *hear and honor the heart of the Father* in this or that life situation.[16] Therefore, our commitment to pursue Christ's empowering presence—an ongoing mentoring relationship with Jesus through the working of the Holy Spirit (John 16:12–15)—cannot help but produce in us the *moral faithfulness* God is looking for.

Third, to be *missionally faithful* requires a *wholistic* rather than truncated understanding of the *missio Dei*: disciple-making, social action, *and* creation care. Moreover, with respect to the disciple-making component, faithfulness before God requires that we maintain *balance*: we must *contend* for the faith once for all entrusted to God's people (Jude 1:3), while also continually *contextualizing* that same faith for various people groups in a way that is both comprehensible and compelling (1 Cor 9:19–23). It is in this way that we embody the *missional faithfulness* God is looking for.

Please note that, while the Scriptures clearly indicate that all three forms of faithfulness matter greatly to God, we have good reason to believe that a genuine missional faithfulness serves to indicate that all three are at work in someone's life. In other words, the three forms of faithfulness are interrelated in a critical way: a *spiritual* faithfulness underwrites the *moral* faithfulness, without which a *missional* faithfulness will founder. Put differently, a missional faithfulness before God derives from and evidences the presence and quality of the other two![17]

The impact of this threefold faithfulness upon one's preaching is huge! There is simply no way to overstate the impact a genuine life-orientation such as this will have on the credibility (*ethos*) of the Christian preacher, and the God-pleasing needfulness (*telos*) of his or her

16. For more on a moral faithfulness, see Tyra, *Pursuing Moral Faithfulness*.

17. For much more on what a missional faithfulness involves, its importance to a God-pleasing lifestyle spirituality, and some customs crucial to its cultivation, see Tyra, *Introduction to Spirituality*, 85–102, 145–158. See also Tyra, *Missional Orthodoxy*, 12–13, 28, 15, 61–63, 66, 68n7, 70, 79, 89–91, 103, 106–8, 110, 164, 212, 220–24, 227, 307, 324, 326–27, 329, 331, 345, 355, 361, 369.

sermons! A preacher whose lifestyle spirituality has him or her actively pursuing a spiritual, moral, and missional faithfulness has veritably clothed himself or herself in the full armor of God (Eph. 6:10–20).[18] It is hard to imagine how someone whose lifestyle is genuinely earmarked by the virtues and behaviors promoted by Paul in this famous discussion could fail to bring to the pulpit a spiritual gravitas (*ethos*) and holy purposefulness (*telos*) that would prove both reassuring and inspirational (*pathos*) to those in the congregation.

Moreover, Jesus said about himself: "I seek not to please myself but him who sent me" (John 5:30). A lifestyle spirituality—the purpose or aim of which is to prove faithful to God, spiritually, morally, and missionally—engenders an ability to bring meaningful (*logos*) messages from God to his people. When our congregations become convinced that the intent of our lives is to honor our Trinitarian God rather than ourselves, they begin looking and listening for God as we preach his word to them.

HOW OUR SPIRITUALITY CUSTOMS CAN CONTRIBUTE TO SACRAMENTAL SERMONS

In his writings, Paul not only encouraged some spirituality-generating convictions and commitments, but some *customs* as well. It is these customs that allow us to make good on the commitments referred to above. Though I am unable here to treat all the customs Paul identified,[19] I will focus in a cursory manner on one spirituality practice related to each of the three commitments. It is my contention that each of the customs I will briefly treat below contribute mightily to the *logos* (meaningfulness), *ethos* (trustworthiness), *pathos* (winsomeness), *telos* (needfulness), and *kairos* (timeliness) of our sermons in such way as to greatly increase the likelihood that they play out in a sacramental, encounter-enabling manner.

18. For more on this notion, see the chapter titled "Full Armor of God" in Tyra, *Dark Side of Discipleship*, 163–96.

19. For more on this topic, see Tyra, *Introduction to Spirituality*, 105–58.

The Impact of Praying in the Spirit on Our Preaching

The first of Paul's three spirituality commitments calls for us to *keep in step* with the Spirit: i.e., to be ever sensitive and responsive to the devotional, lifestyle, and ministry promptings of the Holy Spirit toward a greater Christlikeness (see Gal 5:16–25). Think about it: *how would such a commitment not be basic to a Pauline, fully Trinitarian, "I-Thou," lifestyle spirituality?*

Of course, it is one thing to be aware of Paul's call to keep in step with Spirit; it is another to be intentional about doing it. *Where do we start?*

Though Paul encouraged the readers of his letters to engage in various spiritual practices (e.g., worship, the study of Scripture, community, service, etc.), the cardinal discipline he emphasized was prayer—a practice he referred to fifty-seven times! This extraordinary emphasis on prayer in Paul's writings must be significant! Moreover, it must not escape our notice that the apostle kept insisting that *this crucial custom can and should be performed in a way that is perpetual, ongoing, unceasing* (e.g., see Rom 12:12; Eph 6:18; Phil 4:6; Col 4:2; 1 Thess 5:17). Certainly, the possibility exists that Paul was merely being hyperbolic. *Then again, what if Paul was in touch with a way for theologically real prayer to become a persistent, especially prominent and impactful feature of our day-to-day lives? What if there is a kind of praying that, because it does not require a lot of concentration, can be performed in a virtually perpetual manner?* I believe the biblical evidence suggests that these queries are legitimate. Though several customs need to be engaged in daily for the first of Paul's three commitments to be realized in our lives, the key to cultivating an ongoing sensitivity and responsiveness to the Holy Spirit's promptings is the spirituality practice known as "praying in the Spirit."

In Paul's experience, the role the Holy Spirit played in prayer was hugely significant. In addition to a couple of passages in which Paul indicated that it is the Spirit who assures Christ's followers of their familial status before God by inspiring them to pray in an "I-Thou" manner (Rom 8:15; Gal 4:6), he also provided the readers of his Letter to the Romans with these profound words of encouragement: "In the same way, the Spirit helps us in our weakness. We do not know what we ought to pray for, but *the Spirit himself intercedes for us through wordless groans*" (Rom 8:26, emphasis added). Moreover, Paul referred to this practice again at the conclusion of his "armor of God" discussion located in Ephesians 6:10–20. In that classic spiritual warfare passage Paul exhorts his readers:

> And pray *in the Spirit on all occasions* with all kinds of prayers and requests. With this in mind, be alert and *always keep on praying* for all the Lord's people. Pray also for me, that whenever I speak, words may be given me so that I will fearlessly make known the mystery of the gospel, for which I am an ambassador in chains. Pray that I may declare it fearlessly, as I should. (Eph 6:18–20, emphasis added)

It is not uncommon for biblical scholars to assert that praying in the Spirit was, for Paul, simply unscripted, extemporaneous prayer, or praying in an especially fervent manner.[20] However, I contend that these suggestions do not account for the charismatic and prophetic manner in which Paul seems to have practiced this type of prayer himself. Some very reputable New Testament scholars suggest that Paul likely had in mind the phenomenon of *glossolalic* prayer (see 1 Cor 14:2, 14–19).[21] Others aver that praying in the Spirit can occur literally through "wordless groans."[22] Either way, we must consider the possibility that, for Paul, praying in the Spirit was a pneumatologically real type of praying that not only involves our being sensitive to the Spirit, but *the Spirit praying through us in a prophetic manner*—a kind of praying that does not originate in, and is not limited by, human understanding.[23]

20. For example, see Brown, *Armor of God*, 91–105. See also Borgman and Ventura, *Spiritual Warfare*, 90–92; Beeke, *Fighting Satan*, 56–58.

21. For example, see Dunn, *Jesus and the Spirit*, 239, 241, 245; Fee, *God's Empowering Presence*, 731; Bruce, *Romans*, 165; Barrett, *Epistle to the Romans*, 164, 168. As for what Jude had in mind, see Barton, *1 Peter, 2 Peter, Jude*, 258–59.

22. For example, see Dunn, *Jesus and the Spirit*, 241. See also Wallis, *Pray in the Spirit*, 95–96.

23. See Dunn, *Jesus and the Spirit*, 241. For more on the role the Spirit plays in the prophetic dynamic, see Tyra, *Holy Spirit in Mission*, 40–74; Tyra, *Pursuing Moral Faithfulness*, 166–67, Tyra, *Dark Side of Discipleship*, 192.

Going further, I assert that it is this pneumatologically real understanding of praying in the Spirit that seems to best explain why Paul indicates in Ephesians 6:18 that it can be practiced "on all occasions," and "always." For sure, prayer that is a purely human endeavor will require a level of concentration (cognitive focus) that will make the practice of "continual" prayer an impossibility. But there is also a type of prayer that is more visceral in nature, that does not originate in one's intellect, and therefore does not require a huge amount of concentration. This kind of praying can occur throughout one's waking moments, in between and even during the busiest moments of the day.

I have found that praying in this way engenders a visceral, hopeful waiting on the Lord with listening ears and a receptive heart (e.g., see Ps 77:1–4; 123:1–2).[24] Whether this type of prayer takes the form of *glossolalia,* or a literal "sighing too deep for words," or both, it will ultimately manifest as a *prayerful mood* that continues regardless of any other activities that must be engaged in. This is a *prayerful posture* or *state of being* that is virtually ongoing—a lingering season of hopeful waiting on, and responsiveness to, God.

Make no mistake, this understanding of praying in the Spirit is significant for all Christ-followers. A genuine, ongoing partnering with the Spirit in prayer is critical to keeping in step with the Spirit and, therefore, to a Christian lifestyle spirituality. But here I want to focus on its significance for us preachers in particular. I contend that praying in the Spirit also opens the door to something prophetic occurring during the preaching moment.

For what it is worth, it is my sense that a discernible correlation seems to exist between my praying in the Spirit and the experience of an increased sense of spiritual sensitivity, creativity, and the likelihood of something prophetic occurring during the preaching, teaching, counseling, or writing activity I am preparing for. Please note that I am not claiming that a *direct* correlation has been proved to be true—only a *discernible* correlation. That said, I have found the correlation to be consistent enough for the practice of praying in the Spirit to become

24. See also Num 9:8; Ps 5:3; 27:14; 33:20; 38:15; 40:1; 130:5–6; Isa 30:18; 40:30–31; Lam 3:24–26; Mic 7:7.

an important component in my own everyday spirituality, as well my preaching, teaching, and counseling preparation.

Furthermore, there is some scientific support for the discernible correlation I have just described: evidence garnered from recent research in the field of neurotheology (which studies what is happening in the brain during a religious experience).[25] Some recent studies making use of various types of brain imaging and measurement suggest that praying in the Spirit, though initiated by Christian disciples, does not engage the speech center in the brain. Thus, instead of requiring the cognitive concentration the left side of our brains is responsible for, this type of prayer actually stimulates the right hemisphere of the brain—the seat of our most creative impulses.[26]

This leads me to wonder: Could it be that God created the human brain in such a way that praying in the Spirit can, over time, increase within the disciple a heightened sensitivity to the presence and voice of God, and do so to a greater degree than when humans are meditating or even praying contemplatively in the vernacular?[27] And, could it be that this effect can occur whether our praying in the Spirit takes the form of glossolalia or literal wordless groans, both of which involve partnering with the Spirit in a way that bypasses human understanding and, thus, the language center of the brain located in the left hemisphere?[28] Though one's Christian faith and practice should not hinge on the findings of empirical science, these recently discovered neurolinguistic realities certainly seem to support my contention that *praying in the Spirit may be viewed as highly productive of a distinctive type of spirituality—one that plays out as a lifestyle rather than a set of practices engaged in now and then.* Furthermore, all of this would also seem to suggest a connection between praying in the Spirit and the preparation and delivery of genuinely anointed preaching. If the first

25. Edmonds, "Is the Brain Hardwired for Religion?," para. 4.

26. For example, see Newberg and Waldman, *Born to Believe.*

27. For a much more thorough treatment of this topic, see Tyra, *Introduction to Spirituality,* 117–24.

28. "The human brain is divided into two hemispheres. The left hemisphere is the 'logical brain' and is involved in language and analysis and the right hemisphere is the 'creative brain' involved in daydreaming and imagination." Mandal, "Language and the Human Brain," para. 1.

earmark of such sermons is that they are Spirit-enabled and therefore prophetic in nature, then a spirituality custom that is all about discerning and obeying the Spirit's promptings cannot help but be just what the doctor ordered.

The Impact of Continually Conversing with Christ on Our Preaching

The second commitment at the heart of a Pauline lifestyle spirituality entails what Dallas Willard referred to as the "hot pursuit" of Christ. [29] References to this spirituality practice (which I refer to as the pursuit of Christ's empowering presence) can be found in the writings of spirituality masters both ancient and contemporary.[30] One of the best known advocates for this practice was a seventeenth century French monk named Nicholas Herman (1610–1691), who has come to be known to the world as Brother Lawrence of the Resurrection. In a well-known work titled *The Practice of the Presence of God,* we discover that, for Brother Lawrence, the pursuit of Christ's empowering presence entails an ongoing conversation. Brother Lawrence encourages us to:

- begin each day conversing with the risen Christ (the real Jesus, not just the idea of him), surrendering the entire day to him, asking him, in advance, to be with us each moment of the day, helping us discern what he is up to in it;
- keep an *internal* conversation with Christ going throughout the day, reckoning with his real presence, dedicating our work to him, seeking to serve and honor him in everything we say and do;
- express regret whenever we recognize that we have become distracted from "the pursuit" and have begun to respond to people and situations in our own strength rather than his;

29. Willard, *Renovation of the Heart*, 42–43.

30. For a book-length treatment of the importance of this practice as recorded in the history of Christian spirituality, see Tyra, *Christ's Empowering Presence.* For an abbreviated treatment, see Tyra, *Introduction to Spirituality,* 69–83.

- keep returning to the pursuit of his presence, expressing gratitude for his grace and committing ourselves to both *knowing* his remarkable love and mercy and then *showing* it to others; and then
- conclude the day by taking stock of how well we fared in the pursuit, drifting off to sleep knowing that, Lord willing, we will awake in a few hours to begin the adventure of walking with Christ all over again.[31]

The historical corpus of works devoted to the theme of Christian spirituality reveals that Brother Lawrence was certainly not the only spiritual master to suggest that a continual conversation with Christ is possible. For example, a twentieth-century missionary and mystic named Frank Laubach (1884–1970) reveled in this spirituality practice:

> While a daily devotional hour is vital for saturating our minds with Christ, it is not enough. All during the day, in the chinks of time between the things we find ourselves obliged to do, there are moments when our minds ask: "What next?" In these chinks of time, ask Him:
>
> "Lord, think Thy thoughts in my mind. What is on Thy mind for me to do now?"
>
> When we ask Christ, "What's next?" we tune in and give Him a chance to pour His ideas through our enkindled imagination. If we persist, it becomes a habit. It takes some effort, but it is worth a million times what it costs. It is possible for everybody, everywhere. Even if we are surrounded by throngs of people we can continue to talk silently with our invisible Friend. We need not close our eyes nor change our position nor move our lips.[32]

The idea here is that this is a genuine, ongoing conversation. Throughout the day, regardless of the situation in which we find ourselves, whether expected or unexpected, we may pray: "Okay, Lord, what are you up to now, and how can I cooperate with you in it?" Moreover, because we are uttering this prayer in a theologically real manner, we can genuinely expect the Lord to respond, not necessarily

31. Brother Lawrence, *Practice of the Presence of God*, 25.

32. Laubach, *Man of Prayer*, 245.

in an audible manner, but, as Laubach testifies, via impressions, ideas, and an enkindled imagination. This is why I suggest that the product of "the pursuit" is nothing less than an ongoing mentoring relationship with the risen Christ (John 16:12–15).

The point is that, if the second earmark of genuinely anointed preaching is that it is incarnational (encounter-enabling) in manner, then a spirituality custom that has us, with the help of the Holy Spirit, conversing with Christ all day every day in such a way as to be personally mentored by him, cannot help but inform what we say in our sermons and how we say it!

The Impact of Empathic Listening (To Our Hearers) on Our Preaching

The third commitment of Paul's spirituality calls for us to take seriously that which is necessary to communicate the gospel to our cultural contemporaries in a way that is both comprehensible and compelling. To do this we must endeavor to truly understand our cultural contemporaries, to understand them better perhaps than they understand themselves! A spirituality custom that is crucial in this regard is to converse with and listen to our peers in an empathic manner. This entails our paying attention not only to what they are saying but also the emotion behind it and doing so without judgment or rebuke. It is *empathic listening* that provides our conversation partners with the psychological air they need to breathe, relax, and allow their defensiveness to diminish. This is how we imitate Christ and earn the right to speak into their lives in a winsome manner. In other words, genuinely anointed preaching requires that we not only listen to God, but to our hearers as well. If the third earmark of such preaching is that it is truly transformative in effect precisely because of its missional faithfulness in both message and manner, then a spirituality custom that has us taking pains to truly, deeply understand our hearers, from the inside out, cannot help but be the kind of preaching our missionary God always intended.

NEEDED: A PERSONALITY MORE THAN SKIN DEEP

The problem is that the consumeristic manner in which many contemporary churchgoers approach the preaching moment places a premium on the appearance, wit, and charm of the preacher over a genuine anointing. Thus, there is a certain pressure felt by many preachers to focus more on their preaching style than their spirituality. The question I want to pose as I conclude this chapter is this: Must we choose between a focus on one or the other, or, properly understood, can we consider both to be important?

Years ago, Phillips Brooks, a popular preacher known for his eloquence, defined Christian preaching as "truth poured through personality."[33] While some of the most auspicious homiletical authors of our day find value in this observation, others express concerns.

For his part, Haddon Robinson writes approvingly: "Phillips Brooks was on to something. . . . We affect our message. We may be mouthing a scriptural idea, yet we can remain as impersonal as a telephone recording, as superficial as a radio commercial, or as manipulative as a con man. The audience does not hear a sermon, they hear a person—they hear you."[34]

At the same time, channeling Karl Barth's hesitancy toward all things anthropocentric, William Willimon is less approving of this emphasis on the preacher's personality. He writes:

> Preaching is utterly dependent upon a God who raises the dead and who calls some people to tell about it. If there is no God to make the preacher's sermon "work," then the preacher is the greatest of fools. The messenger is disposable by, dispensable to, and derivative of the message. We have this treasure in earthen vessels. The treasure is more interesting and powerful than the vessel. Today's preachers find themselves in a vulnerable, dangerous situation when a pleasing personality is more important to a congregation than a truthful one, when charm and wit, warmth and "love" become more valued in a preacher than being a person who is willing to stand up and

33. Brooks, *Lectures on Preaching*, 8.
34. Robinson, *Biblical Preaching*, 25–26.

> speak the truth as God has given it. The truth that is communicated through personality (Phillips Brooks definition of preaching) is so much more important than the personality.[35]

Once again, I think there is truth in both camps. While it may be true that Brooks was influenced by the emergence in his day of modern, liberal theology, and may have "tended to stress the personality of the preacher more than the nature of the truth communicated through the personality,"[36] we must also acknowledge that his reference to the importance of personality involved the conviction and character of the preacher as well as his charm and wit. According to Brooks:

> Truth through personality is our description of real preaching. The truth must come really through the person, not merely over his lips, not merely into his understanding and out through his pen. It must come through his character, his affections, his whole intellectual and moral being. It must come genuinely through him.[37]

This likely explains the nuanced manner in which Bryan Chapell approaches the spirituality versus personality debate. He writes:

> Phillips Brooks' oft-cited observation . . . reflects biblical principle as well as common sense. Our fathers taught, "Your actions speak so loudly I can't hear what you say." Today's young people tell us, "Don't talk the talk, if you don't walk the walk." Each maxim merely reflects a higher wisdom that urges Christian leaders to "conduct [themselves] in a manner worthy of the gospel" [cf. Phil 1:27]. Our preaching should reflect the uniqueness of our personalities, but our persons should reflect Christ-likeness in order for his message to spread unhindered.[38]

35. Willimon, *Conversations with Barth*, 243–44. See also, Willimon, *Proclamation and Theology*, 17–19.

36. Willimon, *Proclamation and Theology*, 19. See also Fuller, "Phillips Brooks," 231–38.

37. Brooks, *Lectures on Preaching*, 8.

38. Chapell, *Christ-Centered Preaching*, 27.

I can envision the apostle Paul, despite his avowed avoidance of human wisdom and rhetoric in his preaching (1 Cor 2:1–5), agreeing with both Brooks and Chappell, properly understood. There is a sense in which personality, as it relates to character, is important, very important in our preaching! The passage that serves as the epigraph for this chapter (1 Thess 1:5) seems to indicate that Paul felt that in addition to the anointed nature of his preaching, his own personal conviction and manner of life vouched for the truthfulness and importance of his message. In other words, while our *message* matters, so does our *manner*. Who we are and how we are in the world contributes significantly to the sacred rhetoric—the *logos, ethos, pathos, telos,* and *kairos*—of our preaching. But Paul's understanding of the personality of the preacher went way deeper than a focus on appearance, wit, and charm. It went to character.

This is why I contend that the first step in the process toward the preaching of sacramental sermons is for preachers to live into the prayer presented in Colossians 1:9–10. And to do that we must adopt a certain kind of spirituality—one that immerses us into the Trinitarian realism that is productive of sacramental sermons. Then, like Isaiah (and Paul), we can address those who listen to us preach and teach as one who has been visited by the seraphim with a burning coal from the altar (see Isa 6:1–8). For sure, personality matters, but not one that is only skin deep.

In the next couple of chapters we will continue to talk turkey about the preparation and delivery of sacramental sermons. And yet, these discussions will differ significantly from what one will find in most homiletics textbooks. I would like to think that this book's emphasis on the prophetic nature of the kind of preaching God always intended definitely adds some value to the conversation.

5

The Second Step

Prophetic *Discernment*

If anyone speaks, they should do so as one who speaks the very words of God.

—1 PETER 4:11

WILLIAM WILLIMON ALLUDES TO the power of encounter-enabling sermons to effect change in those who hear, but he does so by drawing attention to a tragic homiletical irony.

> In my experience, preachers, particularly mainline Protestant preachers, tend to have too little faith in preaching rather than too much. And I use the word "faith" here with intention. How curious, among those who make their living talking about God in sermons, to find so little confidence in the ability of our sermons to *render God*. Too many preachers can tell you all the factors responsible for people's inability to *encounter the Word of God* in a sermon—laziness, sin, ignorance, distraction, and so forth, but have no means of accounting for why, despite all of these conventional reasons for not hearing, sometimes people do hear. Some pastoral psychologists have suggested that this curious sort of pastoral lack of confidence in the efficacy may have something to do with the preacher's

> unconscious fear that if preaching really is effective, if preaching is truly God's appointed means for intruding upon the world, then that means that preachers must be considerably more invested in the preaching. If preaching is powerful, for good or ill, then preachers must be willing to exercise more care and responsibility in their preaching. Better to whine about the pointlessness of preaching and its ineffectiveness than to admit its possible power.[1]

The call here seems to be for us preachers to take our preaching seriously. It really is possible for hearers to "encounter the Word of God in a sermon," but for this to happen the preacher must believe this is so and then prepare accordingly.

In truth, the preparation of sermons that aim to "render God" in the sense of enabling a genuine spiritual encounter with Christ is more rather than less involved than when crafting "business as usual" sermons that merely satisfy the need for a weekly homily. The apostle Peter called for those who "speak" or preach to do so carefully, "as one who speaks the very words of God" (1 Pet 4:11). At the very least this is a call for us to base our sermons on a careful exegesis of the written word of God (cf. Acts 7:38; Rom 3:2; Heb 5:12). But it also seems that Peter was, like Paul, open to the notion of preaching that is, or should be, prophetic in nature: sermons made up of words that are literally provided by the Spirit of God (2 Pet 1:21; cf. 2 Cor 2:17; 4:2; Eph 6:19; 1 Thess 2:15).[2] But for us to receive those words, some careful and prayerful cooperation with the Spirit is required. We are at the point in our journey where we must engage in a frank discussion of how the prophetic phenomenon plays out in the process of preparing sacramental sermons.

AN OVERVIEW OF THE PROPHETIC PHENOMENON

In a previous publication that focused on Christian ethics, I argued that God not only provides his people with moral *guidelines* but also

1. Willimon, *Conversations with Barth*, 141, emphasis added.
2. Davids, *First Epistle of Peter*, 161.

Spirit-enabled moral *guidance*.[3] I included in that work a sidebar discussion that focused on what the Bible has to say about the "prophetic phenomenon."[4] In general, the Scriptures seem to describe the prophetic phenomenon as occurring in two stages. The first stage involves *discernment*—the Spirit enabling the prophet to somehow "hear" from God, thus receiving a message and/or ministry assignment from him. The second stage involves *deployment*—the Spirit empowering the prophet to speak and/or act into the lives of people on God's behalf. Most often these two aspects of the prophetic phenomenon occur in tandem: the prophet hears from God, then speaks and/or acts on behalf of God.[5]

Those familiar with the work of Old Testament scholar Walter Brueggemann will be aware that the main way he focuses on the prophetic dynamic is in the second (deployment) sense. Early in his *The Prophetic Imagination,* Brueggemann states: "*The task of prophetic ministry is to nurture, nourish, and evoke a consciousness and perception alternative to the consciousness and perception of the dominant culture around us*."[6] In other words, the role of the prophet is to confront or challenge the enculturation of the faith community and steer it toward a greater faithfulness vis-à-vis its tradition.

Obviously, this discussion of the prophetic phenomenon has implications for us preachers. While I will treat the *deployment* aspect of "prophetic preaching" in the chapter that follows, my focus here is on the *discernment* phase of the prophetic phenomenon—the theologically real "hermeneutical hearing" that preachers must engage in if they are to, with the help of the Holy Spirit, sense the mind and heart of God as they prepare their next, hopefully sacramental, sermon. If this stage is skipped, nothing truly prophetic occurs in our preaching.[7]

3. See Tyra, *Pursuing Moral Faithfulness*, 181–204. For instance, see Ps 143:10; Ezek 36:24–27; Rom 8:1–14 and Gal 5:16–25; Eph 5:17–18; Phil 1:9–11; Col 1:9–10.

4. See Tyra, *Pursuing Moral Faithfulness*, 166–67.

5. For a book-length discussion of this topic, see Tyra, *Holy Spirit in Mission.*

6. See Brueggemann, *Prophetic Imagination,* 3, emphasis original. See also Tisdale, *Prophetic Preaching*, 6–7.

7. See Chapell, *Christ-Centered Preaching*, 61–62.

EXEGESIS AS DISCERNMENT

It is because all Christian preaching really should be understood as prophetic in nature that the endeavor known as *exegesis* is required. According to biblical scholar Bill Mounce, the Greek word from which the English term *exegesis* derives is *exago,* which essentially means "to bring or lead out" (cf. Mark 8:23; 15:20; Luke 24:50). In the broadest sense, to exegete something is to discover and then bring out into the open something that is not readily apparent. There is a sense in which exegesis is essentially an exercise in discernment: "the quality of being able to grasp and comprehend what is obscure."[8]

Now the usual object of the exegetical endeavor for most Christians is the Bible. To exegete a biblical passage is to discover, unpack, bring out into the open the meaning its author vested in it—that is, the meaning the author intended the text's original readers (or hearers) to take away from it.[9]

For sure, biblical exegesis is a crucial component in the hermeneutical hearing I want to advocate for in this chapter. But in addition to a careful exegesis of pertinent biblical texts, a genuinely anointed sermon that is prophetic in nature requires that the one preaching it has faithfully exegeted something even more basic. We must, with the help of the Holy Spirit, exegete or discern the heart (and mind) of God vis-à-vis this preaching moment.

This is an audacious suggestion. Is there biblical and theological support for it? I believe there is.

THE ROLE OF SPIRIT-ENABLED DISCERNMENT IN PAUL'S THEOLOGY OF PREACHING

In 1 Corinthians 1:17—2:16 we find the apostle Paul summarizing his theology of preaching. To understand the reason behind this summary, we must view it as part of a larger pericope which extends from 1:10 to 4:21. Most scholars agree that Paul seems to be on the defensive here, having become aware that a significant segment of the Corinthian

8. See *Merriam-Webster Dictionary,* "discernment."

9. Keller, *Preaching,* 69.

congregation had become critical of him since his departure from Corinth.[10] Apparently, the church had fragmented into various factions that differed in their allegiances to several ministry icons: Paul, Apollos, Peter, and Jesus (1 Cor 1:10–12). One of the last points that Paul makes in this long discussion is to remind the Corinthian congregation that, though they may have had other voices speak into their lives since becoming Christians, his should be considered special because he was the one who fathered them into the faith (1 Cor 4:15–16)! Thus, I contend the evidence indicates that Paul felt the need to justify his preaching (cf. 2 Cor 10:10; 11:6; 13:3), perhaps over against that of Apollos, in particular, who, hailing from Alexandria (Acts 18: 24), may have been better trained in the art of oratory.[11] This is not to say that Apollos had done anything wrong, but that some of the Corinthians were guilty of immaturely pitting him and his preaching style against that of Paul (see Acts 18:27–28).

First Corinthians 1:17—2:16 is pertinent to a discussion of the importance of prophetic discernment for genuinely anointed preaching because of the tack Paul took in explaining his theology of preaching to the Corinthians.[12] As he justified his preaching style over against that of Apollos, he placed a huge amount of weight on the importance of preaching that is truly Spirit-empowered. Presented below is a cursory survey of the main points I see Paul making in this extended, apologetical, sometimes polemical passage.

First, Paul was careful to indicate that preaching was at the heart of his apostolic ministry, and that his intention was to preach the gospel in a way that possessed spiritual power rather than mere human artistry:

10. Fee, *First Epistle to the Corinthians*, 56. Barrett, *First Epistle to the Corinthians*, 43.

11. Though Barton and Osborne do not suggest as I do that Paul had Apollos particularly in mind as he defended his preaching ministry, they do indicate that "Apollos was from Alexandria and had become distinguished for his speaking ability. Oratory and eloquence were highly valued in the culture of the day, so Apollos probably attracted the highly educated and distinguished believers in the congregation." Barton and Osborne, *1 and 2 Corinthians*, 26.

12. This interpretation finds support in Litfin, *Paul's Theology of Preaching*, 53.

> For Christ did not send me to baptize, but to preach the gospel—not with wisdom and eloquence, lest the cross of Christ be emptied of its power. (1 Cor 1:17)[13]

Second, Paul went on to contrast the saving power inherent in God's message concerning Christ with the worldly wisdom hawked by Greek philosophers and Jewish teachers of the law:

> For the message of the cross is foolishness to those who are perishing, but to us who are being saved it is the power of God. For it is written: "I will destroy the wisdom of the wise; the intelligence of the intelligent I will frustrate." Where is the wise person? Where is the teacher of the law? Where is the philosopher of this age? Has not God made foolish the wisdom of the world? For since in the wisdom of God the world through its wisdom did not know him, God was pleased through the foolishness of what was preached to save those who believe. Jews demand signs and Greeks look for wisdom, but we preach Christ crucified: a stumbling block to Jews and foolishness to Gentiles, but to those whom God has called, both Jews and Greeks, Christ the power of God and the wisdom of God. For the foolishness of God is wiser than human wisdom, and the weakness of God is stronger than human strength. (1 Cor 1:18–25)[14]

Third, Paul encouraged the members of the Corinthian church to remember God's penchant for using imperfect things (people) to achieve his purposes in his world, and, therefore, to refrain from

13. We have already noted that Apollos may have been known for his eloquence. Gordon Fee indicates that the Corinthians may have also viewed him as superior to Paul in terms of wisdom. Says Fee: "It is not so much that Apollos himself advocated understanding the gospel in terms of wisdom—although this cannot be ruled out, given his origins in Alexandria, the home of his contemporary, the Jewish Platonist Philo—but that the Corinthians themselves had become enamored with *sophia* and saw Apollos as best fitting their new understanding. This would be especially so if their love of wisdom included a fascination for the values of the Greek philosophical, rhetorical tradition . . ." Fee, *First Epistle to the Corinthians,* 58.

14. According to Fee, it appears that the human wisdom with which the Corinthians were enamored was that "characterized by the Greek philosophical, rhetorical tradition." Fee, *First Epistle to the Corinthians,* 67.

boasting about anything other than what God has done for them in and through Christ:

> Brothers and sisters, think of what you were when you were called. Not many of you were wise by human standards; not many were influential; not many were of noble birth. But God chose the foolish things of the world to shame the wise; God chose the weak things of the world to shame the strong. God chose the lowly things of this world and the despised things—and the things that are not—to nullify the things that are, so that no one may boast before him. It is because of him that you are in Christ Jesus, who has become for us wisdom from God—that is, our righteousness, holiness and redemption. Therefore, as it is written: "Let the one who boasts boast in the Lord." (1 Cor 1:26–31)[15]

Fourth, based on what he had written already, Paul then boldly explained to the Corinthians why he was deliberate in his preaching to focus on the gospel of Christ without relying on arguments that depended on impressive oratory and worldly wisdom (such as that proffered by the Sophists). He wanted their faith to rest on a genuine experience of, and encounter with, the risen Christ rather than *sophisticated* human arguments:

> And so it was with me, brothers and sisters. When I came to you, I did not come with eloquence or human wisdom as I proclaimed to you the testimony about God. For I resolved to know nothing while I was with you except Jesus Christ and him crucified. I came to you in weakness with great fear and trembling. My message and my preaching were not with wise and persuasive words, but with a demonstration of the Spirit's power, so that your faith might not rest on human wisdom, but on God's power. (1 Cor 2:1–5)[16]

15. "Paul tries to get these believers to see that their own existence as Christians, especially with regard to their Christian beginnings, stands in total contradiction to their present "boasting." Fee, *First Epistle to the Corinthians*, 69.

16. See *Merriam-Webster Dictionary*, "sophistication." See also Fee, *First Epistle to the Corinthians*, 95–96; Litfin, *Paul's Theology of Preaching*, 263–71.

Fifth, Paul went on to make clear, however, that it is not like his preaching lacked wisdom. No, especially when preaching to those mature enough to track with him, Paul could speak from and about a divine wisdom that none of the rulers of this world knew anything about, as evidenced by their having completely missed (or failed to discern) what God was up to in Jesus Christ.

> We do, however, speak a message of wisdom among the mature, but not the wisdom of this age or of the rulers of this age, who are coming to nothing. No, we declare God's wisdom, a mystery that has been hidden and that God destined for our glory before time began. None of the rulers of this age understood it, for if they had, they would not have crucified the Lord of glory. (1 Cor 2:6–8)[17]

Sixth, Paul unveils for his Corinthian readership the means by which not only he, but all who are in Christ, can access God's wisdom previously hidden but now revealed. It is the role of the Spirit of God to enable God's people to properly *discern* who God is and what he is up to in the world.

> However, as it is written: "What no eye has seen, what no ear has heard, and what no human mind has conceived"—the things God has prepared for those who love him—these are the things God has revealed to us by his Spirit. The Spirit searches all things, even the deep things of God. For who knows a person's thoughts except their own spirit within them? In the same way no one knows the thoughts of God except the Spirit of God. What we have received is not the spirit of the world,

17. In a footnote, Fee is careful to point out that the use of the pronoun "we" in verses 6 and 7 referred not only to him but to other apostolic preachers. Indeed, Paul may have been attempting to draw his readers into "his own orbit," acknowledging the inclusion of his readers in the community of faith. At the same time, however, given the polemical nature of this pericope, this may have also been an "inclusive-exclusive" usage of the pronoun "we," suggesting some non-differentiation between him and the members of the Corinthian congregation related not to salvation but spiritual maturity, as 1 Corinthians 3:1 later makes clear. See Fee, *First Epistle to the Corinthians,* 108n232.

> but the Spirit who is from God, so that we may understand what God has freely given us. (1 Cor 2:9–12)[18]

Seventh, Paul boldly asserted that his preaching was genuinely anointed, essentially prophetic. His speaking involved words he received directly from the Holy Spirit.

> This is what we speak, not in words taught us by human wisdom but in words taught by the Spirit, explaining spiritual realities with Spirit-taught words. (1 Cor 2:13)[19]

Eighth, Paul went on to explain why those without the Spirit of God would necessarily consider his preaching to be foolish. He may have also been hinting at why some church members might have undervalued his preaching ministry.

> The person without the Spirit does not accept the things that come from the Spirit of God but considers them foolishness, and cannot understand them because they are discerned only through the Spirit. (1 Cor 2:14; cf. 3:1–4)[20]

Finally, Paul indicated how inappropriate it is for people without the Spirit to judge and evaluate the spiritual wisdom possessed by those who are being enabled by the Spirit to discern and make known to others the very "mind of Christ."

18. Fee makes the point that the wisdom of which Paul speaks is not esoteric in nature, focusing on the ontic qualities of God, but focuses on God's economy, what he is up to in the world. Says Fee: "That wisdom in fact is not esoteric knowledge of deeper truths about God; rather it is simply God's own plan for saving his people." See Fee, *First Epistle to the Corinthians,* 120.

19. Acknowledging the possibility of other interpretations which soften the emphasis of the prophetic at work in Paul's preaching, Fee states: "Nonetheless, the grammar would seem to favor the view that Paul is giving further explication of what he has just said. "We speak words taught by the Spirit," he asserts, "which means that we [explain] 'spiritual' things [probably referring to the 'things freely given us by God,' v. 12] by means of, or with, the 'spiritual' words taught us by the Spirit." See Fee, *First Epistle to the Corinthians,* 123.

20. Fee suggests that Paul may indeed have been "setting up the Corinthians for the polemic that will come hard on the heels of this passage (in 3:1–4)." See Fee, *First Epistle to the Corinthians,* 123.

> The person with the Spirit makes judgments about all things, but such a person is not subject to merely human judgments, for, "Who has known the mind of the Lord so as to instruct him?" But we have the mind of Christ. (1 Cor 2:15–16)[21]

In sum, this polemical passage (1 Cor 1:17—2:16), in which Paul seems to have been explaining/defending his ministry in Corinth, provides some substantial support for preaching that is prophetic in nature. Commenting on a key verse (1 Cor 2:13), Bruce Barton and Grant Osborne write:

> Here Paul explained that the gospel message had not been given with *words of human wisdom* because no human wisdom can adequately explain God's wisdom. In order to speak the Spirit's message, believers must *speak words given to us by the Spirit.* In order to *explain spiritual truths,* believers must use *the Spirit's words.* Paul's words are authoritative because their source was the Holy Spirit. Paul was not merely giving his own personal views or his personal impression of what God had said. Under the inspiration of the Holy Spirit, he was writing the very thoughts and words of God.[22]

But Paul not only defended the authority of his preaching in this important passage; he also indicated the crucial role the Holy Spirit plays in helping any preacher discern the very heart and mind of God (i.e., engage in theological exegesis)! Commenting on 1 Corinthians 2:16, New Testament scholar Craig Keener explains:

> Paul's point is not merely that human wisdom cannot fathom God; he also argues the converse, namely, that by the Spirit believers *can* understand God. The full knowledge of God is

21. I will discuss Craig Keener's take on what having the "mind of Christ" entails for Christians below. For his part, Fee suggests that though Paul's reference to "those without Spirit" refers to unbelievers rather than Christians who lack the Spirit, he is at the same time suggesting that the Corinthians, who should know better, are not allowing the Spirit to do his illuminating work in their lives. While it is possible for them to have access to the "mind of Christ" through the work of the Spirit, "they don't." See Fee, *First Epistle to the Corinthians,* 128. See also Keener, *Mind of the Spirit,* 216.

22. Barton and Osborne, *1 and 2 Corinthians*, 44.

> eschatological (1 Co. 13:12), but believers can experience a foretaste of that knowledge in the present. We might describe this knowledge as quantitatively finite, given the finiteness of the human recipients, but qualitatively perfect (in its pure form), because it comes from the Spirit of the infinite God.[23]

Moreover, Keener goes on to offer an experience-based insight into what having the "mind of Christ" may entail for Christians.

> In practice, having the mind of Christ or acting on the basis of Christ living in one (Rom. 8:10; Gal. 2:20) probably includes a range of elements: moral empowerment (as in the context of Gal. 2:20); a theocentric, Christocentric, ecclesiocentric, and missional framework for thinking; periodic personal direction from, or being moved by, the Spirit; periodic experiences of acknowledged divine wisdom; periodic revelatory insights; and so on. One may facilitate such experiences in faith, though the diversity of gifts means that some will experience some aspects of this (such as wisdom or revelatory insights) more than others.[24]

I propose that an implication of this insight is that Christian preachers will benefit from the Spirit-enabled ability to see and feel about things the way Jesus himself does!

So then, according to Paul, with the help of the Holy Spirit, God's heart and Christ's mind can be discerned (exegeted). This extended Pauline passage provides some salient biblical and theological support for my contention that some prophetic discernment is not only possible, but required, if we are to preach in the way God always intended.

HERMENEUTICAL HEARING: TOWARD A PROPHETIC BIBLICAL EXEGESIS

If our goal is to hear and honor the heart of God in our preaching, the first step must be for us to do our due diligence in trying to understand or "hear" what the Spirit of God was encouraging the human authors

23. Keener, *Mind of the Spirit*, 195–96.

24. Keener, *Mind of the Spirit*, 199.

to say in the texts we feel led of the Lord to preach and teach from.[25] That said, there is a difference between a traditional, Enlightenment-influenced approach to biblical exegesis and the kind I have in mind. Let us take a closer look at the following proposition: *If our goal is the preparation of genuinely anointed sermons, some serious, careful, prayerful, Spirit-enabled, "I-Thou" biblical exegesis is crucial!*

Craig Keener's Call for a Spirit-Enabled Biblical Exegesis

As it happens, this is a topic that Craig Keener touches upon in his book *Spirit Hermeneutics: Reading Scripture in Light of Pentecost.* Though hermeneutics—how we read Scripture and apply it to our lives—can be differentiated from the exegetical task—doing our best to discern what the biblical authors were saying through the texts they composed—Keener makes the point that the Holy Spirit can and should be involved at the level of exegesis as well as hermeneutics.[26] But make no mistake, though he identifies as a Pentecostal, Keener goes to great lengths to indicate his commitment to solid, traditional biblical exegesis:

> The common basis for discussion that readers from various vantage points share is the text and (as best we can reconstruct it) how the text would have been heard by the audience for which its author(s) constructed it with ancient vocabulary, idioms, and cultural assumptions.[27]
>
> God did not send Scripture to us in some random way, but in particular languages, cultures, and genres normally already accessible to the first audiences. The message came to us already contextualized, so if we wish to hear it fully, we must hear it first in the shape in which God provided it.[28]

25. Chapell, *Christ-Centered Preaching*, 61–62.
26. Keener, *Spirit Hermeneutics*, 288–89.
27. Keener, *Spirit Hermeneutics*, 87.
28. Keener, *Spirit Hermeneutics*, 102.

> Spirit hermeneutics, then, may be *more* than simply traditional exegesis . . . [y]et it should also not be *less* than traditional exegesis.[29]
>
> The Spirit still speaks today; that is what Scripture leads us to expect. We can be most confident of the Spirit's voice, however, when we attend to what the Spirit has already spoken. The canon provides the opportunity and the responsibility to submit our hearing the Spirit to what the tested prophetic tradition has heard, and thus to grow in hearing correctly.[30]

So, there is no question regarding the vital importance of traditional, carefully executed biblical exegesis.

That said, early in this work (which promotes a Spirit-enabled hermeneutic), Keener states that his approach focuses on the basic question: "How do we hear the Spirit's voice in Scripture?"[31] It is apparent that Keener has in mind the type of Trinitarian realism with its emphasis on an "I-Thou" approach to God, Christ, and the Spirit that I have referred to repeatedly in this book. He also possesses a theologically real understanding of the Scriptures. As a result, he insists that the Scriptures should be read and studied in an experiential as well as intellectual manner. He goes on to explain:

> All Christians should read Scripture as people who are living in the biblical experience . . . as people living by the same Spirit who guided God's people in Scripture. . . .
>
> This means that we are interested in biblical texts not simply for what they teach us about ancient history or ideas . . . but because we expect to share the kind of spiritual experience and relationship with God that we discover in Scripture. Jesus's resurrection is not mere historical datum; it declares that the Jesus we learn about in the Gospels is now the exalted Lord, who has sent his Spirit so that we may continue to experience his presence. . . .
>
> Throughout Scripture we read about people hearing from God, prophesying, and experiencing miracles. Though we

29. Keener, *Spirit Hermeneutics*, 116.

30. Keener, *Spirit Hermeneutics*, 118.

31. Keener, *Spirit Hermeneutics*, 2.

> may not all experience all these activities of the Spirit daily, biblical patterns lead us to expect that the God who empowered these activities throughout Scripture is the God who still empowers them. . . .
>
> While careful study of Scripture helps counter the unbridled subjectivism of popular charismatic excesses, study that does not lead to living out biblical experience in the era of the Spirit misses the point of the biblical texts.[32]

In sum, according to Keener: "when we correctly understand the Scriptures, we find there also repeated testimony to divine encounters and a living relationship with Christ. Recognizing in Scripture the prevalence and promise of divine activity, and expecting the Spirit's presence and pedagogy as we read Scripture, is a Spirit hermeneutic."[33]

So the question I believe Keener would put to those of us who routinely exegete biblical texts in the preparation of sermons is this: *Will our reading and study of the Scriptures be "I-It" in nature—merely technical, conceptual, and formal—or "I-Thou"—personal, experiential, and existentially impactful?* In a chapter titled "Reading Experientially," Keener indicates that a theologically informed approach to Scripture, even for exegetes, will be intentionally "devotional,"[34] "dynamic,"[35] and "missional."[36] In other words, we must strive to read and study the biblical texts with *ears that hear* what the Spirit is saying through them!

To do this, Keener emphasizes the need for Christians to read (hear)[37] Scripture *prayerfully*. He writes;

> Prayer for understanding is certainly a biblical concept (e.g., 1 Kgs 3:9–10; Ps 25:4–5; Dan 2:18–19; Eph 1:17–18; Phil 1:9–10; Col 1:9–10; Phlm 6; Jas 1:5), and this principle certainly applies to understanding Scripture (Dan 9:2–3, 23); prayer for understanding of the law is a frequent refrain in Psalm 119

32. Keener, *Spirit Hermeneutics*, 5.

33. Keener, *Spirit Hermeneutics*, 18.

34. Keener, *Spirit Hermeneutics*, 24–25.

35. Keener, *Spirit Hermeneutics*, 29.

36. Keener, *Spirit Hermeneutics*, 42–43.

37. See Mark 4:9 // Luke 8:8; Mark 4:23; Luke 14:35; Rev 2:17, 29; 3:6, 13, 22; 13:9.

> (119:27, 34, 73, 125, 144, 169). We do not need to wait until there is a passage that we do not understand cognitively, however. When reading Scripture devotionally, we can pray while reading, taking time to praise God for, and prayerfully ponder, what we find there. This approach need not require lingering over every point, but we can pray about the points that offer challenges or special insights to us. The prayer might be a brief whisper before moving on, or wrestling deeply with a matter particularly challenging to us.[38]

Anyone familiar with Keener's exacting yet engaging scholarship will feel the need to take his commitment to a prayerful engagement with God's word very seriously. There is more to be said about what is involved in Spirit-enabled exegesis, but even a cursory interaction with Keener's advocacy for a prayerful, expectant, experiential engagement with the biblical texts will inspire preachers to make sure that they are fully cooperating with the Spirit's desire to help them discern what God might want them to give voice to in this or that biblically based sermon.[39]

Craig Bartholomew and the Importance of Listening to the Scriptures

Though to my knowledge evangelical philosopher and biblical scholar Craig Bartholomew does not identify as a Pentecostal, he, too, might be considered an advocate for the dynamic of hermeneutical hearing. Seeming to argue from a theologically and pneumatologically real perspective, he writes:

> Biblical hermeneutics needs to recover the primacy of creative receptivity, of listening. This is not for a moment to undermine the role of analysis but to insist that listening and analysis are linked. . . . The scant attention to listening in much work on

38. Keener, *Spirit Hermeneutics*, 25.

39. For more on this from a traditional Pentecostal perspective, see the discussion of the need for a "revelational hermeneutic" in Crabtree, *Pentecostal Preaching*, 142–44, as cited in Samuel, *Holy Spirit in Worship Music, Preaching, and the Altar*, 162–65.

> biblical interpretation is an indication of the extent to which biblical studies has been shaped by some of the least attractive aspects of modernity. Starting with listening provides us with an opportunity to redirect biblical hermeneutics along healthier lines.[40]

> It is when we learn how to listen to the Bible that it starts to come alive to us. . . . Any Christian biblical hermeneutic that fails to make the telos or goal of reading the Bible *to listen to God's address to us today* falls short of taking Scripture seriously as God's Word.[41]

As for how Scripture is "listened" to, Bartholomew, like Keener, emphasizes the role of theologically real prayer. He explains:

> If the goal or telos of biblical interpretation is to listen for God's address, then it must begin and end with God. I must begin in prayer with profound dependence upon God and end in hearing and responding to God's speaking.[42]

> The Bible should not be approached neutrally but on our knees with our ears wide open, ready to hear God's address.[43]

So, it seems, both Pentecostals and evangelicals can agree on the need for a prayerful, "I-Thou" rather than "I-It" engagement in exegesis that is especially attentive to the heart of God in the process. Before we move on, however, I will cite additional support for my thesis from a theologian who did not fit neatly into either the Pentecostal or evangelical camp, but for whom genuinely anointed preaching was of paramount importance.

KARL BARTH AND HERMENEUTICAL HEARING

Decades before Keener and Bartholomew, Karl Barth also emphasized the importance of prayerful, Spirit-enabled, theologically real exegesis.

40. Bartholomew, *Introducing Biblical Hermeneutics,* 24.
41. Bartholomew, *Listening to Scripture,* 11–12, emphasis original.
42. Bartholomew, *Listening to Scripture,* 7.
43. Bartholomew, *Listening to Scripture,* 7.

Let us look briefly at some indications of his commitment to exegesis and the value he placed on a Spirit-enabled, theologically real, and, therefore, prayerful approach to it.

Barth's emphasis on exegesis can be discerned, first, in his bibliology—that is, his conception of the Bible as God's speaking. In a chapter titled "Preaching the Bible with Barth," William Willimon observes that over against the liberal view that the Bible is entirely a human product, "Barth describes scripture as primarily a work of God, the very voice of God, an invasion of our world through words."[44] Indeed, Barth's bibliology dramatically impacted his early view of the form sermons should take, and the limited type of homiletical interpretation he considered appropriate. Willimon remarks that "his robust sense of revelation will not allow Barth to do much more than 'exegesis and application.' Any interpretation of scripture ought to be a kind of restatement, a redescription rather than vigorous and imaginative interpretation."[45]

This high view of the authority of Scripture explains the emphasis Barth placed on exegesis in the preparation of sermons. Speaking again of Barth, Willimon relates that

> As he boarded the train to return to Switzerland, victim of the Nazi's purge of the German universities, Barth's parting exhortation to the students and pastors whom he left behind, his last gift to them for the fight ahead, was to urge them toward "exegesis, exegesis and yet more exegesis! Keep to the Word, to the scripture that has been given to us."[46]

Barth was also convinced that the assistance of the Holy Spirit is required for the revelation inspired by the Spirit to be discerned by human preachers. Citing Barth in the process, Willimon writes:

> The luminosity of the biblical text is not a matter of the reader's pious imagination, not a matter of the application of our interpretative skills—be they moral, historical, or exegetical—because "this revelation inspired by the Holy Spirit, can

44. Willimon, *Conversations with Barth*, 23.

45. Willimon, *Conversations with Barth*, 29.

46. Willimon, *Conversations with Barth*, 45. Quote is from Busch, *Karl Barth*, 259.

> become luminous for us only through the same Spirit." Here we see Barth's insistence on the reality of divine agency as a prerequisite for biblical interpretation. Our fertile imaginations are not the key to biblical interpretation but rather the work of the Holy Spirit. The source of any interesting interpretation is prayer.[47]

Willimon also highlights the implications that Barth's theologically real, deeply relational understanding of God can and should have for our sermon preparation. For example, says Willimon:

> For Barth, prayer is not so much our speaking to God, but God's speaking to us. . . . Preaching is not so much what we say about God, but rather what God says about God's self. And Scripture is not so much an account of our history of God, but God's history with us, not our experience of God, but *God's* experience of us! Barth really believes that biblical knowledge is knowledge of a person, a living, communicative person distinct from ourselves.[48]

To be more specific, flowing from the "I-Thou" rather than "I-It" relation to God that Barth championed, is a need for not only a consistent christo-sensitive reading of the Spirit-inspired biblical texts that witness to him,[49] but a vibrant christological realism as well—one that fully expects the real and risen Christ to personally respond to our prayer for discernment by speaking to us from the biblical texts![50]

In other words, Barth (like the apostle Paul) found in the gospel the potential for real relationship with God the Father, made possible by Christ the Son, through the work of the Holy Spirit. And because all relationships involve some measure of ambiguity, a significant amount of humility is required if we are to put ourselves in a place to encounter Christ in our preparation of sermons that, hopefully, will enable their

47. Willimon, *Conversations with Barth*, 23–24. Quote is from Barth, *Church Dogmatics* I/2, 102.

48. Willimon, *Conversations with Barth*, 28, emphasis original.

49. Willimon, *Conversations with Barth*, 33.

50. Willimon, *Conversations with Barth*, 33–39.

hearers to encounter him as well during the preaching moment. Again, citing Barth in the process, Willimon explains:

> Toward the end of his *Homiletics,* after having given his rules for reading scripture, Barth confesses the need humbly to keep biblical mystery as mystery, to remain as an "astonished child":
>
> We should not try to master the text. The Bible will become more and more mysterious to real exegetes. They will see all the depths and distances. They will continually run up against the mystery before which *theology* is like trying to drain the ocean with a spoon. The true exegete will face the text like an astonished child in a wonderful garden, not like an advocate of God who has seen all his files.[51]

In my book *Pursuing Moral Faithfulness,* I include a discussion of why God seems to have built some ambiguity (mystery) into the very nature of the cosmos.[52] In short, my argument is that some ambiguity is divinely purposeful; it is the ambiguities we experience in life that drive us, like Job, to our knees in prayer, crazy-hungry desperate for a genuine, personal, existentially impactful encounter with the living God (see Job 42:1–6). In a similar manner, it is the ever-present mystery we run up against as we wrestle with the biblical texts that remind us that our exegesis must be "I-Thou" rather than "I-It" in the way it is executed.

It would appear that Barth, himself, was convinced that sermon preparation should not only involve the biblical text, but the God of the biblical text, and therefore prayer. We must ever keep in mind the pronounced emphasis Barth placed on "the free and dynamic movement of God that can never be bound to or imprisoned by the proclaimed Word," and his insistence that "it is never in humanity's power 'that our human word should be God's Word.'"[53] This emphasis on the freedom of God in Barth's theology underscores my contention previously that,

51. Willimon, *Conversations with Barth,* 45. Quote is from Barth, *Homiletics,* 128.

52. See Tyra, *Pursuing Moral Faithfulness,* 257–69.

53. Currie, *Only Sacrament Left to Us,* 24. Quotation is from Barth, *Homiletics,* 90.

while a sacramental effect is possible in Christian preaching, it should never be considered inevitable or something that occurs in a formalistic, automatic, essentially magical manner.[54] Instead, it is a wonderful, mysterious possibility realized only through a humble yet hopeful engagement in some serious *prayer*.[55] According to Barth, "It is prayer that puts us in rapport with God and permits us to collaborate with him."[56]

I suspect Craig Keener might agree with Barth regarding the possibility and advisability of an "I-Thou," collaborative relationship with the Holy Spirit when interacting with the word of God. Keener's description of how such a prayer-enabled collaboration with the Spirit routinely plays out in his own scholarship is both instructive and inspiring.

> I believe that the Spirit has often helped me in my exegesis also, often facilitating my cognitive skills (which seems usual in the exegetical process), for example, by striking my attention with all sorts of potential connections as I read the background sources and still more as I wrestle with the text. Yet this also happens by guiding me in ways traditionally considered more "charismatic." Thus, for example, when several decades ago I was struggling with the point of the tabernacle material in Exodus, praying desperately, I felt that God directed me to study ancient Near Eastern temples to understand the symbolism. On a different level, at times various ideas come together and something "clicks" in a special way. I do not want to elevate such insights as if they are perfect or immune to correction: again, "we know in part and prophesy in part" (1 Cor 13:9). I mention them simply to illustrate that I do expect and experience what I believe to be the Spirit's guidance even at the exegetical stage.[57]

54. Some support for this contention can be found in Jonathan Edward's theology of preaching as well. See Carrick, *Preaching of Jonathan Edwards*, 438.

55. Currie, *Only Sacrament Left to Us*, 24–25,40, 43–44, 120. Worthy of note is Currie's suggestion that the importance Barth placed on prayer in the life of the church increased over the course of his academic career. For example, see Cox, *Fire from Heaven*, 107, 112, 135.

56. Barth, *Prayer*, 20, as cited in Currie, *Only Sacrament Left to Us*, 113.

57. Keener, *Spirit Hermeneutics*, 129.

CHIMING IN: MY OWN EXPERIENCE OF HERMENEUTICAL HEARING

For what it is worth, I resonate with the commitment to prayerful exegesis we find in the hermeneutics proffered by Keener, Bartholomew, and Barth. I, too, have found prayer to be critical to the hermeneutical hearing phase of sermon preparation. In the previous chapter I referred to the value of praying "in the Spirit" as I prepare for preaching, teaching, counseling activities. To be even more specific, it has been my experience that entering the preaching moment with a strong sense that I have something to say that is from the Lord correlates with the wisdom provided in Proverbs 2:1–6:

> My son, if you accept my words and store up my commands within you, turning your ear to wisdom and applying your heart to understanding—indeed, if you call out for insight and cry aloud for understanding, and if you look for it as for silver and search for it as for hidden treasure, then you will understand the fear of the LORD and find the knowledge of God. For the LORD gives wisdom; from his mouth come knowledge and understanding.

According to this and many other biblical passages, our God is a speaking God, a loving heavenly Father who is not loathe to speak to his people, providing them with wisdom, knowledge, and understanding.[58] However, according to the Scriptures as a whole, and this passage in particular, *there are some things we must do to put ourselves in a position to hear God's voice.* Most basically, we must "turn our ears" and "apply our hearts." More specifically, we must "call out for insight" and "cry aloud for understanding," while at the same time engaging in some serious study as we "look for it as for silver" and "search for it as for hidden treasure." What is more, all this must be done *at the same time* and *in a theologically real* rather than formalistic manner.

Since we have allowed Keener, Bartholomew, and Barth to encourage us to engage the study of Scripture in a way that is both theologically real and Spirit-enabled, I want to conclude this chapter by elaborating a bit on my own approach to discerning God's heart

58. For more on this, see Adam, *Speaking God's Words*, 15–17, 22–24.

through some theologically real, missionally sensitive, honest-to-God prayer.

Theologically Real Praying

First, I feel the need to elaborate a bit on what it means to pray and study in a theologically real manner. As I have already indicated, a realist understanding of God maintains that he is much more than a philosophical concept or impersonal spiritual force. The God revealed to us in Jesus Christ is a personal, relational, and responsive "heavenly Father." As a result, it is possible for humans to interact with their creator in ways that are personal, relational, and responsive. At the risk of greatly oversimplifying things, I contend that this basic understanding of the reality, relationality, and responsiveness of God suggests at least three prayer principles. First, there is a huge difference between *talking to God* and *talking toward the idea of God.* Second, the goal of prayer should *not* be to simply get something from God, but to honor him. We honor God in prayer when we reckon with his real presence in the moment, and then, while honestly sharing with him our concerns, defer to him and his will (Matt 6:9–10; 26:39 // Mark 14:36), doing our best to discern and align ourselves with his benevolent purposes. Third, we also honor God when, in addition to pouring out our hearts to him, we prayerfully wait upon him, anticipating a response (e.g., Acts 13:1–3). Once again, this is where that prayerful mood or way of being in the world that is created through our praying in the Spirit (either through glossolalia or literal wordless groans) becomes so very important.

It is my contention that praying in this relational, responsive, theologically real manner is fundamental to putting ourselves the position to discern God's heart. That said, there are additional forms of prayer that are also necessary.

Missionally Sensitive Praying

Building on the foundation of theologically real prayer just presented, I will press on to offer that because the Holy Spirit is, as was stated in the Cape Town Commitment, "*the missionary Spirit sent by the missionary*

Father and the missionary Son, breathing life and power into God's missionary Church."[59] Another prayer that should often be on the lips of those seeking to render the Lord a missional faithfulness is this: *Spirit of mission, what are you up to in this ministry context/situation, and how can I cooperate with you in it?* Obviously, such a prayer is especially appropriate during the hermeneutical hearing stage of sermon preparation!

To be more precise, I suggest that, as we approach each preaching endeavor, we wait on God in prayer, seeking discernment regarding:

- what the Holy Spirit is currently up to in the life of this congregation; and
- what message (keeping the original meaning of the biblical texts, and the categorical importance of the threefold faithfulness ever in view) might the Spirit be encouraging me to communicate to this congregation in this upcoming preaching/teaching moment.[60]

Going further still, I will reiterate here how important it is for preachers (and professors) to help church members (and students) fully comprehend just how much our God desires the spiritual, moral, and missional faithfulness we have discussed in previous chapters. Since these three forms of faithfulness align with God's essential attributes—his relational, holy, and sending natures—many if not all the hortatory passages in the New Testament ultimately aim at guiding readers toward an embodied faithfulness in these three aspects of their walk with Christ. This has huge implications for our preaching and teaching. If the goal of the Christian life is for Christ's followers to someday have Jesus look them in the eye and affirm the faithful way they lived for him prior to his *parousia* (Matt 25:21, 23), is it not needful for the human shepherds of God's flock to: (1) have a sense of how well the members of the flock under their care are currently faring with respect to the threefold faithfulness; and (2) to herald Christ's encouragement with respect to the same? The apostles were led by the Spirit to encourage

59. "Cape Town Commitment," para. 1.

60. See the discussions of divine illumination and the application of biblical texts in Keener, *Spirit Hermeneutics*, 12–13 and 31, 77–78, 149–51, 237–38, 249–50; 257–58.

progress toward a spiritual, moral, and missional faithfulness in the letters they sent to the churches. Genuinely anointed preaching will do the same. Therefore, we must develop the habit of praying in a missionally sensitive manner as we prepare each and every sermon we deliver to those who trust us to bring God's word to them. My experience has been that our doing so significantly increases the quality of the sacred rhetoric (*logos, ethos, pathos, telos,* and *kairos*) imbued in our preaching, and, therefore, the likelihood of something prophetic occurring during it. Mark it down: praying in a missionally sensitive manner cannot help but fine-tune our "dialing in" to the heart of our missionary God!

Honest-to-God Praying

The third form of discerning prayer that needs to be engaged in while we prepare our sermons has to do with ourselves—our own spiritual, moral, and missional faithfulness before the Lord. Personally, I have found the Spirit of Christ to be averse to any degree of hypocrisy.[61] He is also super eager to help us overcome the wiles of the evil one.[62] Thus, calls for Christians to remain sincere in their walk with Christ pockmark the book of Acts and epistolary corpus of the New Testament.[63] Striking also are those passages which depict the apostle Paul's hope that the Corinthians, with whom he had such a tempestuous relationship, would, at the end of the day, recognize the sincerity that had been at work in his ministry among them (see 1 Cor 1:12; 2:17; cf. 1 Thess 2:3–12).

I draw attention to this apostolic emphasis on sincerity because, frankly, there have been times when I have preached messages that I thought beforehand might play out in a sacramental manner only to have them founder miserably. When this happens, I have learned to engage in some prayerful introspection. Sometimes I will sense the Spirit

61. For example, see Matthew 6:2, 5, 16; 7:5; 15:7; 22:18; 23:13, 15, 23, 25, 27–29; 24:51.

62. See Eph 6:10–11; Jas 4:7–8; 1 Pet 5:8.

63. See Acts 2:46; Rom 12:9; 2 Cor 6:6; 11:3; 1 Tim 1:5; 3:8; 2 Tim 1:5; Heb 10:22; Jas 3:17.

prompting me to deal with something amiss—the presence of some degree of pride, selfishness, or rebellion in my heart, or some specific occasion where my words, deeds, or thoughts were not pleasing to the Lord. God is gracious and merciful to the max but we have some pretty good reasons to believe that he really does hold his spokespersons to a higher standard of accountability (see Jas 3:1; cf. Ps 66:18; Isa 59:2). Thus, my spirituality takes this prayer of David seriously:

> But who can discern their own errors? Forgive my hidden faults. Keep your servant also from willful sins; may they not rule over me. Then I will be blameless, innocent of great transgression. May these words of my mouth and this meditation of my heart be pleasing in your sight, LORD, my Rock and my Redeemer. (Ps 19:12–14)

Not to overstate the matter, but I have found that after a preaching or teaching endeavor earmarked more by a sense of struggle than spiritual empowerment, some soul-searching will reveal that I had indeed entered into the ministry moment not sufficiently surrendered and yielded to our inherently relational but holy God. It did not take very many experiences of this type to get my attention!

Thus, I have come to recognize the need to check in with the Lord early on during the preparation of a sermon and, again, just prior to the preaching moment. I ask the Holy Spirit to help me discern whether I have acted, spoken, or even engaged in thinking about others in ways that have grieved him (Eph 4:29–32). I also ask myself whether I currently sense genuine intimacy in my walk with Christ, or, instead, some distance. When I sense there is something amiss, my custom is to draw near to the Lord in prayer (both in the Spirit and in the vernacular), humbly surrendering anew everything I have and am to him (Jas 4:7–8), inviting not only his forgiveness, but a palpable restoration of the joy and steadfast spirit David referred to in Psalm 51:12.[64]

I will be honest here: there are times when this type of spiritually renewing prayer has occurred just moments before I began to preach. The good news is that, even then, I have never found the Lord to be slow

64. Of course, such a prayer also includes an appeal for the Lord to bless the ministry endeavor at hand (see Ps 90:17; Prov 16:3).

in his responsiveness to this prayerful appeal. And this is important because of the way the apostle Paul spoke of the dramatic difference between our being controlled *either* by our sinful nature *or* by Christ's Spirit (Rom 8:5–8; Gal 5:16–18). We must be honest with ourselves and acknowledge that it is possible for us to enter the preaching moment more influenced by our flesh than Christ's Spirit! But, at the same time, I will boldly suggest that, if there is a biblically prescribed protocol for recognizing when we are being more influenced by our sinful nature than the Spirit, and then making the shift from flesh to Spirit Paul commends in Galatians 5:13–26, the prayerful interaction described above would be it. The positive effect of this exegesis of my own heart—this personal examination and theologically real interaction with Christ through his Spirit as I prepare for the preaching moment—has been so consistently salutary that I feel comfortable recommending it to others, especially to those just beginning their preaching and teaching ministries.

In sum, the message of this chapter has been that the second step toward the preaching of sacramental sermons is an engagement in hermeneutical hearing—a prophetic discerning of the heart of God. This begins with a Spirit-enabled exegesis or "faithful listening" to what the Spirit is saying through the biblical text(s) the sermon emerges from,[65] but then, building on that, it leads to a prayerful pondering of how we might cooperate with what our missionary God is up to here and now in the lives of people we have been called to shepherd in Christ's name. It also requires something I refer to as "honest-to-God" praying—an exegesis of our hearts before the Lord.

I am not saying that this is the only way to attempt to discern the heart of God for this or that preaching moment. But it is an approach that seems to be theologically informed. It also enjoys support from preachers both ancient and contemporary, and has proven effective in my own experience. This is how we put ourselves in a position to be able to, with the help of the Holy Spirit, speak to others the very words of God (1 Pet 4:11).

65. Willimon, *Conversations with Barth*, 192.

In the next chapter our focus shifts to the actual composition of sermons that end up playing out in a sacramental manner. Once again, there are some things we can do to increase this possibility.

6

The Third Step

Homiletical Moves That Make for Prophetic Preaching

The elders who direct the affairs of the church well are worthy of double honor, especially those whose work is preaching and teaching.

— 1 TIMOTHY 5:17

IT IS MY HOPE that something prophetic happens every time I preach or teach. If genuinely anointed preaching as I have described it is indeed the type God always intended, we should hope that as many of our sermons as possible play out in a sacramental manner.

Repeatedly I have asserted that, though sacramental sermons cannot be conjured, there are things we can do to put ourselves in a place where the Holy Spirit can use us to facilitate them. In this third section of the book, we have been discussing the process involved in the actualization of the sacramental sermon. Having discussed the importance of the preacher's spirituality, and the need for prophetic discernment regarding the heart of God for this or that preaching moment, we come now to the preparation of the sermon itself. *Are there some things we can do to prepare sermons that are more likely to effect a spiritual, transformative encounter between hearers and the risen Christ?* My experience has been that there are!

I promised the editors and publishers of this work a theology of preaching. But I also indicated that I wanted to include a discussion of some practical homiletical matters. The preaching of sacramental sermons is not just a theory; it really happens. While this ministry phenomenon cannot be mastered or controlled, a capacity to engage in it can, with the help of the Holy Spirit, be lived into. It is my hope that this chapter will help this cooperation with the Holy Spirit to occur.

There are literally dozens of academic and popular books that boldly prescribe the "best" way to preach. The word "whiplash" comes to mind, however, when I reflect on the ways these homiletical works differ from one another in the counsel they provide concerning the *purpose*, *style*, and *mechanics* of Christian preaching. For instance, with respect to the *purpose* of preaching, experts differ on whether preaching should involve gospel proclamation, doctrinal instruction, or heresy-defeating apologetics. With respect to the *style* of preaching there is the perennial debate between topical versus expositional, and between conversational versus didactical sermons. With respect to the *mechanics* of preaching, readers are encouraged to choose between a sermon that focuses on one big idea or allowing the biblical text to speak for itself without imposing a subjective, reductionistic take upon it. And then there is the debate regarding what we should take with us into the pulpit: a manuscript, an outline, or no notes at all. These are only a few of the many disputed matters!

This chapter will address such hotly debated homiletical issues, but in a novel manner. The questions I want to introduce into the conversation are these: *How does the prophetic phenomenon figure into these discussions? What difference, if any, does a "desperate dependence" on the Holy Spirit make during the preparation and delivery of sermons we hope will play out in a sacramental manner? How might our engagement in the art of homiletics be impacted if we take seriously the possibility of a Spirit-enabled and, therefore, "sacred" rhetoric?*

THE METHOD TO MY MADNESS

Several decades of experience in the sanctuary and university classroom, accompanied by a commitment to preaching and teaching that aims at effecting sacramental encounters with the risen Christ, have allowed me to identify some homiletical/pedagogical moves that seem to earmark sermons and lectures that do just that. Some of these moves—those related to the prophetic discernment of God's heart for this or that sermon—were addressed in the previous chapter. The practical counsel in this chapter will build on that previous discussion, identifying some additional homiletical choices I believe we should take seriously if our goal is preaching imbued with the prophetic dynamic. The irony is that we may discover here that there is no "right side" in the debates which populate many homiletical treatises. (Karl Barth famously asserted that there is no final word with respect to anything, including homiletics.)[1] I offer that, instead of striving to be "correct" with respect to the purpose, style, and mechanics of our preaching, *our primary preoccupation ought to be those homiletical moves the Spirit prompts us to make when composing and delivering a sermon.*

We should also, I suggest, give some thoughtful consideration to the relationship between the homiletical moves we make at the behest of the Spirit and the *logos, ethos, pathos, telos,* and *kairos* of our sermons. In chapter 4 we acknowledged the possibility that giving attention to these rhetorical matters can be something the apostle Paul might approve of, his invective against worldly wisdom and oratory in 1 Corinthians 2 notwithstanding. Indeed, we went on in chapter 4 to consider how a Pauline, fully Trinitarian, "I-Thou," lifestyle spirituality will impact who we are, what we say, and how we say it in such a way as to add significant value to our preaching endeavor. Here I want to go further, making the bold observation that the very best sermons I have heard preached, and have preached myself, were aided by the Holy Spirit to be:

- clear, coherent, meaningful (*logos*);
- credible, sincere, trustworthy (*ethos*);

1. See Willimon, *Conversations with Barth,* 159.

- winsome, compelling, viscerally impactful (*pathos*);
- crucial, essential, needful (*telos*); and
- timely, appropriate, providential (*kairos*).

This is why the collection of Spirit-enabled homiletical moves presented below is organized according to these five rhetorical attributes, and why the discussion of many of these moves will include additional commentary intended to clarify the correlations. This dual criterion—Spirit prompting and rhetorical impact—will help us make some critical choices when preparing sermons: choices that might increase the likelihood that our sermons will play out in a Spirit-enabled, sacramental manner.

SOME SUGGESTED HOMILETICAL MOVES: AN ANNOTATED CHECKLIST

There is nothing like the exhilaration and sense of fulfillment that follows the delivery of a sermon you have reason to believe was genuinely anointed by the Holy Spirit and, as a result, did indeed affect at least one hearer in a prophetic, incarnational, truly transformative manner. For what it is worth, here are some homiletical moves I consider crucial to the kind of preaching this book is about.[2]

Preaching Choices That Can Contribute to the Logos (Meaningfulness) of Our Sermons

It is one thing to structure a sermon in such a way as to encourage hearers to go away pondering some things not fully explained. Jesus' use of parables and deliberately provocative questions and statements (see John 3:1–10) bear this out. It is another thing, however, for those who hear our sermons to routinely go away with virtually no clue as to what the sermon was about. While not all hearers will be equally quick

2. I was pleased to discover, after composing this chapter, that many of the items in the "checklist" provided here find support in Dietrich Bonhoeffer's "Criteria for Evaluating the Sermon" as a postscript to his lectures on preaching. See Fant, *Bonhoeffer*, 178–79.

on the uptake, and there can be spiritual reasons why some hearers will seem obtuse with respect to the messages we bring (see 2 Cor 4:4; Titus 3:9–11), Jesus never encouraged his hearers to define truth on their own, or for themselves. Because of his ambition to always honor what he heard the Father saying (John 12:48–50; 14:24) and to emulate what he saw the Father doing (John 5:17, 19), there was always substance and direction in Jesus' interactions with others, even if their awareness of this meaningfulness evolved over time and ended up dismantling their previously held "idolatrous certainties."[3]

I have argued elsewhere that the Matthean version of Jesus' most famous sermon—the Sermon on the Mount (Matt 5–7)—rather than being a hodgepodge of various dominical sayings and teachings, possesses an often overlooked through-line. In a nutshell, Jesus was laying out for his followers, in this first teaching section of Matthew's Gospel, what is involved in a real, trust-based relationship with God, rather than a fear-based, overly scrupulous devotion to rules and rituals based on human traditions. In the process, Jesus kept using the religious leaders of his day (especially the Pharisees) as anti-models or negative examples of the spiritual, moral, and missional faithfulness God desires and deserves. The sermon begins with an edgy, attention-arresting introduction wherein he announced the spiritual attitudes and actions God is really looking for—attitudes and actions that were noticeably lacking in the lives of the Pharisees (Matt 5:1–12; cf. 23:1–36). The sermon concludes with Jesus calling for his hearers to be careful to put into practice what they had heard him preach (Matt 7:21–27). Then we find an editorial comment from the pen of the evangelist that indicated that the crowds much preferred Jesus' teaching over that of the teachers of the law, for what he taught possessed a sense of authority the scribes and Pharisees lacked (Matt 7: 29). Perhaps the heart of the sermon is located in Matthew 5:20 where we hear Jesus say: "For I tell you that unless your righteousness surpasses that of the Pharisees and the teachers of the law, you will certainly not enter the kingdom of heaven."

Space here will not permit a rehearsal of the full argument, but I contend that simply reading through Matthew 5–7 with this thesis will

3. See Alter, *Resurrection Psychology*, 98, 102–3, as cited in Tyra, *Defeating Pharisaism*, 72–73.

be game-changing with respect to our understanding and appreciation of what the Matthean Jesus was up to in the sermon, and what Matthew was up to in his telling of the Jesus story as a whole. The dominical "homily" we refer to as the Sermon on the Mount—grounded in, and profoundly reflective of, God's relational, holy, and missional nature—very definitely possessed a particular theme, and moved in a distinct direction, in a sometimes obvious, sometimes subtle, but ultimately discernible manner.[4]

This would suggest that those who preach in Christ's name likewise have an obligation to make sure that our sermons possess substance and direction.[5] If we, as preachers, are not clear where our sermon is supposed to go, we should not be surprised if we lose hearers along the way (1 Cor 14:8–11). I have benefited much from the adage, "If there is mist in the pulpit, there will be fog in the pew." We preachers must be crystal clear, ourselves, regarding the substance and direction of our sermon—i.e., what we sense the Spirit would have the hearers of this message know, feel, and do (either immediately or ultimately) as a result of it. The method by which we seek to enable hearers to gain a biblically informed understanding of God's heart for them via this or that sermon may vary (e.g., conversation versus exhortation, with or without notes, etc.). But it is never wise nor responsible to be nonchalant regarding the essential coherence (*logos*) of our sermons. And while it is true that the Holy Spirit may call some audibles that we must respond to during the preaching of a sermon, this does not mean that we should enter the moment without a clear, empowering sense of divine direction. Another adage counsels, "If the pilot of a ship doesn't know where he's going, no wind is the right wind."

So, regardless of the nature or style of this or that sermon, the first few moves on my checklist—those related to the *logos* quality of it—are these:

- *Am I, myself, as clear as can be about the direction of this sermon: what God would have my hearers know, feel, and do (either immediately or ultimately) as a result of it?*

4. For a much more comprehensive discussion of this thesis, see Tyra, *Defeating Pharisaism*, 79–189.

5. For more on this, see Robinson, *Biblical Preaching*, 33–50; 101–13.

- *Have I invested sufficient effort in the composition of the sermon's introduction and conclusion, recognizing how important these two components are to helping my hearers understand the sermon's substance and direction?*[6]
- *Does the body of my sermon, as currently constructed, possess a through-line and the right balance between description and prescription, proposition and illustration, explicit assertions and implicit suggestions: rhetorical moves that will help my hearers track with me throughout the sermon without me becoming overly pedantic in the process?*
- *Have I prayerfully (and carefully) created some clear points of possible application that, while not overly patronizing, veritably make it impossible for hearers to go away from the preaching event not knowing what the sermon was about or what God might have been up to in it?*

Preaching Choices That Contribute to the Ethos (Trustworthiness) of Our Sermons

The need for every sermon we preach to possess a clear sense of divine direction leads us to consider yet another set of homiletical moves, the first of which is:

- *Have I taken care to create a sermon that will not only "get to Jesus" thematically, but experientially as well?*

Tim Keller was an especially effective contemporary proponent of the need for every sermon to "get to Christ" and the good news concerning him. He exhorted the readers of his *Preaching*:

> Every time you expound a Bible text, you are not finished unless you demonstrate how it shows us that we cannot save ourselves and that only Jesus can. That means we must preach Christ from every text, which is the same as saying we must

6. For more on this, see Chapell, *Christ-Centered Preaching*, 227–57; Robinson, *Biblical Preaching*, 165–82.

> preach the gospel every time and not just settle for general inspiration or moralizing.[7]

Keller's missional sensitivity is apparent when he argues that getting to Jesus thematically in each sermon is crucial to helping hearers escape the antinomianism and moralism that, ironically, are both rife in contemporary culture.[8] To do this, says Keller, we must get to Jesus—preach the gospel—in every sermon we preach.

Certainly, such a missional sensitivity will contribute to the *logos* of our sermons—a meaningful message that is near and dear to the heart of our missionary God. At the same time, however, I will dare to suggest that we take the idea of "getting to Jesus" further. What if the Spirit of Christ is not only eager to help us preachers "get to Jesus" *thematically* in each sermon, but *experientially* as well? That is, what if "getting to Jesus" involves a Spirit-enabled ability to embody in ourselves those qualities of Christ the people of his day found so compelling: his *wisdom, courage, compassion,* and *anointing*? In other words, perhaps the dynamic of "getting to Jesus" can be understood in two ways: one that impacts the *logos* (substance, meaningfulness, coherence) of our sermons, the other their *ethos* (credibility, trustworthiness)!

Some support for such a supposition can be found in the way the apostle Paul encouraged the Galatian Christians to understand that by keeping in step with the Spirit (Gal 5:25) they would begin to embody the Christ-virtues of "love, joy, peace, patience, kindness, goodness, faithfulness, gentleness and self-control" (Gal 5:22–23). So, it is not out of bounds to think that the Spirit of Jesus might be eager to help those of us who preach Christ to exude the *wisdom, courage, compassion,* and *anointing/authority* that earmarked his public ministry. If a Spirit-enabled embodiment of Jesus' ministry virtues is even a possibility, is it not something we should prayerfully pursue? Indeed, as I pray in the Spirit prior to each preaching moment, allowing the Spirit of Jesus to pray through me according to the will of the Father, my heart is hoping that one effect may be that I am enabled to "bring Christ's presence, personality, and power with me" into the preaching moment.

7. Keller, *Preaching*, 48.

8. Keller, *Preaching*, 52–63.

Once again, Tim Keller is of service:

> People do not simply experience your words, arguments, and appeals as disembodied messages; they are always sensing and evaluating the source. . . . They are looking for love, humility, conviction, joy, and power—for some integrity and congruence between what you are saying and who you are. Audiences are able to sense what kind of energy—or lack thereof—lies behind the speaking. . . .
>
> To be sure, your listeners are responding to your skills, preparation, character, and conviction. . . . But for the act of preaching in particular, there's something even more central to persuasion: your listener's sense of the Holy Spirit working in and through you.[9]

So I suggest we become intentional about asking the Holy Spirit to help us take "getting to Jesus" to the next level. Certainly, the influence of the Spirit on not only what we say but how we say it—so that our hearers are reminded of Jesus even as we preach in his name—will contribute to the ethos of our sermons.[10]

Going further still, and focusing especially now on the *authority* at work in Jesus' ministry, I offer a related checklist item:

- *Have I done my due diligence to prepare a sermon that might function in people's lives with authority—as the word of God proclaimed—without me having to make this suggestion myself?*

I have already indicated that the author of the "first Gospel" considered it important to report that the crowd's appreciation of Jesus' Sermon on the Mount was due in large part to the fact that the homily exuded genuine spiritual authority—an authorization provided by God's Spirit to speak and act in his name.[11] This raises two critical questions: *Can Christ's inherent spiritual authority genuinely imbue the*

9. Keller, *Preaching*, 191–92.

10. See Chapell, *Christ-Centered Preaching*, 94, 222.

11. The anointing or authority at work in Jesus' ministry—his ability to speak and act on God's behalf—is a theme that shows up in both implicit and explicit ways throughout Matthew's telling of the Jesus story (e.g., see Matt 8:5–10; 9:6–8, 32–34; 10:1; 21:23–27; 28:18).

sermons of those who are called to preach in his name? If so, what can we preachers do to put ourselves in a place whereby we might experience this imparted spiritual authority?

I contend that Karl Barth's understandings of revelation as event (God's speaking) and the threefold form of the Word of God, suggest that this remarkable phenomenon can occur.[12] Barth scholar Kurt Anders Richardson explains: "Barth wanted his readers to focus on *the active revelation of God's Word,* which God is *constantly accomplishing* through Scripture, and *the preaching of Scripture by the power of the Holy Spirit.*"[13] Barth saw this revelatory event as taking place in three forms: the Word of God *revealed* (Jesus Christ); the word of God *written* (the Scriptures); and the word of God *proclaimed* (Proclamation).[14] But Barth maintained that there is an order of priority within this threefold expression of the word of God. The word of God proclaimed is contingent upon the word of God written, which is contingent upon the Word of God revealed. This explains Barth's insistence that true proclamation is contingent upon the Word of God. Says Barth: "For so far as proclamation really rests upon the recollection of the revelation attested in the Bible and is therefore the obedient repetition of the Biblical witness, it is no less the Word of God than the Bible."[15] In other words, though it may seem too messy for some, the preparation of the sermon is genuinely grounded in a theologically real conversation with Christ the living Word, by means of a faithful listening to his voice in the biblical text(s)—the written word—might convey Christ's own authority/anointing.[16] This means that hearers would not only sense Christ's authority underwriting the sermon, but also an innate

12. A summary discussion of these topics which aims to be accessible to those only beginning their study of Barth can be found in Franke, *Barth for Armchair Theologians,* 115–23. Another brief summary of Barth's takes on these topics is available in Bromiley, *Introduction to the Theology of Karl Barth,* 6–8. For a more thorough discussion of Barth's perspective on revelation in general, see Chia, *Revelation and Theology,* 129–60. For a nuanced discussion of Barth's concept of revelation as event/encounter in particular, see Hart, "Revelation," 45–55.

13. Richardson, *Reading Karl Barth,* 106.

14. Richardson, *Reading Karl Barth,* 88–24.

15. Barth, *Church Dogmatics,* I/2, 136, as cited in Lischer, *Theology of Preaching,* 59.

16. For more on this, see Willimon, *Conversations with Barth,* 230–31.

compulsion to call upon him for the spiritual enablement necessary to live into its message.

Obviously, were this phenomenon to occur with some degree of frequency in a local church, the impact would be great. Our hearers might eventually begin to approach preaching/teaching events in an expectant, receptive, even reverent manner. I will have more to say about how congregations can be enabled to discern and respond to sacramental sermons in the next chapter. At this point, however, the question is: *How might our hearers begin to suspect that they can trust their preacher to proclaim to them a word that might actually come from the heart of God without the preacher making this claim for him- or herself?*

Karl Barth made it very clear that, were a preacher to "reach out beyond himself, to put himself with his word about God in the place of God, it would be blasphemous rebellion."[17] So that approach is a nonstarter. At the same time, though, as we have seen, he also argued that there will be a prophetic aspect to true proclamation. This is why Barth emphasized the ability of (and need for) congregations to accurately gauge the degree of intimate interaction between their preacher and God. William Willimon describes Barth's perspective: "When the preacher speaks, what is spoken is testimony to the sort of conversation and interaction that the preacher has had with the incarnate Word."[18] Put differently, according to Barth, our preaching can be experienced as the word of God when it is truly *generated* by an engagement in "faithful listening" to the Bible's Spirit-inspired witness to the living Word, Jesus Christ.[19]

On the one hand, this means that a preacher must do more than simply cite a biblical text at the beginning of a homily. Whether a sermon is stand-alone or part of a topical or expositional series, it must *emerge* or *derive its life* from the biblical witness to Christ. It only makes sense to assume, then, that the same Spirit who inspired that written witness to Christ would want the sermons we preach to be genuinely grounded in, rather than merely introduced by, one or more canonical texts. On the other hand, the larger point I am making is this: *To the*

17. Barth, *Church Dogmatics,* I/1, 52–53.

18. Willimon, *Conversations with Barth,* 193.

19. Willimon, *Conversations with Barth,* 192.

degree we do more than use the Bible as a launching pad or diving board into our sermons—to the degree we genuinely engage in the kind of faithful listening Barth advocated for, and humbly, discreetly, faithfully allow the Spirit to speak through us in a prophetic manner during the preaching moment—it is possible for congregants to eventually gain the impression that our sermons are indeed products of theologically real conversations with Christ and the Scriptures. When this occurs, the *ethos* of our preaching, and the capacity of any given sermon to effect a sacramental encounter with Christ, the living Word, is greatly enhanced. We do not have to announce to the congregation that we have been in touch with Jesus and have been authorized to speak for him. The Holy Spirit will do this for us!

Preaching Choices That Contribute to the Pathos (Winsomeness) of Our Sermons

Students in online synchronous class sessions will sometimes respond to what they are hearing in the lecture by typing a single word into the chat forum: *Fire!* I will not necessarily be aware of this at the time, but it is gratifying to see these comments later, after the class session has concluded. It is with this in mind that I add another item to our self-reflection checklist:

- *Will this sermon, while faithful to the biblical text(s), strike hearers as fresh, thought-provoking, compelling, and important rather than stale, clichéd, or hackneyed?*

Tim Keller provided support for this preaching move/concern when he stressed the need for preachers to communicate in a way that is *memorable* in its *insight*. He writes:

> Rather than telling the listeners things they already know in terms they know, a memorable address is filled with fresh, insightful ways of conveying concepts—concepts the listeners may already know at one level but find new and interesting. "I

> never heard it put that way before" is what they say or think afterward. [20]

We should note that Keller's encouragement was *not* for us to come up with new concepts that may be at odds with the intentions of the biblical authors. The call, instead, was to communicate the mind and hearts of the biblical authors in ways that are unexpected and arresting rather than tired and boring. As well, we can endeavor to apply biblical texts to the lives of contemporary hearers in ways that, while not specified by the biblical authors, are not incongruous with the understanding the biblical authors had of who God is and what he is about.

It is in this sense that creativity can be considered an earmark of anointing. I still remember a compliment I once received from a church member who was, literally, a rocket scientist. He appreciated the fact that my sermons did not seem to be simple recitations of information provided in biblical commentaries. Later in my preaching ministry, another parishioner commented on the way my illustrative material, while faithful to Scripture, seemed to indicate a familiarity with extrabiblical literary works. That said, while I concur with the emphasis Keller placed on the need for preachers to be well-read,[21] I will also contend, once again, that one of the benefits of praying in the Spirit during my preparation of sermons has been the many creative "epiphanies" the Spirit has provided over the years. If we allow him, the Holy Spirit who inspired the Scriptures can help us notice details in and connections between biblical texts not previously recognized, and communicate insights in memorable, impactful ways.

Going further, and keeping the winsomeness of our sermons in mind, another important homiletical move is to be very intentional about speaking to both the head and heart of our hearers. Interestingly, Karl Barth argued that it is unnecessary for preachers to shoulder the burden of "finding the right word, the right technique, and the right form in order that a sermon 'works.' . . . That task belongs to the Holy Spirit."[22] This assertion was based on Barth's view that true divine

20. Keller, *Preaching*, 177.

21. Keller, *Preaching*, 177.

22. Willimon, *Conversations with Barth*, 128.

proclamation—the spoken word that is grounded in the written word, which points to the living Word—is self-authenticating and cannot fail to accomplish what our speaking, self-revealing God intends (Jer 23:29; Isa 55:10–11.) On the other hand, Tim Keller insisted that preachers should be sensitive to this issue. He suggested rather stridently that:

> Preaching cannot simply be accurate and sound. It must capture the listener's interest and imaginations; it must be compelling and penetrate to their hearts. It is possible to merely assert and confront and feel we have been very "valiant for truth," but if you are dry or tedious, people will not repent and believe the right doctrine you present. We must preach so that, as in the first sermon on Pentecost, hearers are "cut to the heart" (Acts 2:37).[23]

Is there any way we can reconcile the apparently competing counsels provided by Barth and Keller regarding this homiletical choice? I believe Barth was right to say that it is the Holy Spirit's job to enliven the preached word in such a way as to convince and convict (John 16:18). But Keller was also right to suggest that the words of the preacher matter, as Peter's sermon in Acts 2 makes evident. What I will offer is that while Keller focuses on the need for preachers to reach people's hearts by presenting to them the "beauty of Christ,"[24] it has been my experience that the creative ways we do this can be the result of our praying for the Holy Spirit's anointing upon the preparation and delivery of the sermon. In an online article titled "Karl Barth and the Phenomenon of Prophetic Preaching," I explained how that my experience over the years has been that, in addition to the startling degree of serendipity that has occurred during the collection of resources for some sermons, and the sense that, quite often, the Holy Spirit seems to "speak through me" while preaching, the dead giveaway that something prophetic is occurring in the preaching moment is that the Spirit moves in my listeners' hearts in an especially powerful manner.[25] Thus, both Barth and Keller were correct. But I contend that a pneumatological posture of

23. Keller, *Preaching*, 157.

24. Keller, *Preaching*, 162.

25. Tyra, "Karl Barth and the Phenomenon of Prophetic Preaching," para. 13.

expectation rather than presumption is key to our experiencing, in a more frequent rather than occasional manner, the kind of anointing that causes sermons to reach the hearts of hearers. Thus, another item in my checklist of homiletical moves that make for prophetic preaching is this:

- *How intentional have I been in seeking the Holy Spirit's assistance at speaking to the heart of my hearers in this sermon? Have I prayed with a sense of expectancy for the experience of creative epiphanies while preparing this sermon? Have I prayed in the Spirit as part of my preparation for the preaching moment, inviting the Holy Spirit to speak through me during it?*

Praying in the Spirit for creative insights to come to us during the preparation and delivery of sermons and lectures really is a thing—a game-changing homiletical, pedagogical move! It can dramatically impact the *pathos* (winsomeness, visceral impact) of our sermons. Should we not be open to *all* the assistance the Holy Spirit will provide as we endeavor to preach God's word in the manner he always intended?

Preaching Choices That Contribute to the Telos (Needfulness) of Our Sermons

Earlier in this chapter I referred to the adage, "If there is a mist in the pulpit, there will be a fog in the pew" to make the point that we must be crystal clear with respect to the meaning (*logos*) of our sermons. If we are not sure of the sermon's message, how can we expect our hearers to be? I am also convinced that we preachers must believe deeply in the needfulness (*telos*) our sermons. If we are not thoroughly convinced of each sermon's importance, why should we expect anyone to take it seriously?

The good news is that if our sermon preparation process has included the kind of hermeneutical hearing that enables us to sense the heart of God in this or that biblical passage and, therefore, this or that sermon, the *telos* characteristic of those sermons should be readily apparent. On the other hand, the fact that genuinely anointed sermons are prophetic in nature, and may strike our hearers as challenging as well as comforting, means that there will be times when we find ourselves somewhat reticent to obey the Spirit's homiletical prompting. It happens! What do we do then? How can we be assured that a message we know will be especially provocative is so important/needful that it must be delivered regardless of the consequences? As well, in what manner should we deliver an especially challenging word from the Lord?

Jesus' preaching ministry provides us with a paradigm for how to act at such times even though, because of his intimacy with the Father, his certainty regarding the importance and needfulness of this or that message was never in doubt. There were, however, occasions when Jesus' faithfulness to the heart of the Father called for him to preach messages that not only put his life in jeopardy but, perhaps more importantly, broke his heart. As a case in point, consider the public dressing down of the scribes and Pharisees by Jesus in Matthew 23. This strikes me as a glaring example of an important, needful message from the heart of the Father that the human Jesus might have wished he did not have to deliver. I believe we can extrapolate from this preaching scenario some criteria by which we can discern whether a challenging message really is from the Father's heart and, therefore, too important not to deliver. Inversely, it may also produce within us some deep reflection regarding an important difference between Jesus' preaching ministry and ours, highlighting for us the manner in which we imperfect preachers are called to communicate difficult truths to fellow sinners.

Some especially powerful verses in Matthew's record of this stunning sermon are these:

> "Woe to you, teachers of the law and Pharisees, you hypocrites! You shut the door of the kingdom of heaven in people's faces. You yourselves do not enter, nor will you let those enter who are trying to." (Matt 23:13)

> "Woe to you, teachers of the law and Pharisees, you hypocrites! You travel over land and sea to win a single convert, and when you have succeeded, you make them twice as much a child of hell as you are." (Matt 23:15)

> "Woe to you, teachers of the law and Pharisees, you hypocrites! You clean the outside of the cup and dish, but inside they are full of greed and self-indulgence." (Matt 23:25)
>
> "Woe to you, teachers of the law and Pharisees, you hypocrites! You are like whitewashed tombs, which look beautiful on the outside but on the inside are full of the bones of the dead and everything unclean." (Matt 23:27)
>
> "You snakes! You brood of vipers! How will you escape being condemned to hell?" (Matt 23:33)

Matthew 23 surely underscores how very serious Jesus was about heralding the heart of the Father even when the sermon was liable to rile people who could make his life very uncomfortable. Sermons that are prophetic in nature can have this effect. Two questions come to mind: (1) *Why did Jesus consider this message to be so important that it needed to be delivered despite the consequences?* (2) *What manner-related lesson(s) can we take away from this sermon: are we to emulate the manner in which Jesus delivered this sermon, or take care not to?*

As to the first question, in my book, *Defeating Pharisaism: Recovering Jesus' Disciple-Making Method,* I cite the work of Margaret Alter titled *Resurrection Psychology: An Understanding of Human Personality Based on the Life and Teachings of Jesus.* According to Alter, behind the Pharisees' devotion to rules and rituals was a fear-based pursuit of psychological safety.[26] Thus, it was essentially idolatrous in that it replaced a personal God with a set of moral commands and rabbinic traditions to be obeyed and observed in a formalistic manner. Alter explains: "If, in fact, we have nailed down a perfect code to be followed in detail, we do not need to interact with the God of freedom. Indeed, if we possess a code to which we can cling, we embrace an illusion of safety: we know good and evil; we have become 'like God' (Gen 3)."[27] What is more, the Pharisees sought to impose this essentially idolatrous religion of rules and rituals on the *am ha-aretz* (people of the land). If Alter's argument holds, it explains why Jesus felt the need to not simply quarrel with

26. Alter, *Resurrection Psychology*, 24, 31.

27. Alter, *Resurrection Psychology*, 35.

the Pharisees, but to upbraid them publicly in the sternest of tones.[28] The religious formalism of the Pharisees, which, in turn, produced a rigorous legalism, separatism, judgmentalism, dogmatism, pugilism, hypocrisy, etc., was and is completely antithetical to an intimate, interactive, trust- and love-based relationship with our Creator whose image we bear, [29] as well as the spiritual, moral, and missional faithfulness our God desires and deserves.[30] The fact that the Pharisees were not only engaging in an egregious form of idolatry themselves, but also traveling land and sea to make converts, explains why Jesus felt the need to confront the Pharisees in a public manner. The scalding rebuke of the scribes and Pharisees presented in Matthew 23 was and is a super-important, badly needful message from the heart of the Father!

That said, I also believe that Jesus was, ironically, showing mercy to the Pharisees, speaking to and about them in ways that not only warned onlookers, but also served to throw cold water in the faces of his antagonists, putting them on their heels, nudging them toward some badly needed theological and personal reflection. Viewing Nicodemus as a Johannine paradigm for what Jesus was up to, I believe a case can be made for the idea that the way Jesus interacted with the legalistic, pugilistic, formalistic religionists of his day was designed to actually reach as many of them as possible. The Spirit of mission led Jesus to do that which was necessary to unseat the Pharisees' "idolatrous certainties," replacing them with haunting questions that might cause at least some of them, like Nicodemus, to experience life-changing personal encounters with God's primary sacrament (e.g., see John 3:1–21). I do not believe for a moment that Jesus enjoyed upbraiding the Pharisees. But he was willing to do it, as these passages from the first Gospel make clear: Matthew 5–7; 12:22–37, 38–45; 15:1–20; 21:45; 23:1–39.[31]

28. Alter, *Resurrection Psychology*, 31–32.

29. For more on the problem Jesus had with the Pharisees, see Tyra, *Defeating Pharisaism*, 44–50.

30. For more on the relation between Pharisaism and a spiritual faithfulness, see Tyra, *Getting Real*, 76–77.

31. Though space will not permit me to elaborate here, I propose that because we find in the fourth Gospel the language of both responsibility (e.g., John 5:24, 39, 44, 46–47) and election (e.g., 6:35–40), Jesus was likely using the latter in a missional manner. Rather than being merely dismissive, Jesus was speaking to the "Jews" in

His own embodiment of a spiritual, moral, and missional faithfulness before the Father, as well as the threefold faithfulness of his followers through the ages, required these prophetic sermons.

The point is that preaching prophetically is serious business and not for the faint of heart. On any given occasion, hearing the very words of God proclaimed to them will be, for some, comforting, encouraging, strengthening (1 Cor 14:3), and for others, anything but. We must, like Jesus, be faithful heralds of God's heart in any case!

And yet, with respect to the second question posed above, let me be clear: I am *not* suggesting that we imitate the harsh invective Jesus directed toward the Pharisees. In my mind, only the incarnate Son of God can be truly righteous in his indignation (Jas 1:20). Yeshua hamashiach was up to something in the lives of the Pharisees and those sermon auditors who were being profoundly, negatively influenced by them. At the very least, this should be our rule of thumb: *Anything and anyone that stands in the way of our hearers cultivating a spiritual, moral, and missional faithfulness before the Father needs to be confronted—vigorously!* But we must always speak this and all spiritual truths in a manner which errs on the side of mercy rather than judgment and condemnation when it comes to the persons involved (see Matt 7:1–5; Eph 6:12; Jas 2:12–13; 3:17–18).

In sum, to be genuinely prophetic, our sermons can and must possess a sense of weightiness and genuine needfulness. Our hearers should *never* sense that the purpose (*telos*) of any sermon delivered by us might have been simply to entertain, impress, or fulfill an obligatory ecclesial task. Instead, our demeanor and rhetoric should instill confidence in our hearers regarding our commitment to *honor the heart of God every single time we preach his word!* As well, they should sense our deep conviction that any sermon that succeeds at encouraging and enabling hearers to someday hear Jesus say to them "Well done, good and faithful servant" is straight from God's heart and therefore super necessary! It is with these thoughts in mind that I proffer the following collection of self-reflection questions:

---

such a way as to produce some necessary uncertainty in their minds regarding their current status before God, a testing, haunting uncertainty that would ultimately draw some of them (like Nicodemus) to him.

- *Honestly, was my aim when preparing this message to do my best to honor God's heart discerned through a diligent, prayerful engagement in hermeneutical hearing, or was it, rather, to merely entertain, impress, or fulfill an obligation?*
- *Does this sermon portray Jesus' commitment (or that of some other biblical character) to render to God a spiritual, moral, and missional faithfulness? Does it seek to encourage and enable its hearers to make progress in their own ability to render to God the threefold faithfulness he desires and deserves?*
- *To what degree will this sermon provide a prophetic deconstruction of religious and culturally pervasive beliefs and values that Satan uses, in every age, to blind people to the truth of the Christian gospel (2 Cor 4:3–4) and seduce them away from a sincere and pure devotion to Christ and his mission (2 Cor 11:3)?*
- *To what degree does this sermon model for hearers a commitment to communicating both grace and truth (John 1:17), and always speaking the truth in love (Eph 4:15)?*

Preaching Choices That Contribute to the Kairos (Timeliness) of Our Sermons

Prophetic preaching will, by definition, always be timely and profoundly pertinent. But sometimes sermons can strike hearers as eerily prescient. They will wonder how their preachers know what they know and will readily acknowledge that what was proclaimed in the message they just heard was precisely what they needed to hear at that moment in their lives. Preaching that is truly prophetic does more than dispense sound but generic wisdom anyone would do well to keep in mind. It seems to provide specific insight regarding what God would have his people know, feel, and do just now. To a large degree, it is the *kairos* attribute of a sermon—its timeliness and remarkable pertinence—that causes it to play out in a sacramental, encounter-effecting manner.

My experience has been that this dynamic can occur in ways both subtle and dramatic. If we spend time during the preparation of the sermon praying in the Spirit—i.e., allowing the Spirit to pray for and through us according to God's will (Rom 8:26–27)—we may be enabled by the Spirit to compose a sermon that derives not only from the biblical text but also the mind of Christ (1 Cor 2:9–16). As a result, our sermon might take up matters at work in people's lives that are unbeknownst to us but that God knows need to be addressed. Thus, we end up speaking to people in a way that is rich with *kairos:* timeliness, relevance, pertinence.

But there is another, less subtle, more dramatic way the prophetic nature of a sermon might manifest itself. Sometimes the rhetorical attribute known as *kairos* may become evident when, mid-sermon, we find ourselves, as it were, *being carried along by the Holy Spirit* (1 Pet 1:21)—saying things we did not know we knew, explaining things in ways not planned or rehearsed, evidencing feelings and emotions that catch even us by surprise, with the result that the attention of hearers is arrested in a way that seems supernatural. I dare say most preachers, even those who do not identify as Pentecostal or Charismatic, have experienced this amazing phenomenon: prophetic, incarnational, truly transformative preaching. Testimonies abound to lives being changed as a result.

The question is: *What, if anything, can preachers do to put themselves in a position to deliver sermons that, in this more dramatic manner, strike hearers as being genuinely providential?* The answer to this question is baked into the preceding paragraph with its reference to our "being carried along by the Holy Spirit."

In the final chapter of *Preaching and Preachers,* the very evangelical Martyn Lloyd-Jones writes: "I have kept and reserved to this last lecture what is after all the greatest essential in connection with preaching, and that is the unction and the anointing of the Holy Spirit."[32] Later in the chapter Lloyd-Jones exclaims: "You can have knowledge, and you can be meticulous in your preparation; but without the unction of the Holy Spirit you will have no power, and your preaching will not be effective."[33]

32. Lloyd-Jones, *Preaching and Preachers*, 307.

33. Lloyd-Jones, *Preaching and Preachers*, 321.

Perhaps it was because he knew that his non-Pentecostal readers would benefit from it, that Lloyd-Jones proceeded to clarify what is meant by this notion of an "unction" or "anointing" of or by Spirit.

> It is the Holy Spirit falling upon the preacher in a special manner. It is an access of power. It is God giving power, and enabling, through the Spirit, to the preacher in order that he [or she] may do this work in a manner that lifts up beyond the efforts and endeavor of [humans] to a position in which the preacher is being used by the Spirit and becomes the channel through whom the Spirit works.[34]

In an earlier discussion (chapter 2), we took note of the way Lloyd-Jones spoke of preachers being amazed at what the Spirit was saying and doing through them as they preached. He boldly referred to the Spirit using preachers as willing, enthralled instruments, channels, and vehicles during the preaching moment.[35]

He then went further to describe, in an equally exuberant manner, the effect that a genuinely anointed sermon has on its hearers, writing: "They sense it at once; they can tell the difference immediately. They are gripped, they become serious. . . . They know at once that something quite unusual and exceptional is happening. As a result, they begin to delight in the things of God and they want more and more teaching."[36]

Finally, Lloyd-Jones articulated this crucial query: "What then are we to do about this?"[37] Remember, Lloyd-Jones was an evangelical writing primarily for evangelicals. Still, he offered some bold counsel, displaying in the process the pneumatological realism I believe was at work in his theology and preaching ministry. He wrote:

> There is only one obvious conclusion. Seek Him! Seek Him! What can we do without Him? Seek Him! Seek Him always. But go beyond seeking Him; expect Him. Do you expect anything to happen when you get up to preach in a pulpit? Or do you just say to yourself, "Well, I have prepared my address, I

34. Lloyd-Jones, *Preaching and Preachers*, 306.
35. Lloyd-Jones, *Preaching and Preachers*, 326.
36. Lloyd-Jones, *Preaching and Preachers*, 326.
37. Lloyd-Jones, *Preaching and Preachers*, 326.

> am going to give them this address; some of them will appreciate it and some will not"? Are you expecting it to be the turning point in someone's life? Are you expecting anyone to have a climactic experience? That is what preaching is meant to do. That is what you find in the Bible and in the subsequent history of the Church. Seek this power, expect this power, yearn for this power; and when the power comes, yield to Him. Do not resist. Forget all about your sermon if necessary. Let Him loose you, let him manifest His power in you and through you. I am certain, as I have said several times before, that nothing but a return of this power of the Spirit on our preaching is going to avail us anything. This makes true preaching, and it is the greatest need of all today—never more so. Nothing can substitute for this.[38]

It is with these words ringing in our ears that I proffer this final trio of items for our sermon prep checklist:

- *Honestly, to what degree has the preparation of this sermon been earmarked by a "desperate dependence on the Spirit"? To what degree have I genuinely sought the Spirit and his anointing?*
- *As I approach this coming preaching moment, is there a sense of hopeful expectation within me that something prophetic will occur?*
- *Have I specifically indicated to the Spirit that he is welcome to speak through me, evincing Christ in the process, not only arresting the attention of my hearers, but also convincing and convicting them in a supernatural manner, pleasing God the Father as a result?*

It is my hope that the collection of homiletical moves in this chapter will *move* us toward that focus on the Spirit-enablement and rhetorical impact I have found to be genuinely helpful in the preparation of sermons that play out in a sacramental manner. I will bring this provocative discussion to a close with some words of wisdom provided by the late Tim Keller. After presenting a checklist of his own (characteristics of preaching from the heart), Keller shared with his readers these perspective-providing, ultimately encouraging remarks:

38. Lloyd-Jones, *Preaching and Preachers*, 326–27.

> Feeling overwhelmed? Me too. However, a key to developing these traits is not to directly try to have them. Instead, glory in your infirmities so his power may be made perfect in weakness (2 Corinthians 12:9). This is a discipline by which you constantly remind yourself of what you are under your own power. It leads to desperate dependence on the Spirit—but along with this desperation will come the joyful freedom of knowing that in the end nothing in preaching rests on your eloquence, your wisdom, or your ability. Nothing ever has! Every success and blessing and fruit you have ever borne has been from him.
>
> Tremendous freedom comes when we can laugh at ourselves and whisper to him, "So! It's been you all along!" In some ways that day will be the true beginning of your career as a preacher and teacher of God's Word.[39]

I concur with Keller. Though the task of preaching—especially the kind of preaching God always intended—can seem overwhelming, the truth is we are never really alone or on our own. The Holy Spirit and the risen Christ want to enable us to discern God's heart and then empower us to preach sermons that make a difference in the lives of our hearers. Knowing this, remembering this, living into this awareness, is crucial to the pursuit of genuinely anointed preaching! So, I must inquire: Are you in?

The final stop in our journey is just ahead. There are some things we can do to help our congregants experience an anointing of their own—one that is also crucial to the experience of sacramental sermons. It may be that I have saved the best for last!

39. Keller, *Preaching*, 206–7.

7

The Fourth Step

Preparing the Congregation

And we also thank God continually because, when you received the word of God, which you heard from us, you accepted it not as a human word, but as it actually is, the word of God, which is indeed at work in you who believe.
— 1 Thessalonians 2:13

Barth scholar Aaron Smith attempts to explain why the Swiss parson-turned-theologian was so obsessed with the preaching task. Citing Barth in the process, Smith writes:

> The sermon is instructive for Barth because of its existential poignancy. "On Sunday morning when the bells ring to call the congregation and minister to church, there is in the air an *expectancy* that something great, crucial, and even momentous is to *happen*." It is not, of course, that everyone feels or is equally conscious of this anticipation, but that does not alter the fact that "*expectancy* is inherent in the whole situation."
>
> The sermon is wreathed in readiness. For what? Not merely for edification, entertainment, or instruction, Barth says, but to hear and confess that "God *is* present. The whole situation witnesses, cries, simply shouts of it, even when in

> minister or people there arises questioning, wretchedness, or despair." It is to hear and interrogate the biblical claim that God is in fact present even in the midst of doubting and wretched humanity that people come to church and the minister climbs the pulpit.[1]

According to Smith, Barth was convinced that people came to church hoping against hope for an encounter—to experience a sacramental sermon.

On the other hand, William Willimon suggests that Barth's theology of crisis[2] could make him less optimistic regarding the manner in which churchgoers approach the preaching moment. Using a much more caustic tone, this mainline Protestant preacher channels Barth as he writes:

> The congregation is the Body of Christ, that gathering whom God has convened to hear the royal proclamation, but the congregation is full of the same incomprehension, cowardice, disbelief, and rebellion that is found in any human gathering when it is assaulted by the Word. We preachers meet no resistance to the Word that was not first encountered in our own hearts. As Barth might put it, the church is just full of "religion" and therefore full of idolatry and credulity, resistance and artful dodging of the Word. Though the church may say it wants to hear the Word of God—to be addressed by their Lord and Savior—the church lies. Perhaps resistance to the Word is even more pronounced in the church because the church knows firsthand that (1) God's Word is always a summons, an address, a vocation and an obligation, and (2) God has great work in mind for the church, and therefore the church is justified in feeling some fear and consternation in

1. Aaron Smith, *Theology of the Third Article*, 39. The quotations are from Barth, "Need and Promise of Christian Preaching," 104, emphasis original.

2. Barth scholar Ronald Allen describes Barth's theology of crisis: "For Barth, the word of God through preaching creates a crisis in the congregation in which listeners should recognize the ways they fail to embrace God's purposes, while offering the congregation the grace necessary to turn away from the idolatries of modern life (including liberal theology) and to turn toward the coming world of God." See Allen, "Preaching as Spark for Discovery in Theology," 140.

> the face of that vocation and therefore is full of resistance to that Word. Church therefore tends to be not only training in discipleship but also in various techniques for avoiding the Word of God.[3]

Okay, so which take on Barth's view of churchgoers is the correct one? Do most congregants approach the preaching moment eager to hear from God, or do they arrive with their defenses up, uneasy and wary? I suspect that, as with most either/or propositions, there is truth in both, and support for each can be found in Barth's dialectical theology.

That said, I want to focus here on *how preachers can partner with the Holy Spirit in the cultivation of ecclesial environments that are rich with a sense of pneumatological expectancy.* The Gospels are replete with stories that depict Jesus commenting approvingly on the hopeful faith exercised by supplicants (e.g., Matt 8:10; 9:20–22; 15:21–28; Luke 7:1–10). Likewise, the prayer meeting that occasioned the outpouring of the Holy Spirit and emergence of the Christian church as such (Acts 2:1–41) seems to have been earmarked by a significant degree of spiritual expectancy. The "hundred and twenty" (Acts 1:15) in the upper room on the day of Pentecost were not simply praying, they were "waiting" on the Lord,[4] praying with an intense expectation precipitated by Jesus' instructions (Acts 1:4–5, 8).

This explains, I believe, why it is in ecclesial environments that are characterized by the hope and expectation that sermons might play out in a sacramental manner. This is not simply wish fulfillment or shared psychosis; it is the theologically real connection that exists in God's economy between expectancy and experience!

Recently I was asked to Zoom into an online session of a Doctor of Ministry course being taught by a professor friend. One of my books had been assigned as required reading and I was to interact with students regarding it. Near the end of the discussion, a student inquired about my next publishing project. In my response to this query I indicated that I was currently working on a theology of preaching from a

3. Willimon, *Conversations with Barth*, 244–45.

4. See, for example, Ps 27:14; 33:20; 37:7; 38:15; 130:5–6; Lam 3:24–26; Mic 7:7; Isa 40:31 (KJV).

Spirit-empowered perspective. The next day I received an email from another student on that Zoom call—one that included these remarks:

> It was great having you in our class today . . . I was excited to hear about your new book on Prophetic Preaching. My former pastor . . . preached in a way that I considered prophetic. There was an obvious moving of the Spirit in my heart and I heard from the Lord every time. I knew that when I came to service, I would be hearing from the Lord. That is what I want [in my own preaching] . . . people to experience the presence of the Lord in a way that does not happen in the world, where they will recognize that the Lord is here, alive in the midst, speaking to them personally.

This student, already a church leader herself, describes in retrospect an ecclesial environment she remembers fondly: one in which churchgoers eagerly approached preaching/teaching moments with a sense of eager expectancy. She describes a church setting in which a pneumatological realism is at work: people are aware of the activity of the Holy Spirit around and within. More precisely, they sense the presence of the Lord during the preaching event, speaking to them personally through their preacher. Like the church members in Thessalonica to whom Paul wrote, they are eager and able to receive a genuinely anointed sermon for what it actually is: not merely a human word, but the word of God (1 Thess 2:13).

Of course, there are no perfect churches, preachers, or sermons. Still, I am convinced that, as this DMin student's fond reflection indicates, *it is possible to cultivate ecclesial settings in which prophetic, incarnational, truly transformative preaching occurs with some degree of frequency.* We have talked at length in previous chapters about the preparation of *preachers* and *sermons* if the word proclaimed is to play out in a sacramental manner. In this final chapter we will engage in a serious discussion of what church leaders can do to prepare their *congregations* for this phenomenon.

To be more specific, in this final chapter, I want to discuss three important matters:

- how to help congregants eagerly *anticipate* genuinely anointed sermons;
- how to help congregants *discern* when and how the risen Christ is speaking to them through a genuinely anointed sermon; and
- how to enable churchgoers to *process* genuinely anointed sermons in such a way as to become doers of the word rather than hearers only.

What we are about to discover is that sermons that play out in a sacramental manner not only require an anointing on the preacher, but on the audience as well. This chapter is about how we as church leaders can help congregants experience this anointing. I propose that there are three church leadership moves that make for prophetic preaching—sermons that function as what Barth referred to as the "Word of God proclaimed."

HELPING OUR CONGREGANTS ANTICIPATE THE WORD OF GOD PROCLAIMED

The student referred to above indicated in her email that she fondly remembered attending preaching events with a sense of anticipation in place. She genuinely believed she might experience a "moving of the Spirit" in her heart as her pastor preached the word. As I would say, her pneumatological posture was one of expectancy rather than presumption or indifference. In other words, there was a pneumatological realism at work in her walk with Christ! Our goal as preachers should be to see the pews of our churches packed with folks who similarly possess a robust, realist doctrine of the Holy Spirit.

The place to start is to make the congregation aware of the biblical support for such a pneumatology. For the sake of space, I am going to focus here on how it is possible to argue that the apostle Paul, himself, supported a pneumatological realism. The trick is to do this in a way that is not too nerdy. I have found Gordon Fee's *Paul, the Spirit, and the People of God* to be helpful in this regard. Three discussions in particular need to be noted if we are to help our hearers understand Paul's pneumatology.

Paul and the Personhood and Divinity of the Holy Spirit

Foundational to Paul's doctrine of the Holy Spirit was his perspective regarding the Spirit's personhood and divinity. Thus, the first thing we must do is help congregants understand that the way Paul ascribes certain behaviors to the Holy Spirit suggests that he should be viewed as a person rather than a mere force. According to the apostle, he is a divine being who makes moves in our lives that need to be responded to in an "I-Thou," interactive manner. For example, Paul says of the Spirit:

- he searches (1 Cor 2:10)
- he knows (1 Cor 2:11)
- he teaches (1 Cor 2:13)
- he dwells (Rom 8:11; 1 Cor 3:16; 2 Tim 1:14)
- he accomplishes (1 Cor 12:11)
- he gives life (2 Cor 3:6)
- he cries out (Gal 4:6)
- he leads (Rom 8:14; Gal 5:18)
- he bears witness (Rom 8:16)
- he desires (Gal 5:17)
- he helps (Rom 8:26)
- he intercedes (Rom 8:26–27)
- he works (Rom 8:28)
- he strengthens (Eph 3:16)
- he grieves (Eph 4:30)[5]

Clearly, the Paul conceived of the Spirit in a personal rather than impersonal manner.[6]

Many churchgoers do not seem to be alert to the distinction: why it is important for them to understand and experience the Holy Spirit

5. Fee, *Paul, the Spirit, and the People of God*, 27.

6. Fee, *Paul, the Spirit, and the People of God*, 22.

in an "I-Thou" rather than "I-It" manner. We can and must help them see and experience the difference!

It is also important that our congregants acknowledge the full divinity (and authority) of the Holy Spirit. Fee draws attention to the sixteen times Paul refers to the Holy Spirit as the "Spirit of God" or its equivalent, and the several times he likewise has the Holy Spirit in mind when he refers to the "Spirit of Christ" or its equivalent (see Acts 16:7; Rom 8:9; Gal 4:6; Phil 1:19).[7] Fee concludes that the way Paul associates the Spirit with God the Father and Christ the Son indicates that he believed the Holy Spirit to be fully God—the third person of the Holy Trinity.[8] This too is an important component of Paul's robust doctrine of the Holy Spirit. The truth is that the Holy Spirits merits the same kind of respect, reverence, and obedience that is owing to God the Father and Christ the Son (see Matt 12:31–32; Acts 5:1–11)!

Paul and the Importance of the Holy Spirit to the Christian Life

Moreover, a truly robust, biblically informed doctrine of the Spirit requires a vivid awareness of the full scope of the Spirit's work in our lives. This, in turn, results in an adequate appraisal of just how crucial the Spirit is to the cultivation of a spiritual, moral, and missional faithfulness before God. Sadly, I have interacted with many students and veteran church members who are not sufficiently dialed in here.

In chapter 3 I explained that one of the things missing from a non-realist doctrine of the Spirit is a proper understanding how important the Spirit is to absolutely *every* aspect of the Christian life. Wanting this chapter to provide some practical assistance, I present below a bulleted list of roles the Holy Spirit plays in our lives. I utilize this outline when introducing non-theology majors to the doctrine of the Holy Spirit. It succeeds in raising eyebrows and awareness of the need to get real with respect to Christ's Spirit.[9] The list could also be used in the local church to encourage congregants to do the same.

According to Jesus and his apostles, it's the Holy Spirit's job to

7. Fee, *Paul, the Spirit, and the People of God*, 28.
8. Fee, *Paul, the Spirit, and the People of God*, 28.
9. An annotated version of this list can be found in Tyra, *Getting Real*, 125–30.

- enable us to experience the *new birth* and *new life in Christ* (John 3:3–8; 6:44; 16:7–11; Eph 2:18, 22; 3:16–17; and Gal 5:25);
- assure us that we've become God's children (Rom 8:15–16; Gal 4:6);
- lead us into a deeper and ongoing interaction with the risen Christ (John 14:15–26; 16:12–15);
- serve as a guarantee of our heavenly inheritance (2 Cor 1:22; 5:5; Gal 4:6–7; Eph 1:13–14; 4:30);
- inspire us toward a vital, joyful, prophetic, theologically real worship experience (John 4:24; Eph 5:18–20);
- manifest the risen Christ's presence and power in our lives in various edifying, community-building, ministry-engendering ways (1 Cor 12:4–8; 14:24–25);
- empower us to obey God's moral commands (Rom 8:1–4) by enabling us to overcome our habituated sinful tendencies (Gal 5:16–21), and producing within us the character traits and ethical virtues of Jesus instead (Gal 5:22–25);
- intercede for us and through us according to the will of the Father (Rom 8:26–27);
- empower us to boldly bear witness to the risen Christ (Acts 1:8; cf. Matt 10:18–20);
- provide us with an amazingly precise degree of ministry guidance (Acts 10:17–20; 13:1–3; 16:6–10);
- motivate us to stand firm in the faith and to intercede for others in this regard (Eph 6:10–18, cf. Jude 1:17–21; 2 Tim 1:13–14); and
- endow us, time and again, with a dynamic, despair-defeating sense of hope (Rom 15:13).

The upshot is this: to create an *environment of expectancy* with respect to the Spirit, church members must be continually reminded of how crucial the Spirit of Jesus is to true Christian discipleship. We simply must take the Spirit seriously to experience the Christian life in its fullness. This awareness is at the heart a pneumatological realism!

Paul and the Experiential Manner Early Christians Interacted with the Holy Spirit

And yet, there is one more bit of New Testament support for a realist rather than non-realist understanding of the Holy Spirit that we must make our congregants aware of. I am referring to the way the apostle Paul seemed to suggest that Christ's followers can and should experience the Spirit in real, immediate, personal, phenomenal, life-story-shaping ways. Once again, Gordon Fee is of great assistance.

> The Spirit is God's way of being present, powerfully present, in our lives and communities as we await the consummation of the kingdom of God. Precisely because he understood the Spirit as God's personal presence, Paul also understood the Spirit always in terms of an empowering presence; whatever else, for Paul the Spirit was an experienced reality.[10]
>
> This dynamic, evidential dimension of life in the Spirit probably more than anything else separates believers in later church history from those in Paul's churches. Whatever else, the Spirit was *experienced* in Paul's churches; *he was not simply part of a phrase in the creed.*[11]
>
> *One reads Paul poorly who does not recognize that for him the presence of the Spirit, as an experienced and living reality, was the crucial matter for Christian life, from beginning to end.*[12]
>
> In the final analysis, in every aspect of this theology—at least what is basic to his theology—the Spirit plays a leading role. To be sure, the Spirit is not *the* center for Paul—Christ is, ever and always—but the Spirit stands close to the center, making Christ known and empowering all genuinely Christian life and experience. For this reason, the Spirit must play a much more vital role in our thinking about Paul's theology than tends to be the case.[13]

10. Fee, *Paul, the Spirit, and the People of God*, xxi (emphasis original).
11. Fee, *Paul, the Spirit, and the People of God*, 144 (emphasis original).
12. Fee, *Paul, the Spirit, and the People of God*, xiii (emphasis original).
13. Fee, *Paul, the Spirit, and the People of God*, 180 (emphasis original).

According to Fee, the Paul's doctrine of the Holy Spirit held that Christians are to experience him in ways that are intimate, interactive, immediate, palpable, and existentially impactful. There is no way Paul would have signed off on a merely conceptual or formalistic doctrine of the Holy Spirit!

This is how, over time, we preachers can make the biblical case for a pneumatological realism: by emphasizing, time and again, the New Testament (Pauline) support for:

- the personhood, agency, and divinity of the Spirit;
- the tremendous importance of the Spirit to the Christian life; and
- the experiential (rather than merely conceptual or formalistic) manner in which the early Christians engaged with the Spirit.

And it should not escape our notice that this emphasis on the experiential, existentially impactful interactions we can expect to have with Christ's Spirit will generate a sense of eager anticipation (rather than boredom or cynicism) when we hear the written word preached. A pneumatological realism makes it possible for genuinely anointed sermons grounded in the written word, to become for us the word of God proclaimed (1 Thess 2:13; cf. 1 Pet 4:11). To the degree an ecclesial setting is earmarked by an embrace of pneumatological realism, congregants will be enabled by the Spirit to attend worship gatherings eagerly anticipating the preaching moment!

HELPING OUR CONGREGANTS HEAR THE WORD OF GOD PROCLAIMED

Important as it is for church leaders to encourage churchgoers toward the embrace of a robust, biblically informed, and Christ-honoring doctrine of the Holy Spirit, we must do more than teach sound doctrine. Our aim must be to see this doctrine be *realized* in the lives of those whose souls we have been called to care for. To do this, in addition to encouraging our congregants to embrace Paul's *pneumatology*, we must also encourage them to adopt his *spirituality*.

Paul's Spirituality in Review

To review, the spirituality practiced and promoted by Paul was grounded (rooted) in some theological *convictions* that were either produced or strengthened by his conversion experience on the road to Damascus (Acts 9:1–22). These theological convictions generated three prominent spirituality *commitments*, which then mandated the spirituality *customs* (or practices/disciplines) we find Paul referring to repeatedly in his writings. All of this produced in Paul a distinctive way of being in the world that was Spirit-enabled, Christ-honoring, and God-the-father pleasing because of the way it enabled a lifestyle earmarked by a spiritual, moral, and missional faithfulness (see Col 1:9–12).

Paul's Spirituality and the Spiritual-Hearing Impaired

I have argued that when preachers engage in a sincere practice of Paul's spirituality, it elicits an anointing: a Spirit-enabled hermeneutical hearing and homiletical preparation that contributes to the *logos* (meaningfulness), *ethos* (trustworthiness), *pathos* (winsomeness), *telos* (needfulness), and *kairos* (timeliness) of their sermons.

Here, however, I want to discuss why it is critical for us preachers to encourage our congregants to adopt this same Pauline, fully Trinitarian, "I-Thou," lifestyle spirituality. When those who are regularly exposed to genuinely anointed sermons practice the same "I-Thou" spirituality that produced them, they may experience an anointing themselves—a Spirit-enabled ability to really hear in these sermons the voice of Jesus.

Here is how this works. First, Paul's lifestyle spirituality enables congregants to engage in all four of the cardinal components of Christian discipleship—worship, nurture, community, and mission—in a *comprehensive*, *ongoing*, and *theologically real* manner. And, because these four primary discipleship dynamics are interrelated, a theologically real engagement in all of them makes for a more balanced and empowered walk with Christ. Indeed, an "I-Thou" rather than "I-It" approach to these spiritual formation activities is a game-changer, making our experience of worship, nurture, community, and mission personal and dynamic rather than merely formalistic.

Second, this theologically real approach to all the cardinal components of Christian discipleship creates the possibility of sacramental encounters with the living Jesus as we engage in each of them. Indeed, the second *commitment* in Paul's spirituality entails the pursuit of a Spirit-enabled, ongoing mentoring relationship with Christ. This means that every time a Christ-follower participates in a worship gathering, he or she will be praying in the Spirit, sensitive to Christ's presence and the promptings provided by his Spirit. As the sermon is preached, the congregant practicing Paul's spirituality will be leaning forward, open to being enabled by the Holy Spirit to sense Jesus speaking through the sermon directly to their hearts. Put simply, the practice of Paul's spirituality will equip good-hearted churchgoers (Matt 5:8)[14] with *ears that hear.*[15] How does one place a value on this?

HELPING OUR CONGREGANTS ACTUALLY DO THE WORD OF GOD PROCLAIMED

On the other hand, really hearing the word of God proclaimed does not stop there. The Bible bears witness to the Holy Spirit's penchant for using God's people to achieve God's missional purposes in the world. As previously indicated, there is evidence in the Scriptures that the coming of the Spirit into people's lives imparts an anointing I refer to as prophetic capacity. This prophetic capacity entails the Spirit-enabled ability to:

- hear God's voice;
- receive ministry assignments from him; and
- then speak and act into the lives of people on God's behalf;
- achieving God's missional purposes in the world as a result.[16]

14. Cf. Ps 78:37; 101:4; Prov 11:20; 15:14; 16:5; 18:12; 26:23; Isa 46:12; Acts 8:21.

15. Mark 4:9 // Luke 8:8; Mark 4:23; Luke 14:35; Rev 2:7, 11, 17, 29; 3:6, 13, 22; 13:9.

16. See Tyra, *Holy Spirit in Mission*, 98; Tyra, *Getting Real*, 111–12.

This prophetic phenomenon was at the heart of the missional faithfulness that Jesus himself rendered to the Father. The prophetic, responsive, "hearing-then-doing" nature of Jesus' intimate, interactive relationship with the Father is evidenced in those Johannine passages where we find him asserting that everything he does is at the behest of his Father (see John 14:10, 31), because he only does the kinds of things he sees his Father doing (see John 5:19; 10:37) and only says the kinds of things he hears his Father saying (see John 5:30; 8:28; 12:49; 14:24; 15:15). Because Jesus sends us in the same manner that he himself was sent (John 20:21), I consider it important to help congregants understand that a closed-loop or "touch-all-the-bases" experience of prophetic Christian preaching requires Spirit-enabled discernment and deployment (hearing and doing) on the part of sermon hearers. This is why Jesus was careful to warn his disciples to "consider carefully what you hear" (Mark 4:20–25). The miracle/privilege of hearing the word of God proclaimed entails some ministry responsibility.

The New Testament passage that functions for me as the paradigm for this closed-loop, touch-all-the-bases, "hearing-then-doing" relationship with the word of God is Acts 9:10–22. Having heard the word of God, Ananias found himself being tasked by the Holy Spirit to function prophetically in the life of Saul of Tarsus. Though reluctant at first, God has his way and Ananias faithfully speaks and acts into the life of a dazed and confused Saul of Tarsus in such a way as to make (and begin the formation) of a new disciple for Jesus. Indeed, as a result of Ananias's hearing then doing, the church was blessed by the ministry of the apostle Paul, who went on to engage in a prophetic, "hearing-then-doing" ministry of his own![17]

So we see that the same anointing that provides the capacity to hear the word of God entails a responsibility then to do the word of God. This is why I consider it imperative to provide congregants with a process by which they can put themselves in a position to do the very best job possible of acting on whatever it is they "hear" the Lord saying

17. For a much more thorough discussion of the essential "prophethood" of all Spirit-filled Christian believers, see the chapters titled "Would God that All the Lord's People Were Prophets," and "You Shall Receive Power" in Tyra, *Holy Spirit in Mission*, 39–74 and 75–101.

to them in this or that sermon. While some congregants may not need help in this regard, many will. It goes without saying that the goal of a caring shepherd will be to help as many churchgoers as possible become doers of the word, and not hearers only (Jas 1:22–25).

Toward this end, one of the lessons I, as a pastor/teacher, have learned over the years is the value of a small group experience that enables congregants to *process* and then *live into* the word of God genuinely presented to them during preaching/teaching moments. I have in mind here a contemporized, synthesized version of John Wesley's system of interlocking groups: a disciple-making method that radically impacted the church in eighteenth-century England, and millions of Christ-followers globally since. [18]

In *John Wesley's Class Meeting: A Model for Making Disciples*, D. Michael Henderson describes the "method" behind the discipling movement that came to be known as "Methodism."

> Wesley's unique "method" combined several interlocking group techniques to construct a ladder of personal spiritual improvement. All sincere Christians, whatever their intelligence or background, could work up that ladder by faithful participation, from one level of spiritual maturity to the next. The "rungs" on Wesley's ladder of Christian discipleship were small interactive groups—the class meeting, the band . . . and the society. Each group within the system was designed to accomplish a specific developmental purpose, and each group had its own carefully defined roles and procedures to ensure that the central objectives were accomplished.[19]

Though I believe that the image of web rather than a ladder is more apt with respect to our lived experience, I agree with the observation that Wesley correctly recognized that there is a critical difference between providing churchgoers with some discrete disciple-making events, and being intentional about the cultivation of an ecclesial disciple-making environment.[20] Contemporary church leaders who

18. See Henderson, *John Wesley's Class Meeting*, 110–11.

19. See Henderson, *John Wesley's Class Meeting*, 11.

20. See Tyra, *Defeating Pharisaism*, 205–6; 220–21.

recognize this, and whose goal is to form "all-in" disciples rather than "almost Christians," need to give Wesley's small-group approach to spiritual formation a careful look.[21]

At the risk of oversimplifying, the key to Wesley's success at making disciples, I believe, was the way he made it possible for folks to experience all four components of Christian discipleship—worship, nurture, community, and mission—every week. What is more, these disciples were immersed into an ecclesial environment rich with the earmarks of genuine Christian community: *support* and *accountability*. While this required Wesley's converts to participate in several small group meetings each week (society, class, and band meetings), this engagement in theologically real worship, nurture, community, and mission, in settings rich with both support and accountability, produced some genuine life transformation in the lives of a huge number of people. History indicates that the thousands of ordinary people who responded to Wesley's field preaching then began to evidence growth toward a spiritual, moral, and missional faithfulness as they transitioned from merely hearing the word preached to them, to living into it. The key was the way Wesley's system of interlocking groups sought to replicate in his place and day the ecclesial dynamics we read of in Acts 2:42–47.[22]

And yet, the catch is: How do we contemporary church leaders employ Wesley's disciple-making method when the lifestyles of our congregants simply will not allow for multiple small group meetings each week? I am convinced that the Holy Spirit wants to help us, in our place and day, cultivate ecclesial environments that replicate Acts 2:42–47.

Once again, wanting this chapter to be practical as well as theoretical, I will share a success story from my own pastoral experience. In the last church I pastored, just prior to becoming a full-time professor and author, I had the opportunity to implement some of the lessons learned from my study of Wesley's approach to making disciples even though my Southern California congregants lived in scattered

21. For more on this, see Tyra, *Defeating Pharisaism*, 222–238.

22. See Henderson, *John Wesley's Class Meeting*, 12. See also Tyra, *Defeating Pharisaism*, 222–23.

locations at some distance from one another and the church's meeting site. In short, I found a way to expose the bulk of my congregation, each Sunday morning, to the cognitive, behavioral, and affective experiences that occurred in Wesley's society, class, and band meetings respectively.

Following the worship gathering each Sunday morning—a worship gathering that included the type of preaching/teaching that occurred in Wesley's "society" meetings[23]—the congregation adjourned for a fifteen-minute period of conversation with one another, and friendly interaction with first-time attenders. But then, rather than leave the premises after this brief bit of fellowship and assimilation ministry, most of the congregation would gather once again, in small groups scattered throughout the worship space, to process together what they heard God saying to them that morning through the sermon.[24] First, they briefly checked in with one another in a way reminiscent of the sharing that took place in Wesley's "class" meetings.[25] Then, replicating the sharing method utilized in Wesley's "band" meetings,[26] they would engage in a season of communal *sermon processing* as each of them shared from the heart responses to the following queries:

1. What, in your view, was the main message to the congregation presented in the sermon we just heard?
2. Which of the main themes (big ideas) addressed in the sermon do you consider to be especially important and applicable to your life?
3. What specific thing(s), if any, is Jesus calling you to do between now and next Sunday in order to respond obediently to the message proclaimed through this sermon?

23. See Tyra, *Defeating Pharisaism*, 223–24.

24. Though my focus here is on the influence of Wesley's interlocking groups, one may recall my suggestion in chapter 2 that one of the main objectives of the conventicles (small groups) promoted by Philipp Jacob Spener in his work *Pia Desideria* was the processing of sermons. The influence of Pietism on Wesley's conversion and ecclesiology is widely attested.

25. See Tyra, *Defeating Pharisaism*, 224–26.

26. See Tyra, *Defeating Pharisaism*, 231–32.

4. In what specific ways should the rest of us be praying for you as you attempt to live out what you heard the Lord saying to you today?

5. Do you give us permission to ask you next week how you did this week at being a doer rather than a mere hearer of the word?

These small group sessions, approximately forty-five to sixty minutes long, would conclude with members praying together about the week ahead. Tears, hugs, and words of affirmation were always abundant.

Now, one of the values of planting a church is the increased ability on the part of church leaders to influence from the get-go the congregation's nascent ecclesiology. Having planted this church a decade earlier, its leadership team had succeeded in encouraging the congregation *not* to think of itself as a church with some small groups, but, rather, as a church made up of small groups. In other words, the value of each member belonging to a circle of spiritually sincere friends who would provide them with ample amounts of mercy-saturated support and accountability was salient in the church's DNA. For this reason, on any given Sunday, at least 80 percent of the congregation was in the habit of participating in what their pastor, who moonlighted as a professor of biblical and practical theology, referred to as "sermon-processing sessions." Honestly, I can report that in my twenty-eight years of pastoral ministry I never witnessed a more impactful season of spiritual formation on a church-wide scale. *There is something special about beginning each week engaging in theologically real versions of worship, nurture, community, and mission!* At the risk of some redundancy, I will opine that it is hard to overstate the value of congregants spending some quality time each week:

attending to the preaching and teaching of God's Word in an expectant, receptive manner;

prayerfully pondering what the Lord might be up to in it;

prayerfully discerning what the Holy Spirit may be prompting them to do through it;

speaking this out loud to a circle of trusted friends, requesting prayer in the process; and then giving these spiritual friends permission to inquire next week how it went.

I personally found the awareness-raising impact of these sermon-processing sessions upon my own walk with Christ to be remarkable. I heard the same from congregants. We all seemed to be experiencing what Wesley had in mind when he developed his disciple-making method. We were actually becoming doers of God's word rather than merely hearers of it!

Whether an intentional engagement in sermon processing happens immediately after the preaching moment or later in the week, on one's own or as a group exercise, I recommend it heartily. The bottom line is that we preachers can be proactive about helping our hearers attend the preaching/teaching of God's word in a doubly anointed manner: prayerfully *hearing* the Lord's voice in the sermon, and then faithfully *living into* that message going forward. In other words, we preachers can cooperate with the Holy Spirit's desire to help all of Christ's followers cultivate ears to hear what he is saying to the churches (Rev 2:11, 17; 3:6, 13, 22).

Karl Barth knew that the difference between congregants who respond to preaching with dread and defensiveness, and those for whom the ringing of the church bells evokes a sense of eager anticipation, is the working of the Holy Spirit in their lives. What this means is that there is something we preachers can do to help our hearers experience the dual anointing (discerning and doing) that will enable them to benefit fully from prophetic preaching. Though we cannot force anyone to embrace a pneumatological realism, adopt a Spirit-sensitive, Christ-honoring, and God-the-Father–pleasing spirituality, or participate in "sermon-processing sessions," we can make sure they understand how doing so could literally change their lives, and how eager the Spirit is to help this happen. This is how we prepare the congregation to hear and respond to the kind of teaching God always intended. The question is: What will we do with this information?

Conclusion

Now to him who is able to do immeasurably more than all we ask or imagine, according to his power that is at work within us, to him be glory in the church and in Christ Jesus throughout all generations, for ever and ever! Amen.
—EPHESIANS 3:20–21

AS I HAVE INDICATED elsewhere, I am convinced that the apostle Paul's lifestyle spirituality not only functions as a *missional* spirituality, but a *mental health* spirituality (Rom 8:15; 2 Tim 1:7), a *warfare* spirituality (Eph 6:10–20), a *holiness* spirituality (Heb 12:14), a *faithfulness* spirituality (Matt 25:21, 23), and, ultimately, an eschatological *readiness* spirituality (Matt 22:44).[1] This is a bold assertion, yet I will double-down on it here, suggesting that such a spirituality, at work in the lives of preachers and congregants, can facilitate sermons that effect sacramental encounters with Christ which, in turn, enable a spiritual, moral, and missional faithfulness in the lives of everyone concerned.

Earlier I noted how Dallas Willard, after describing the value and effect of pursuing Christ's empowering presence, posed the question: "What are we to say of anyone who thinks they have something more important to do than that?"[2] The query was, of course, rhetorical. Willard's point was clear: absolutely nothing is more important than a Spirit-enabled, "hot pursuit" of the risen Christ!

1. See Tyra, *Introduction to Spirituality*, 175–76.
2. Willard, *Renovation of the Heart*, 42–43.

When you think of it, this is what sacramental sermons are about: genuinely anointed preaching that effects empowering encounters with the risen Jesus. Hearing, discerning, and then doing the Word of God proclaimed in a genuinely anointed manner is one of the most important spiritual disciplines we can engage in! So I conclude this work with a rhetorical question of my own: *If this is truly the kind of preaching God always intended, how could any preacher think they have something more important to do than this?*

In this book I have:

- argued for an expanded understanding of sacramental sermons;
- specified what sacramental sermons do;
- identified the realist, Trinitarian theology that underwrites such sermons;
- analyzed the earmarks of genuinely anointed preaching;
- surveyed the biblical-theological support for prophetic, incarnational, truly transformative preaching;
- insisted upon the need for such preaching in this secular age; and
- addressed in a novel manner the preparation, delivery, and processing of sermons that play out in a prophetic, sacramental manner.

More than once I have boldly indicated that the aim of this work is to inspire preachers—veterans and novices—toward the kind of preaching God always intended. In other words, my ambition has been to provide a biblically and theologically informed vision for preaching that is worth our giving our lives to. Is it possible for a book to be sacramental in its effect? I sincerely and audaciously hope so, buoyed by Paul's reminder to the Ephesian believers that our Trinitarian God "is able to do immeasurably more than all we ask or imagine, according to his power that is at work within us!" This being the case, let us do our best to neither sell him short nor let him down.

Thank you for completing this journey with me. I hope you found it worthwhile. If so, let us eagerly, like never before, commit ourselves to this sacred calling. We can do this! While sacramental sermons cannot be conjured, there are things we can do to increase the frequency of their occurrence. Indeed, I am praying just now for all of us as I write these concluding words. May everyone who reads and acts on them experience a genuine anointing upon their preaching. May we all find ourselves divinely enabled to cooperate with the Holy Spirit in the facilitation of sermons that are prophetic in nature, incarnational in manner, and truly transformative in effect. This is the difference a theologically, christologically, and pneumatologically real approach to the preaching task can make.

Coram deo!

Bibliography

Adam, Peter. *Speaking God's Words: A Practical Theology of Preaching.* Vancouver: Regent College Publishing, 2004.

Allen, Ronald J. "Preaching as Spark for Discovery in Theology." In *Homiletical Theology: Preaching as Doing Theology,* edited by David Schnasa Jacobsen, 129–51. Eugene, OR: Cascade, 2015.

Alter, Margaret G. *Resurrection Psychology: An Understanding of Human Personality Based on the Life and Teachings of Jesus.* Chicago: Loyola University Press, 1994.

Anderson, Ray. *The Soul of Ministry: Forming Leaders for God's People.* Louisville: Westminster John Knox, 1997.

Augustine. *Teaching Christianity.* Translated by Edmund Hill, edited by John E. Rotelle. The Works of Saint Augustine, vol. 1/11. Hyde Park, NY: New City, 1996.

Barna Group. "Six Reasons Young Christians Leave Church." September 28, 2011. https://www.barna.com/research/six-reasons-young-christians-leave-church.

Barrett, C. K. *The Epistle to the Romans.* Harper's New Testament Commentaries. New York: Harper & Row, 1957.

———. *The First Epistle to the Corinthians.* Harpers New Testament Commentaries. New York, HarperCollins, 1968.

Barth, Karl. *Church Dogmatics* I/1. Edited by Thomas F. Torrance and G. W. Bromiley, translated by G. W. Bromiley. Peabody, MA: Hendrickson, 2010.

———. *Church Dogmatics* I/2. Edited by Thomas F. Torrance and G. W. Bromiley, translated by G. W. Bromiley. Peabody, MA: Hendrickson, 2010.

———. *Church Dogmatics* II/1. Edited by Thomas F. Torrance and G. W. Bromiley, translated by G. W. Bromiley. Peabody, MA: Hendrickson, 2010.

———. *Dogmatics in Outline.* New York: Harper & Row, 1959.

———. *Evangelical Theology: An Introduction.* Grand Rapids: Eerdmans, 1963.

———. *The Göttingen Dogmatics: Instruction in the Christian Religion.* Grand Rapids: Eerdmans, 1991.

———. *Homiletics.* Louisville: Westminster John Knox, 1991.

———. "The Need and Promise of Christian Preaching." In *The Word of God and the Word of Man,* 97–135. New York: Harper & Row, 1957.

———. *Prayer.* Louisville: Westminster John Knox, 2002.

Bartholomew, Craig G. *Introducing Biblical Hermeneutics: A Comprehensive Framework for Hearing God in Scripture.* Grand Rapids: Baker Academic, 2023.

———. *Listening to Scripture: An Introduction to Interpreting Scripture.* Grand Rapids: Baker Academic, 2023.

Barton, Bruce B. *1 Peter, 2 Peter, Jude.* Life Application Bible Commentary. Wheaton, IL: Tyndale, 1995.

Barton, Bruce B., and Grant R. Osborne. *1 and 2 Corinthians.* Life Application Bible Commentary. Wheaton, IL: Tyndale, 1999.

Barton, Bruce B., et al. *Romans.* Life Application Bible Commentary. Wheaton, IL: Tyndale, 1992.

Baum, Gregory. *The Twentieth Century: A Theological Overview.* Maryknoll, NY: Orbis, 1999.

Beeke, Joel R. *Fighting Satan: Knowing His Weaknesses, Strategies, and Defeat.* Grand Rapids: Reformation Heritage, 2015.

Berger, Peter. *Sacred Canopy: Elements of a Sociological Theory of Religion.* New York: Anchor, 1990.

Boersma, Hans. *Sacramental Preaching: Sermons on the Hidden Presence of Christ.* Grand Rapids: Baker Academic, 2018.

———. *Scripture as Real Presence: Sacramental Exegesis in the Early Church.* Grand Rapids: Baker Academic, 2018.

Bonhoeffer, Dietrich. *London, 1933–1935.* Minneapolis: Fortress, 2007.

———. *Theological Education at Finkenwalde, 1935–1937.* Minneapolis: Fortress, 2013.

———. *Worldly Preaching.* Finkenwalde Lectures on Homiletics. Translated by Clyde E. Fant. Nashville: Thomas Nelson, 1975.

Borgman, Brian, and Rob Ventura. *Spiritual Warfare: A Biblical and Balanced Perspective.* Grand Rapids: Reformation Heritage, 2014.

Bridgers, Lynn. *American Religious Experience: A Concise History.* Lanham, MD: Rowman & Littlefield, 2006.

Bromiley, Geoffrey W. *Introduction to the Theology of Karl Barth.* Grand Rapids: Eerdmans, 1979.

Brooks, Phillips. *Lectures on Preaching.* New York: Dutton, 1877.

Brother Lawrence. *The Practice of the Presence of God with Spiritual Maxims.* Grand Rapids: Spire, 1967.

Brown, Gregory. *The Armor of God: Standing Firm in Spiritual Warfare.* 2nd ed. Self-published, 2017.

Bruce, F. F. *Romans.* Tyndale New Testament Commentaries. Downers Grove, IL: InterVarsity, 1985.

Brueggemann, Walter. *The Prophetic Imagination.* 2nd ed. Minneapolis: Fortress, 2001.

Brunner, Emil. *The Misunderstanding of the Church.* Cambridge: Lutterworth, 1952.

———. *Truth as Encounter.* Philadelphia: Westminster, 1963.

Buber, Martin. *I and Thou.* Translated by Ronald Gregor Smith. New York: Touchstone, 1971.

Busch, Eberhard. *Karl Barth: His Life from Letters and Autobiographical Texts.* Minneapolis: Fortress, 1976.

Calvin, John. "Commentary on Exodus 24:5." In *Corpus Reformatorum,* vol. 24, 658–60. Halle: C. A. Schwetschke and Son, 1834.

———. *Institutes of the Christian Religion.* Edited by J. T. McNeill and F. L. Battles. Library of Christian Classics 20–21. Philadelphia: Westminster, 1960.

"Cape Town Commitment." Lausanne Movement. https://lausanne.org/statement/ctcommitment#p1-5.

Caroll, B. H., and J. B. Cranfill. *Sermons and Life-Sketch of B. H. Carroll.* Philadelphia: American Baptist, 1895.

Carrick, John. *The Imperative of Preaching: A Theology of Sacred Rhetoric.* Carlisle, PA: Banner of Truth, 2020.

———. *The Preaching of Jonathan Edwards.* Carlisle, PA: Banner of Truth, 2008.

Carroll, Thomas K. *Preaching the Word.* Eugene, OR: Wipf and Stock, 1984.

Chadwick, Henry. *The Early Church.* New York: Penguin, 1967.

Chapell, Bryan. *Christ-Centered Preaching: Redeeming the Expository Sermon.* Grand Rapids: Baker, 1994.

Chauvet, Louis-Marie. *Symbol and Sacrament: A Sacramental Reinterpretation of Christian Existence.* Translated by Patrick Madigan and Madeleine Beaumont. Collegeville, MN: Liturgical, 1995.

Chesterton, G. K. "The Five Deaths of the Faith." In *The Everlasting Man.* https://www3.nd.edu/~afreddos/courses/The%20Grade%20-%20Christmas%20Seminar/EverlastingMan.pdf.

Chia, Roland. *Revelation and Theology: The Knowledge of God in Balthasar and Barth.* New York: Peter Lang, 1999.

Clements, Keith W. "Dietrich Bonhoeffer: Costly Preaching." In *A Legacy of Preaching: Enlightenment to the Present Day,* edited by Benjamin K.

Forrest, Kevin L. King, Bill Curtis, and Dwayne Millioni, 308–22. Grand Rapids: Zondervan, 2018.

Cox, Harvey. *Fire from Heaven: the Rise of Pentecostal Spirituality and the Reshaping of Religion in the Twenty-First Century.* Cambridge: Da Capo, 2001.

———. *The Secular City: Secularization and Urbanization in Theological Perspective.* New York: MacMillan, 1965.

Crabtree, Fred. *Pentecostal Preaching: Empowering Your Pulpit with the Holy Spirit.* Springfield, MO: Gospel, 2003.

Currie, Thomas Christian. *The Only Sacrament Left to Us: The Threefold Word of God in the Theology and Ecclesiology of Karl Barth.* Eugene, OR: Pickwick, 2015.

Davids, Peter H. *The First Epistle of Peter.* The New International Commentary on the New Testament. Grand Rapids: Eerdmans, 1990.

Dean, Kenda Creasy. *Almost Christian: What the Faith of our Teenagers is Telling the American Church.* New York: Oxford University Press, 2010.

"Discernment." *Merriam-Webster Dictionary.* https://www.merriam-webster.com/dictionary/discernment.

Dunn, James D. G. *Jesus and the Spirit: A Study of the Religious and Charismatic Experience of Jesus and the First Century Christians as Reflected in the New Testament.* Grand Rapids: Eerdmans, 1997.

Edmonds, Molly. "Is the Brain Hardwired for Religion?" How Stuff Works. https://science.howstuffworks.com/life/inside-the-mind/human-brain/brain-religion.htm.

Edwards O. C., Jr. *A History of Preaching.* Nashville: Abingdon, 2004.

Fant, Clyde E. *Bonhoeffer: Worldly Preaching.* Nashville: Thomas Nelson, 1975.

Fee, Gordon D. *The First Epistle to the Corinthians.* The New International Commentary on the New Testament. Grand Rapids: Eerdmans, 2014.

———. *God's Empowering Presence: The Holy Spirit in the Letters of Paul.* Peabody, MA: Hendrickson, 1994.

———. *Paul, the Spirit, and the People of God.* Peabody, MA: Hendrickson, 1996.

Flett, John G. *The Witness of God: The Trinity,* Missio Dei, *Karl Barth, and the Nature of Christian Community.* Grand Rapids: Eerdmans, 2010.

Forrest, Benjamin K., Kevin L. King, Bill Curtis, and Dwayne Millioni, eds. *A Legacy of Preaching: Enlightenment to the Present Day.* Grand Rapids: Zondervan, 2018.

Franke, John R. *Barth for Armchair Theologians.* Louisville: Westminster John Knox.

Foulkes, Francis. *Ephesians,* Tyndale New Testament Commentaries. Downers Grove, IL: InterVarsity, 1983.

Fudge, Thomas. "Hussite Theology and the Law of God." In *The Cambridge Companion to Reformation Theology*, edited by David Bagchi and David C. Steinmetz, 22–27. Cambridge: Cambridge University Press, 2004.

Fuller, Charles W. "Phillips Brooks: Preaching the Personality of the Preacher." In *A Legacy of Preaching: Enlightenment to the Present Day*, edited by Benjamin K. Forrest, Kevin L. King, Bill Curtis, and Dwayne Millioni, 228–40. Grand Rapids: Zondervan, 2018.

Gambo, David N. *Spirit-Empowered Witness: A Lukan Theology of Preaching.* Carlisle, Cumbria, UK: Langham, 2022.

Greear, J. D. "Tim Keller's Friendship Transformed My Preaching;" *Christianity Today*, August 28, 2023. https://www.christianitytoday.com/ct/2023/tim-keller-issue/tim-keller-ministry-preaching-friendship.html.

Green, Chris E. W. *Toward a Pentecostal Theology of the Lord's Supper: Foretasting the Kingdom.* Cleveland, TN: CPT, 2012.

———. "Transfiguring Preaching: Salvation, Mediation, and Proclamation." In *Toward a Pentecostal Theology of Preaching*, edited by Lee Roy Martin, 64–81. Cleveland, TN: CPT, 2015.

Green, Roger J. "Catherine Booth: Preacher of Holiness." In *A Legacy of Preaching: Enlightenment to the Present Day*, edited by Benjamin K. Forrest, Kevin L. King, Bill Curtis, and Dwayne Millioni, 88–101. Grand Rapids: Zondervan, 2018.

Griffiths, Jonathan I. *Preaching in the New Testament: An Exegetical and Biblical-Theological Study.* Downers Grove: IL: InterVarsity, 2017.

Hahn, Scott. "The Eucharistic Theology of Early Church Fathers." St. Paul Center for Biblical Theology, April 28, 2011. https://stpaulcenter.com/the-eucharistic-theology-of-early-church-fathers1/.

Hansen, Collin, ed. *Our Secular Age: Ten Years of Reading and Applying Charles Taylor.* Deerfield, IL: The Gospel Coalition, 2017.

Harrison, Everett F. *The Apostolic Church.* Grand Rapids: Eerdmans, 1985.

Hart, Trevor. "Revelation." In *The Cambridge Companion to Karl Barth*, edited by John Webster, 37–56. Cambridge: Cambridge University Press, 2000.

Hartog, Paul A. "John Chrysostom: Golden-Mouthed Preacher." In *A Legacy of Preaching: Apostles to the Revivalists*, edited by Benjamin K. Forrest, Kevin L. King, Bill Curtis, and Dwayne Millioni, 126–45. Grand Rapids: Zondervan, 2018.

———. "Melito of Sardis: Proclaiming Christ the Lamb." In *A Legacy of Preaching: Apostles to the Revivalists*, edited by Benjamin K. Forrest, Kevin L. King, Bill Curtis, and Dwayne Millioni, 64–80. Grand Rapids: Zondervan, 2018.

Henderson, D. Michael. *John Wesley's Class Meeting: A Model for Making Disciples.* Nappanee, IN: Evangel, 1997.

Hoare, Elizabeth. "Bernard of Clairvaux: Preaching to Foster a Love and Devotion to God." In *A Legacy of Preaching: Apostles to the Revivalists,* edited by Benjamin K. Forrest, Kevin L. King, Bill Curtis, and Dwayne Millioni, 177–90. Grand Rapids: Zondervan, 2018.

Holder, Timothy D. "Francis of Assisi: Using Words and Life to Preach the Gospel." In *A Legacy of Preaching: Apostles to the Revivalists,* edited by Benjamin K. Forrest, Kevin L. King, Bill Curtis, and Dwayne Millioni, 191–202. Grand Rapids: Zondervan, 2018.

Horn, Trent. "Will the Real St. Francis Please Stand Up?" Catholic Answers, September 29, 2020. https://www.catholic.com/audio/cot/will-the-real-st-francis-please-stand-up.

Howell, Mark A. "John Huss: Forerunner to the Reformation." In *A Legacy of Preaching: Apostles to the Revivalists,* edited by Benjamin K. Forrest, Kevin L. King, Bill Curtis, and Dwayne Millioni, 246–59. Grand Rapids: Zondervan, 2018.

Hunsberger, George R. "Starting Points, Trajectories and Outcomes in Proposals for a Missional Hermeneutic: Mapping the Conversation." Gospel and Our Culture Network, January 28, 2009. https://gocn.org/library/the-gospel-and-our-culture-eseries-no-2/.

Hunsinger, George. "The Mediator of Communion: Karl Barth's Doctrine of the Holy Spirit." In *The Cambridge Companion to Karl Barth,* edited by John Webster, 177–94. Cambridge: Cambridge University Press, 2000.

Irenaeus. *On the Apostolic Preaching.* Yonkers, NY: St. Vladimir's Seminary Press, 2003.

John, J. "Heroes of the Faith: Phoebe Palmer." CanonJJohn. https://canonjjohn.com/2022/06/25/heroes-of-the-faith-phoebe-palmer/.

Johns, Cheryl Bridges. *Re-Enchanting the Text: Discovering the Bible as Sacred, Dangerous, and Mysterious.* Grand Rapids: Baker Academic, 2023.

Kärkkäinen, Veli-Matti. *Pneumatology: The Holy Spirit in Ecumenical, International, and Contextual Perspective.* Grand Rapids: Baker Academic, 2002.

Keane, James T. "Philosopher for a Secular Age: Charles Taylor's Influence in the Catholic Church." *America,* March 21, 2023. https://www.americamagazine.org/arts-culture/2023/03/21/cbc-column-charles-taylor-244944.

Keener, Craig. *The Mind of the Spirit: Paul's Approach to Transformed Thinking.* Grand Rapids: Baker Academic, 2016.

———. *Spirit Hermeneutics: Reading Scripture in Light of Pentecost.* Grand Rapids: Eerdmans, 2017.

Keller, Timothy. *Preaching: Communicating Faith in an Age of Skepticism.* New York: Penguin, 2015.

Kelley, Noah Warren. "James K. A. Smith: 'Desiring the Kingdom.'" Earthen Vessels, July 8, 2013. https://kelleys4christ.wordpress.com/2013/07/08/james-k-a-smith-desiring-the-kingdom/.

Knapp, Henry M. "John Owen: Preaching for the Glory of God." In *A Legacy of Preaching: Apostles to the Revivalists,* edited by Benjamin K. Forrest, Kevin L. King, Bill Curtis, and Dwayne Millioni, 393–411. Grand Rapids: Zondervan, 2018.

Kolb, Robert. "Martin Luther: Preaching a Theology of the Cross." In *A Legacy of Preaching: Apostles to the Revivalists,* edited by Benjamin K. Forrest, Kevin L. King, Bill Curtis, and Dwayne Millioni, 279–93. Grand Rapids: Zondervan, 2018.

Lane, Anthony N. S. "John Calvin: Preaching the Glorious Christ." In *A Legacy of Preaching: Apostles to the Revivalists,* edited by Benjamin K. Forrest, Kevin L. King, Bill Curtis, and Dwayne Millioni, 344–59. Grand Rapids: Zondervan, 2018.

Larson, Viola. "John Calvin On The Sacraments: A Summary." *Theology Matters,* Vol. 13, No. 4 (September/October 2007). https://theologymatters.com/wp-content/uploads/2020/03/07Vol13-No4-TM.pdf.

Laubach, Frank C. *Man of Prayer: Selected Writings of a World Missionary.* Syracuse: Laubach Literacy International, 1990.

Lewis, C. S. *Mere Christianity.* New York: HarperOne, 2015.

Lischer, Richard. *A Theology of Preaching: The Dynamics of the Gospel.* Eugene, OR: Wipf and Stock, 2001.

Litfin, Duane. *Paul's Theology of Preaching: The Apostle's Challenge to the Art of Persuasion in Ancient Corinth.* Downers Grove, IL: IVP Academic, 2015.

Lloyd-Jones, Martyn. *Preaching and Preachers.* London: Hodder and Stoughton, 1998.

Long, Thomas G. "And How Shall They Hear?" In *Listening to the Word,* edited by Gail R. O'Day and Thomas G. Long, 167–88. Nashville: Abingdon, 1993.

Loyer, Kenneth. *God's Love through the Spirit: The Holy Spirit in Thomas Aquinas and John Wesley.* Washington, DC: Catholic University of America Press, 2014.

Macchia, Frank D. "Services of the Word—Pentecostal." In *New SCM Dictionary of Liturgy and Worship,* edited by Paul F. Bradshaw, 452–54. London: SCM Press, 2005.

———. *Tongues of Fire: A Systematic Theology of the Christian Faith.* Eugene, OR: Cascade, 2023.

Mandal, Ananya. "Language and the Human Brain." News: Medical, Life Sciences, June 20, 2023. https://www.news-medical.net/health/Language-and-the-Human-Brain.aspx.

Marsh, John. "Was Wesley an Anglican? Implications for Mission." Asbury Seminary. https://place.asburyseminary.edu/cgi/viewcontent.cgi?article=1191&context=gcrj.

Marshall, I. Howard. *The Epistles of John.* The New International Commentary on the New Testament. Grand Rapids: Eerdmans, 1978.

Martin, Ralph P. *Worship in the Early Church.* Grand Rapids: Eerdmans, 1974.

Matz, Robert, and Jerry Sutton, "B. H. Carroll: Preaching Sermons Saturated with Scripture." In *A Legacy of Preaching: Enlightenment to the Present Day,* edited by Benjamin K. Forrest, Kevin L. King, Bill Curtis, and Dwayne Millioni, 257–72. Grand Rapids: Zondervan, 2018.

McDermott, Gerald R. "Jonathan Edwards: Preaching the Beauty of Holiness." In *A Legacy of Preaching: Apostles to the Revivalists,* edited by Benjamin K. Forrest, Kevin L. King, Bill Curtis, and Dwayne Millioni, 459–78. Grand Rapids: Zondervan, 2018.

Millioni, Dwayne. "William Perkins: Prince of Puritan Preaching." In *A Legacy of Preaching: Apostles to the Revivalists,* edited by Benjamin K. Forrest, Kevin L. King, Bill Curtis, and Dwayne Millioni, 363–77. Grand Rapids: Zondervan, 2018.

Moltmann, Jürgen, *The Spirit of Life: A Universal Affirmation.* Translated by Margaret Kohl. Minneapolis: Fortress, 1992.

Morgan, Jonathan. "Basil of Caesarea: The Preacher as the Mouthpiece of Christ." In *A Legacy of Preaching: Apostles to the Revivalists,* edited by Benjamin K. Forrest, Kevin L. King, Bill Curtis, and Dwayne Millioni, 111–25. Grand Rapids: Zondervan, 2018

Neuhaus, Richard John. *Freedom for Ministry.* Grand Rapids: Eerdmans, 1992.

Newberg, Andrew, and Mark Robert Waldman. *Born to Believe: God, Science, and the Origin of Ordinary and Extraordinary Beliefs.* New York: Free Press, 2006.

Noble, Alan. "The Disruptive Witness of Art." In *Our Secular Age: Ten Years of Reading and Applying Charles Taylor,* edited by Collin Hansen, 135–45. Deerfield, IL: The Gospel Coalition, 2017.

Olson, Roger E. *The Story of Christian Theology.* Downers Grove, IL: IVP Academic, 1999.

Olson, Roger E., and Christian T. Collins Winn. *Reclaiming Pietism: Retrieving an Evangelical Tradition.* Grand Rapids: Eerdmans, 2015.

Ott, Heinrich. *Theology and Preaching.* Philadelphia: Westminster, 1961.

Pace, Julian. "On Pietists and Preaching." God's Glory: Neighbor's Good. https://julianpace.com/2021/03/02/on-pietists-and-preaching-2/.

———. "Pietist Credentials of John Wesley." Wesleyscholar.com, September 26, 2020. https://wesleyscholar.com/pietist-credentials-of-john-wesley/.

Palmer, Phoebe. *The Way of Holiness with Notes by the Way; Being a Narrative of Religious Experience Resulting from a Determination to be a Bible Christian.* Salem, OH: Schmul, 1988.

Pasquarello, Michael, III. "John Wesley: Homiletic Theologian." In *A Legacy of Preaching: Apostles to the Revivalists,* edited by Benjamin K. Forrest, Kevin L. King, Bill Curtis, and Dwayne Millioni, 479–500. Grand Rapids: Zondervan, 2018.

Perkins, William. *The Art of Prophesying.* Carlisle, PA: The Banner of Truth, 2011.

"Phoebe Palmer: Mother of the Holiness Movement." CBE International. https://www.cbeinternational.org/resource/phoebe-palmer/.

"Pietism." *Encyclopedia Britannica,* January 25, 2022. https://www.britannica.com/topic/Pietism.

"Protestant Orthodoxy." *Encyclopedia Britannica,* September 22, 2006. https://www.britannica.com/topic/Protestant-Orthodoxy.

"Puritanism." *Encyclopedia Britannica,* March 29, 2024. https://www.britannica.com/topic/Puritanism.

Rahner, Karl. *Theological Investigations, Vol. IV.* Translated by Kevin Smyth. London: Darton, Longman & Todd, 1974.

———. "The Word and the Eucharist." In *Theological Investigations, Vol. IV,* translated by Kevin Smyth, 273–98. Baltimore: Helicon, 1966.

Reaves, Dylan. "Peter Berger and the Rise and Fall of the Theory of Secularization." *Denison Journal of Religion,* vol. 11 , article 3. http://digitalcommons.denison.edu/religion/vol11/iss1/3.

"Revivalism." *Encyclopedia Britannica,* December 7, 2023. https://www.britannica.com/topic/revivalism-Christianity.

Richardson, Kurt Anders. *Reading Karl Barth: New Directions for American Theology.* Grand Rapids: Baker Academic, 2004.

Roberts, Alastair. "Liturgical Piety." In *Our Secular Age: Ten Years of Reading and Applying Charles Taylor,* edited by Collin Hansen, 63–73. Deerfield, IL: The Gospel Coalition, 2017.

Robinson, Haddon. *Biblical Preaching: The Development and Delivery of Expository Messages.* Grand Rapids: Baker Academic, 2001.

Rodriguez, Rene. *Amplify Your Influence: Transform How You Communicate and Lead.* Hoboken: NJ, John Wiley & Sons, 2022.

Root, Andrew. *Faith Formation in a Secular Age: Responding to the Church's Obsession with Youthfulness.* Grand Rapids: Baker Academic, 2017.

Samuel, Josh P. S. *The Holy Spirit in Worship Music, Preaching, and the Altar: Renewing Pentecostal Worship.* Cleveland, TN: CPT, 2018.

Schmaus, Michael. *Dogma 5: The Church as Sacrament.* New York: Rowan and Littlefield, 1975.

———. "The Word as Salvific Activity in the Church." In *Dogma 5: The Church as Sacrament,* translated by Patrick Kerans, 16–19. New York: Society of St. Paul, 1969.

Schmemann, Alexander. *Introduction to Liturgical Theology.* Translated by Asheleigh E. Moorhouse. Crestwood, NY: St. Vladimir's Seminary Press, 2003.

Schwanda, Tom. "The Legacy of John Huss." C. S. Lewis Institute. https://www.cslewisinstitute.org/resources/the-legacy-of-john-hus/.

Smith, Aaron T. *A Theology of the Third Article: Karl Barth and the Spirit of the Word.* Minneapolis: Fortress, 2014.

Smith, Gordon T. *Evangelical, Sacramental and Pentecostal: Why the Church Should Be All Three.* Downers Grove, IL: IVP Academic, 2017.

Smith, Gregory, et al. "Decline of Christianity in the U.S. Has Slowed, May Have Leveled Off." Pew Research Center, February 26, 2025. https://www.pewresearch.org/religion/2025/02/26/decline-of-christianity-in-the-us-has-slowed-may-have-leveled-off/.

Smith, James K. A. *Desiring the Kingdom: Worship, Worldview and Cultural Formation.* Grand Rapids: Baker Academic, 2009.

———. *How (Not) to be Secular: Reading Charles Taylor.* Grand Rapids: Eerdmans, 2014.

———. *Imagining the Kingdom: How Worship Works.* Grand Rapids: Baker Academic, 2013.

Smither, Edward L. "Augustine of Hippo: Agape-Driven, Christocentric Preaching." In *A Legacy of Preaching: Apostles to the Revivalists,* edited by Benjamin K. Forrest, Kevin L. King, Bill Curtis, and Dwayne Millioni, 146–56. Grand Rapids: Zondervan, 2018.

"Sophistication." *Merriam-Webster Dictionary.* https://www.merriam-webster.com/dictionary/sophistication.

Spener, Philipp Jacob. *Pia Desideria.* Translated by Theodore G. Tappert. Minneapolis: Fortress, 1964.

Spinka, Matthew. *John Hus at the Council of Constance.* New York: Columbia University Press, 1965.

Stott, John. "The Privilege of Preaching." JohnStott.org. https://johnstott.org/work/the-privilege-of-preaching/.

Taylor, Charles. *A Secular Age.* Cambridge: Harvard University Press, 2007.

Taylor, Justin. "An Interview with James K. A. Smith on How (Not) to be Secular and How (to) Read Charles Taylor." *The Gospel Coalition,* May 1, 2014. https://www.thegospelcoalition.org/blogs/justin-taylor/an-interview-with-james-k-a-smith-on-how-not-to-be-secular-and-how-to-read-charles-taylor/.

Tedeschi, Mary. "Religion in the Secular City, by Harvey Cox." *Commentary,* August 1, 2010. http://www.commentarymagazine.com/viewarticle.cfm/religion-in-the-secular-city--by-harvey-cox-6849.

Tennent, Timothy C. *Invitation to World Missions: A Trinitarian Missiology for the Twenty-First Century.* Grand Rapids: Kregel Academic, 2010.

Thompson, Mark D. "The Declarative God: Toward a *Theological* Description of Preaching." In *Theology is for Preaching: Biblical Foundations, Method, and Practice,* edited by Chase R. Kuhn and Paul Grimmond, 18–33. Bellingham, WA: Lexham, 2021.

Thuswaldner, Gregor. "A Conversation with Peter L. Berger: 'How My Views Have Changed.'" *The Cresset,* Lent 2014. http://thecresset.org/2014/Lent/Thuswaldner_L14.html.

Tisdale, Leonora Tubbs. *Prophetic Preaching: A Pastoral Approach.* Louisville: Westminster John Knox, 2010.

Tomberlin, Daniel. *Pentecostal Sacraments: Experiencing God at the Altar.* Cleveland, TN: Cherohala, 2019.

Torrance, T. F. *Reality and Evangelical Theology.* Downers Grove, IL: InterVarsity, 1999.

Trueman, Carl. "D. Martyn Lloyd-Jones: Preaching *of* the Word and Preacher *for* the Word." In *A Legacy of Preaching: Enlightenment to the Present Day,* edited by Benjamin K. Forrest, Kevin L. King, Bill Curtis, and Dwayne Millioni, 323–38. Grand Rapids: Zondervan, 2018.

Tyra, Gary. *Christ's Empowering Presence: The Pursuit of God through the Ages.* Downers Grove, IL: InterVarsity, 2011.

———. *The Dark Side of Discipleship: Why and How the New Testament Encourages Christians to Deal with the Devil.* Eugene, OR: Cascade, 2020.

———. *Defeating Pharisaism: Recovering Jesus' Disciple-Making Method.* Downers Grove, IL: InterVarsity, 2009.

———. "From Sola Scriptura to the Sacramental Sermon: Karl Barth and the Phenomenon of Prophetic Preaching." Academica.edu, October 7, 2025. https://www.academia.edu/33690368/From_Sola_Scriptura_to_the_Sacramental_Sermon_Karl_Barth_and_the_Phenomenon_of_Prophetic_Preaching.

———. *Getting Real: Pneumatological Realism and the Spiritual, Moral, and Ministry Formation of Contemporary Christians.* Eugene, OR: Cascade, 2018.

———. *The Holy Spirit in Mission: Prophetic Speech and Action in Christian Witness.* Downers Grove, IL: IVP Academic, 2011.

———. *Introduction to Spirituality: Cultivating a Lifestyle of Faithfulness.* Grand Rapids: Baker Academic, 2023.

———. "Karl Barth and the Phenomenon of Prophetic Preaching." *Preaching Today.* https://www.preachingtoday.com/your-soul/power-of-holy-spirit/karl-barth-and-phenomenon-of-prophetic-preaching.html.

———. *A Missional Orthodoxy: Theology and Ministry in a Post-Christian Context.* Downers Grove, IL: IVP Academic, 2013.

———. "Proclaiming Christ's Victory over Sinful Personal Desires." *Enrichment Journal*. https://ministry.journeyonline.org/proclaiming-christs-victory-over-sinful-personal-desires/.

———. *Pursuing Moral Faithfulness: Ethics and Christian Discipleship*. Downers Grove, IL: IVP Academic, 2015.

———. "Revelation as Encounter: Karl Barth, Pneumatological Realism, and the Pentecostal Notion of *Prophetic* Preaching." In *Karl Barth and Pentecostal Theology: A Convergence of the Word and the Spirit*. Edited by Frank D. Macchia, Terry L. Cross, and Andrew K. Gabriel, 29–44. New York: T & T Clark, 2024.

Van Gelder, Craig, and Dwight J. Zscheile. *The Missional Church in Perspective: Mapping Trends and Shaping the Conversation*. Grand Rapids: Baker Academic, 2011.

Volz, Carl A. "The Genius of Chrysostom's Preaching." Christian History Institute. https://christianhistoryinstitute.org/magazine/article/genius-of-chrysostoms-preaching.

Wainwright, Geoffrey. "Preaching as Worship." *Greek Orthodox Theological Review* 28 (1983) 325–36.

Wallace, Ronald S. *Calvin's Doctrine of the Word and Sacrament*. Eugene, OR: Wipf & Stock, 1997.

Wallis, Arthur. *Pray in the Spirit*. Fort Washington, PA: CLC, 1970.

Wax, Trevin. "Mission in a Secular Age: A Conversation with James K. A. Smith." *The Gospel Coalition*, November 12, 2014. https://www.thegospelcoalition.org/blogs/trevin-wax/mission-in-a-secular-age-a-conversation-with-james-k-a-smith/.

Webster, John. "Foreword." In *Trinitarian Theology after Barth*, edited by Myk Habets and Phillip Tolliday, ix–x. Cambridge: James Clarke and Co., 2012.

White, Charles Edward. "Holiness Fire Starter." Christian History Institute. https://christianhistoryinstitute.org/magazine/article/holiness-fire-starter.

Willard, Dallas. *Renovation of the Heart: Putting on the Character of Christ*. Colorado Springs: NavPress, 2002.

Willimon, William H. *Conversations with Barth on Preaching*. Nashville: Abingdon, 2006.

———. *Proclamation and Theology*. Nashville: Abingdon, 2005.

Wilson, Andrew. *Spirit and Sacrament: An Invitation to Eucharismatic Worship*. Grand Rapids, Zondervan, 2018.

Wogaman, J. Philip. *Speaking the Truth in Love: Prophetic Preaching in a Broken World*. Louisville: Westminster John Knox, 1998.

General Index

Scripture Index

OLD TESTAMENT

Isaiah

Jeremiah

Lamentations

Ezekiel

Daniel

Joel

Micah

NEW TESTAMENT

Matthew

Mark

Luke

John

Acts

Romans

1 Corinthians

2 Corinthians

1 John

Jude

Revelation

www.ingramcontent.com/pod-product-compliance
Lightning Source LLC
LaVergne TN
LVHW090512110826
845146LV00003B/822

9798385221011